Universities into the 21st Century

Series Editors: Noel Entwistle and Roger King

Further titles are in preparation

Learning Development in Higher Education

Edited by
Peter Hartley
John Hilsdon
Christine Keenan
Sandra Sinfield
Michelle Verity

palgrave
macmillan

First published 2011 by
PALGRAVE MACMILLAN

Palgrave Macmillan in the UK is an imprint of Macmillan Publishers Limited, registered in England, company number 785998, of Houndmills, Basingstoke, Hampshire RG21 6XS.

Palgrave Macmillan in the US is a division of St Martin's Press LLC, 175 Fifth Avenue, New York, NY 10010.

Palgrave Macmillan is the global academic imprint of the above companies and has companies and representatives throughout the world.

Palgrave® and Macmillan® are registered trademarks in the United States, the United Kingdom, Europe and other countries

ISBN 978-0-230-24148-0

This book is printed on paper suitable for recycling and made from fully managed and sustained forest sources. Logging, pulping and manufacturing processes are expected to conform to the environmental regulations of the country of origin.

A catalogue record for this book is available from the British Library.

A catalog record for this book is available from the Library of Congress.

10 9 8 7 6 5 4 3 2 1
20 19 18 17 16 15 14 13 12 11

Printed and bound in Great Britain by
CPI Antony Rowe, Chippenham and Eastbourne

Contents

Dedication

During the time that this book was being written, Ralph, a homeless man, was brutally murdered in a suburb of Bournemouth. His killers were a group of bored children. This book is dedicated to his memory with the hope that through education we can all contribute to making this a better and safer world.

Acknowledgements

This book is one of the outcomes from the LearnHigher Centre for Excellence in Learning and Teaching (CETL), funded by the Higher Education Funding Council (HEFCE), 2005/2010. We wish to acknowledge the efforts of all the staff in the partner institutions who contributed to the CETL's success. We do not have the space to include all the important individual contributions but must mention Jill Armstrong, who led the original bid and then the partnership through its formative years.

Series Editors' Preface

The series is designed to fill a niche between publications about universities and colleges that focus exclusively on the practical concerns of university teachers, managers or policy makers and those which are written with an academic, research-based audience in mind that provide detailed evidence, argument and conclusions. The books in this series are intended to build upon evidence and conceptual frameworks in discussing issues that are of direct interest to those concerned with universities. The issues in the series will cover a broad range, from the activities of teachers and students, to wider developments in policy, at local, national and international levels.

The current pressures on academic and administrative staff, and university managers, mean that only rarely can they justify the time needed to read lengthy descriptions of research findings. The aim, therefore, is to produce compact, readable books that in many parts provide a synthesis and overview of often seemingly disparate issues.

Some of the books, such as the first in the series, *The University in the Global Age*, are deliberately broad in focus and conceptualization, looking at the system as a whole in an international perspective, and are a collection of integrated chapters, written by specialist authors. In other books, such as *Research and Teaching: Beyond the Divide*, the author looks within universities at a specific issue to examine what constitutes 'best practice' through a lens of available theory and research evidence.

Underpinning arguments where appropriate with research-based conceptual analysis makes the books more convincing to an academic audience, while the link to 'good practice and policy' avoids the remoteness that comes from an over-abstract approach. The series will thus appeal not just to those working within higher education, but also to a wider audience interested in knowing more about an organization that is attracting increasing government and media attention.

NOEL ENTWISTLE
ROGER KING

Notes on the Contributors

John Ackroyd is lecturer in Philosophy and Social Studies in the School of Childhood and Early Years at Leeds Metropolitan University.

Ann Barlow is Head of the Researcher Development Team in the Humanities Faculty at the University of Manchester.

Rebecca Bell is a Learning and Teaching Officer in the Library and Learning Resources department at Nottingham Trent University.

Julia Braham is Senior Academic Skills Development Officer in the Skills@Library team at the University of Leeds.

Tom Burns is Senior Lecturer in Learning Development at London Metropolitan University.

Val Chapman is a National Teaching Fellow and Director of the Centre for Inclusive Learning Support at the University of Worcester.

Becka Currant is a National Teaching Fellow and Dean of Students at the University of Bradford.

Neil Currant is Academic Development Advisor in the Learning Development Unit at the University of Salford.

Carol Elston is e-Learning Support Officer in the Skills@Library team at the University of Leeds.

Ed Foster is Study Support Coordinator in the Library and Learning Resources Department at Nottingham Trent University.

Mundeep Gill formerly a Learning Adviser in the Academic Practice Development Unit at Brunel University, is now Senior Tutor of the Science Foundation Programme at the University of Reading.

Bob Glass is Undergraduate Programme Leader in the Department of Information and Communications at Manchester Metropolitan University.

Martin Greenhow is Senior Lecturer in Mathematics in the Department of Mathematical Sciences at Brunel University.

Andy Hagyard is Learning and Teaching Coordinator in the Centre for Educational Research and Development at the University of Lincoln.

Kathy Harrington is Director of the Write Now Centre for Excellence in Teaching and Learning at London Metropolitan University.

Peter Hartley is a National Teaching Fellow and Professor of Education Development in the Educational Development Unit at the University of Bradford.

John Hilsdon is a National Teaching Fellow and Head of Learning Development at the University of Plymouth.

Debbie Holley, formally at London Metropolitan University Business School, is Principal Lecturer in the Faculty of Education at Anglia Ruskin University.

Kate Hoskins is Senior Lecturer in Education at Roehampton University.

Christine Keenan is a Learning and Teaching Fellow at Bournemouth University.

Sarah Lawther is Learning and Teaching Officer in the Library and Learning Resources Department at Nottingham Trent University.

Jane McNeil is Deputy Head of the Centre for Academic Standards and Quality at Nottingham Trent University.

Linda Murray now works as a Consultant in Academic Practice. She was formerly Director of the Academic Practice Development Unit at Brunel University.

Peter O'Neill is Senior Lecturer in Academic Writing at London Metropolitan University.

Alyssa Phillips is Director of Combined Studies at the University of Manchester.

Pauline Ridley is Senior Lecturer in the Centre for Learning and Teaching at the University of Brighton

Martin Sedgley is Effective Learning Advisor in the School of Management at the University of Bradford.

Kim Shahabudin is Study Adviser in the Study Advice and Maths Support team at the University of Reading.

Sandra Sinfield is University Teaching Fellow and Coordinator for Learning Development at London Metropolitan University.

Paul Trowler is Professor of Higher Education in the Department of Educational Research at the University of Lancaster.

Judy Turner is Study Adviser in the Study Advice and Maths Support team at the University of Reading and a Chartered Psychologist.

Michelle Verity is Head of Student Enterprise and Development at York St John University.

Sue Watling is Learning and Teaching Coordinator in the Centre for Educational Research and Development at the University of Lincoln.

Introduction

This book provides a comprehensive overview of the growing field of learning development (LD) in higher education (HE) and demonstrates its impact on student learning through specific examples and case studies. It was edited and written by staff who were involved in the UK's largest collaborative Centre for Excellence in Teaching and Learning (CETL) – LearnHigher – one of the network of 74 Centres which were established by the Higher Education Funding Council for England (HEFCE) to run for five years from 2005. A brief history of this development is given below, before we introduce the sections and chapters in this book.

Learning development is an emergent field in HE, which has attracted interest from practitioners, teachers and researchers in a number of disciplines. It is typically defined to include areas of practice such as study skills, academic advice, lifelong learning, and learning support. While we might all subscribe to a general definition of learning develop ment in terms of its support for student learning, this book does not disguise differences in perspective and approach between colleagues. We have included discussion of major issues and challenges – including the proposition that in some circumstances learning development may be part of the problem rather than the solution!

Learning development has emerged and grown in the context of struc- tural convergence between traditional universities, polytechnics and other higher education institutions (HEIs) in the UK, and as a response to the widening of participation in HE programmes since the early 1990s. This growth has been influenced by a range of external and internal systems and processes, all reflected in the examples and case studies in this book, including teaching approaches, pedagogic theories, institu- tional values and policies, student support systems, student motivation, and strategies for supporting and encouraging students to engage successfully with their learning.

The work of practitioners in learning development has become more important strategically in UK HE over recent years. The political agenda has moved from concerns with access to higher education (that domi- nated the late 1990s) to issues relating to enhancing the student learning experience, improving student retention, and enabling students to become more independent and effective learners, all at a time of dramatically increased pressures on resources.

▶ Aims and objectives

This book aims to:

- explore changing concepts of learning development, including its role in higher education as a change agent;

- discuss a broad range of learning development strategies, both in theory and in practice;

- demonstrate the impact of learning development on the student learning experience;

- consider the impact of new technologies on student learning and development, and the major implications for learning development;

- identify strategic themes, current challenges and likely new directions in this field.

▶ Who should read this book?

This book includes important examples and insights for a number of audiences, including:

- Learning developers, both nationally and internationally, who are looking for demonstrations of effective and innovative practice.

- Lecturers and course/programme leaders, who need to be aware of the range and different types of support that learning development can offer their students.

- University managers, who are looking to provide the best learning support for students in terms of both effective structures and specific initiatives.

▶ Background and context

A brief history of CETLs

'Centres of excellence' were first proposed as one of several initiatives to boost the quality of teaching, in the UK Government's White Paper, 'The Future of Higher Education' (2003). After consultation, the Higher Education Funding Council for England invited bids for 'Centres for Excellence in Teaching and Learning'. This funding was to 'represent a future investment to develop good practice further for the benefit of students and for quality enhancement in the sector more generally'(HEFCE, 2003, p. 3). The purpose of CETLs was to:

> reward excellent teaching practice and to invest in that practice further in order to increase and deepen its impact across a wider teaching and learning community. (HEFCE, 2004, p. 1)

Seventy-four Centres for Excellence in Teaching and Learning (CETLs) were established within higher education institutions (HEIs) throughout England, Wales and Northern Ireland. This initiative was the largest ever single-funded intervention in teaching and learning in the history of UK higher education, receiving £350 million over five years. The CETL policy was clearly an instrument that relied on economic means to incentivise and, indeed, the considerable financial size of the initiative made the sector sit up and take notice. HEFCE later reported that all English HEIs were represented in at least one bid.

How LearnHigher came about

LearnHigher was a collaboration between learning development professionals in sixteen English HE institutions and the Higher Education Academy. This network included several National Teaching Fellows and covered twenty areas of learning development, such as academic writing, group work, reading, note-making, and personal development planning. LearnHigher was committed to improve student learning through practice-led enquiry and to build a research base in the effective use of learning development resources (see full details at www.learnhigher.ac.uk).

The network grew from an existing collaboration between practitioners from the sixteen HEIs, including staff from various roles and levels in their institutions concerned with supporting students' learning. Previous funding initiatives (such as FDTL – Fund for the Development of Teaching and Learning – and TQEF – Teaching Quality Enhancement

Fund) had resulted in pockets of staff with expertise in particular areas of learning development as well as a number of 'excellent' resources produced to support learners. Staff from different institutions had expressed an interest in sharing their expertise and resources and the CETL initiative provided the catalyst to realise these ambitions. Learn-Higher also aimed to address two other key issues facing the sector:

- how to develop a better understanding of learning development theory and practice (and to promote this), and
- how to make good quality-assured learning development resources easier to access.

The CETL was set up to pool existing expertise and provide an accessible central resource for students and staff across HE. The LearnHigher network of 'Learning Area Coordinators' and the central team based at Liverpool Hope University began sharing existing resources and developing new ones, theorising about effective learning development practices and driving up the quality of the resulting outputs of the collaboration. Learning Area Coordinators were tasked with working with further networks of practitioners with an interest or expertise in that particular area, further sharing expertise and embedding enhanced practice.

▶ Structure of this book

Section A: Defining learning development

This section discusses what we mean by 'learning development', how it emerged and how it has changed and developed in recent years. It includes exploration of different approaches to learning development and a consideration of its contested interpretations and status in HE.

John Hilsdon describes how a specific learning development perspective was born from within the field of educational development in the 1990s, and how, from its inception, this approach called for whole-institution policies to develop skills for learning for all students, rather than a remedial model providing support for those perceived as 'needy'. He explores how learning development has evolved by drawing upon theoretical ideas around academic literacies, and values-based approaches aimed at accessible higher education provision for all with the ability to benefit. The history of the Learning Development in Higher Education Network (LDHEN) and related activities up to the present are described, including plans for future developments involving the continuation of LearnHigher activity.

Linda Murray and Bob Glass report on recent surveys conducted among learning developers. They describe their findings in terms of what learning developers do, how they are employed, and what perceptions are held about them in their institutions. They reveal considerable variation and differences in the ways learning development is understood and organised, and reflect on whether the learning development 'community of practice' can call itself a profession.

Asking the important question — Is learning development part of the problem? – Ann Barlow, John Ackroyd and Alyssa Phillips offer a view of the history of the university and its purposes based on philosophical ideas and their interpretation. They report on their work with Combined Honours students and identify views and expectations that might help inform learning developers, and encourage them to support independent learning as opposed to conveying simply techniques to 'pass the course'.

Finally, Sandra Sinfield, Debbie Holley, Tom Burns, Kate Hoskins, Peter O'Neill and Katherine Harrington present a view of learning development as socio-political practice. They argue for the emancipatory potential of learning development and describe how their work with three Centres for Excellence in Teaching and Learning focused on empowering students to be actively involved in all aspects of learning.

Section B: Supporting Students in Transition

This section looks at approaches taken by learning developers to improve a range of student transition experiences. The chapters include references and links to learning resources and case studies, providing examples of how a learning development approach can work with, and empower, students at various points of transition in their academic journey.

A key theme throughout this section is that of enabling students to understand their relationship with their own learning, showing how students can be empowered to maximise their learning. Another significant theme is the power of peer, social, and tutor relationships in the learning process and the important role played by learning developers in facilitating these relationships through their understandings and insights into the learning processes of their students.

Christine Keenan reflects on how personal development planning (PDP) approaches can be integrated into learning activities to enable students to manage their transition into HE more effectively. She reviews three approaches to supporting students in transition: firstly, a resource offering pre-induction learning activities which provides an introduction to university life; secondly, empowering students to build their own PDP; and thirdly, a 20-credit Academic Practice Unit which develops generic and discipline-based learning skills.

Ed Foster, Sarah Lawther and Jane McNeil develop this theme by looking at the experience of students as they arrive at university. Following a brief overview of transition literature, they reflect on research undertaken at Nottingham Trent University (NTU) on the importance of understanding students' prior learning experiences to gain insight into how they make sense of the new learning environment. Finally, they provide examples of how learning developers at NTU are contributing to strategic change in supporting students in transition.

Judy Turner makes a strong case for one-to-one academic advice for students. She analyses the experiences of a mature student, a postgraduate student, a student with additional learning needs, and an international student – all of whom experienced problems that made them consider withdrawing from their courses. She provides evidence to support a view that, despite increasing economic constraints in HE, one-to-one support from professional academic advisers can make all the difference to student success and retention.

Martin Sedgley reflects on the transition of international Masters' students and the problems often faced by these students when tackling assignments in the UK. He describes a collaborative partnership approach, the Assignment Success Programme from the University of Bradford, where academics and learning developers work together to support students' understanding and communication of disciplinary discourses.

Finally, Val Chapman offers some thought-provoking questions and ideas for inclusive practice in a variety of transition situations with students who have a disability. An overview of legislative requirements and definitions of inclusion leads on to discussion of strategies which enable disabled students to progress successfully.

Section C: Developing Effective Academic Practice

This section demonstrates how specific learning development initiatives can enhance students' academic practices throughout their course and in key areas of both disciplinary study and transferable skills. The chapters identify important implications for both university teaching and the efforts of learning developers.

Mundeep Gill and Martin Greenhow demonstrate how they build

students' confidence in mathematics and numeracy, reviewing key issues that students face and examples of strategies and resources that have been used in response. Using Brunel University as a case study, they advocate a blended use of resources, ranging from diagnostic tests and confidence logs to their Maths Café. They focus on their Mathletics CAA system and demonstrate the significant impact of correctly implemented computer-aided assessment.

Rebecca Bell summarises major current issues concerning student academic writing and reviews the three major approaches which have been proposed to resolve them. She then evaluates the approach adopted by one UK University (Nottingham Trent) to address these problems in a way which effectively complements established methods. Using a communities of practice approach, learning developers have forged new and more productive relationships with academic teaching staff

Carol Elston, Peter Hartley and Julia Braham evaluate their flexible web-based resource which is designed to improve the effectiveness of students working in groups – the award-winning 'Making Groupwork Work'. The design of this resource gives considerable scope for further development and it has been produced to allow both individual independent use by students and integration into curriculum delivery.

Andy Hagyard and Sue Watling examine the general development of research-based learning in higher education and then analyse the experience of one university which introduced a research bursary scheme for undergraduate students to kickstart this development. They then identify important implications for both university teaching in general and learning development in particular.

Finally, Pauline Ridley argues that visual knowledge and skills are an essential element of all subject disciplines in higher education. She describes her approach, developed through LearnHigher, working with subject staff both to raise awareness of the visual dimension of their subjects, and to explore how these skills can be taught and assessed. Curriculum innovation through funded projects and initiatives, involving still and moving images and student drawing, has demonstrated significant impact in a range of disciplines.

Section D: Students and Technology

Any discussion of technology and its impact/influence on the twenty-first-century student opens up hotly contested debates amongst academics, ranging from over-arching social agendas to specific educational practice, including, in the UK: the socio-political landscape and legacy of 'managerialist' policies; diminishing resources and widening participation; how and when students should be in the classroom; whether the classroom should be a formal or informal place of learning; and how we might best use specific devices (for example, capturing students' use of mobile devices and effectively blending the learning experience).

Whatever your view, you will find the mapping of the policy landscape (from Debbie Holley, Tom Burns, Sandra Sinfield and Bob Glass) a useful starting point. The materials they showcase also offer useful ideas about reinvigorating pedagogy. Neil Currant, Becka Currant and Peter Hartley focus on student use of technology in order to refute some popular myths regarding the 'digital native'. They propose a typology of students reflecting different incorporation of digital technologies which have very different implications for tutors and learning developers.

Finally, Kim Shahabudin explores problems that students may encounter in juggling their complex lives and demonstrates simple and effective ways of using technology to support revision, reading and independent learning.

Section E: Looking Into the Future
This last section looks both backward and forward to reflect on how learning development has changed and matured, to identify current challenges, and to suggest likely future directions. Different perspectives are offered from colleagues involved in the management and evaluation of LearnHigher as it developed (Chapter 18) and from network members who are further developing this work in the post-CETL environment (Chapter 19).

Michelle Verity and Paul Trowler argue that LearnHigher was an important and influential stage for learning development in the UK (with important lessons for learning development in other educational systems), moving from a relatively uncoordinated enterprise with pockets of innovation and experimentation to a strong collaborative focus on strategic development and institutional support. However, they conclude that the strategic issues are not yet resolved and anticipate increasing pressures on learning developers to adopt 'contingent' approaches which simply reflect local management priorities.

John Hilsdon, Christine Keenan and Sandra Sinfield show how initiatives triggered by LearnHigher will continue to develop under the auspices of ALDinHE (the Association for Learning Developers in Higher Education). They argue that the collaborative ethos established by LearnHigher (which always included considerable interchange with partners not formally represented in the CETL), plus the growing international collaborations between learning developers, will maintain the pressure and support for approaches to learning development which can look beyond immediate institutional 'crises'. Short term measures to solve crises, such as 'fixing retention problems', will not be successful in the long term unless they can meaningfully contribute improvement in student engagement and learning, which is the strategic imperative of learning developers in all contexts. They call for learning development to engage in further research, to build upon models of good practice, and to develop itself as a discipline within higher education.

▶ References

HEFCE (2003) Centres for Excellence in Teaching and Learning: Formal consultation. Available at: www.hefce.ac.uk/Pubs/hefce/2003/03_36.htm (last accessed 21/3/2010).

HEFCE (2004) Centres for Excellence in Teaching and Learning: Invitation to bid for funds. Available at: www.hefce.ac.uk/pubs/hefce/2004/04_05/ (last accessed 21/3/2010).

Section A

Defining Learning Development

1 What is Learning Development?

John Hilsdon

▶ Summary

A growing number of those who focus on students' learning in UK universities are choosing to describe their work as 'learning development'. As successive governments have sought to increase participation in higher education (HE), it has been widely acknowledged that initiatives to support and enhance learning for all university students are of growing importance. This chapter reviews what we mean by 'learning development' and analyses its influences and progress, exemplified by the growth of the UK Learning Development in Higher Education Network (LDHEN) since 2003. This reveals a movement of practitioners with powerful and transformative visions of learning, and of what a modern university is for.

▶ Introduction

When people ask what I do for a living, the answer, 'I'm a learning developer', rarely passes without question as to what one of those might be! In my mind, various images arise. There is the tutorial room where, together with one student, or sometimes a small group of students, we sit discussing how to make sense of an essay question, or a project task. Another is of the lecture theatre, where the learning developer speaks to a hundred or more students about how to undertake critical analysis of a particular topic. Then again, there is the meeting room where the learning developer is working with one or more academic colleagues to devise group activities to get students more involved in learning a set of concepts or processes, or to undertake a reading task more effectively.

There are other images: at a computer replying to students' emails with comments on their work; writing and editing online study guides; struggling to interpret a set of data for a journal paper or conference workshop; or at a committee meeting where the learning developer is explaining that, for example, because of the importance of context in learning, it would be more effective to direct students' attention to key features of lab reports as an embedded activity on their course, rather than offering them a generic session on 'writing skills'.

In other words, learning development is a complex set of multi-disciplinary and cross-disciplinary academic roles and functions, involving teaching, tutoring, research, and the design and production of learning materials, as well as involvement in staff development, policy-making and other consultative activities. Learning development work in UK universities can be traced back to the 1970s (see, for example, Gibbs, 1977) where it evolved as part of or alongside other areas of practice, including tutoring and student counselling (Wheeler, 1983; Peelo, 1994) and educational development (ED) (Land, 2004; Gosling, 2008). The thinking which shaped ED from its outset was aimed at improving student learning as well as teaching (Gibbs, 1988, 1992). This has also been most influential in the emergence of learning development; indeed, as Rust (2009) argues, the rationale for ED and learning development to work together is very powerful.

Nonetheless, learning development has arisen as a field of practice in the UK, within or alongside ED, with some distinguishing features: notably the emphasis on examining how students experience and make sense of learning activities and academic practices. Despite the increasing currency of the term 'learning development' to describe the kinds of activity mentioned above, its status and meaning remain contested (Cash and Hilsdon, 2008). Such complexities reflect debates about the nature and purposes of contemporary HE under conditions of diminishing resources per student, and managerial strategies to direct specialised 'support' to students, rather than making more radical or embedded (and potentially more expensive) changes to courses, teaching and assessment (Mroz, 2009).

▶ The context for learning development

Since the 1980s there has been huge growth and change in higher education throughout the industrialised world, in the wake of global economic, social and technological changes (Knapper and Cropley, 2000; Trow, 2005). In the UK, drives to expand the sector have led to the development of many new universities (the majority being former polytechnics) to meet rising government targets for the percentages of school leavers who engage in higher education. As a consequence, growing numbers of UK university students are now from social and cultural backgrounds where university study was previously uncommon, and are sometimes still termed 'non-traditional'!

These changes have been accompanied by various government initiatives designed to influence the development of thinking and practice within universities, emphasising their role in producing skilled graduates for the UK's workforce. The discourses associated with student needs have identified, on the one hand, their increasingly diverse socio-cultural characteristics (described as 'specific learning needs'; needs of 'mature learners' and 'non-traditional entrants'; 'lifelong learning'; etc.), and on the other, focused on identifying 'key skills', 'transferable skills', 'graduate skills' and, more recently, 'higher level skills'. The latter reflects the growing preoccupation in HE policy formulation with the perceived needs of employers and the UK economy (Smith, Wolstencroft and Southern, 1989; NCIHE, 1997; Department for Education and Skills, 2006). This is illustrated in the 'Leitch Review':

China and India are turning out 4 million graduates a year. The UK turns out 250,000. ... For too long the supply-side in education – the colleges and universities, the qualifications bodies, the funding bodies ... has dominated. 'What young people want' rather than 'what employers need'. ... A move to a system that gives employers the strongest voice is now essential. (Department for Education and Skills, 2006)

Within this context of social, political and economic factors, communities of practice in HE have evolved aiming to focus attention on student learning. Such groups have included educational and staff developers; researchers; study skills tutors; library and careers staff; counsellors; widening participation and disability specialists; and English as a Second Language teachers, among others. This chapter outlines how a 'learning development' perspective has emerged (Gosling, 1995; Simpson, 1996; Cottrell, 2001; Hilsdon, 2004) from among these groupings.

Though originally associated with the development of a 'skills curriculum' (Cottrell, 2001) learning development also highlights social and experiential factors in learning, such as discussions which generate opportunities for students to interpret and make sense of the practices and language(s) of higher education. Examining these and making more explicit some of their 'rules' serves to counter exclusive or alienating aspects of HE study (Mann, 2001; Archer et al., 2003). For this reason the 'developmental' aspects of learning development are multi-faceted. They include how individuals learn; how context affects learning; how students' social identity relates to their experience of higher education; and the impact of institutional policies, pedagogy and practice.

From 2003 onwards, an email discussion group, the Learning Development in Higher Education Network (LDHEN), has acted as a focus for the growing learning development community. From within this network came the successful bid to establish the Centre for Excellence in Teaching and Learning, LearnHigher. The establishment of the Association for Learning Development in Higher Education (ALDinHE) followed in 2007, and the *Journal of Learning Development in Higher Education* in 2008. Learning developers in the UK have thus created a very active community of practice; indeed, this book is a good indicator of the progress being made by that community.

▶ Choosing the term 'learning development'

As noted above, the phrase 'learning development' is used increasingly in the UK to describe the work of practitioners in HE whose primary focus is student learning. In 2002, Sandra Sinfield (one of the co-authors of this book) and I convened a small group of colleagues in 'study support' and similar roles in several new UK universities, to provide a forum for talking about our work via an email distribution list. This became the JISC-mail group (LDHEN) referred to above. Although our job titles were variously styled as 'learning support', 'learning skills' or 'study skills', for example, we deliberately chose the name 'learning development' for the group, motivated by a desire to focus on the broad range of processes involved in learning at university. What united us most strongly was our commitment to work with students to help them make sense of the seemingly mysterious and alienating practices of academia; and to work with academics to rationalise and clarify such practices (Lillis, 2001).

Although we were unaware of it at the time, the phrase 'learning development' was in use before the genesis of LDHEN, and attempts to theorise a learning development approach were already underway, for example, at the University of East London, among staff working to widen participation and access to HE (Wolfendale and Corbett, 1996; Gosling, 1995; Simpson, 1996; Wailey, 1996; Cottrell, 2001). This work distinguishes learning development from a more traditional study skills focus.

Key to this is opposition to a 'deficit' model. Rather than seeing students and their needs as problematic, learning development identifies aspects of learning environments which are inadequate or alienating.

This learning development perspective seeks to promote reflective activities, encouraging and empowering students to analyse and assess their own development. Pioneering work at the educational development unit at Oxford Polytechnic, and research by, among others, Entwistle and Ramsden (1983), Gibbs (1988), and Boud (1986), had shown that a focus on active, student-centred learning was needed for all students, not just those deemed 'at risk'. Changes in course design and teaching practices were implied, emphasising students' participation and involvement in their own assessment. Supporting such changes, Wailey (1996) argued that engagement with the discourse of academic disciplines should be an explicit part of what goes on in HE classes.

In the 1980s and 1990s, the growing field of educational development (ED), charged with 'helping academic staff to accommodate and cope with the massive changes in HE' (Land, 2004, p. 2), directed attention to these issues. In some cases, members of ED units also undertook what we refer to as learning development, providing study support for students directly. As D'Andrea and Gosling pointed out (2001), there are significant advantages in combining the provision of student-focused work on skills for learning, with development activities and courses for staff. This provides ongoing experience and data for developers to use in drawing academics' attention to how their students learn. In such cases, ED and learning development activities inform each other in a 'holistic' fashion (D'Andrea and Gosling, 2001).

Unfortunately, as Gosling (2008) reported, this situation (i.e. educational and learning development working jointly as part of academic practice units) is the exception rather than the rule. The creation of significant numbers of specialised learning support posts in HE from the 1990s made it less likely that ED units would make such provision directly. These new posts – often not based on academic contracts – reflect the rise of market-oriented models for providing 'services' to students, as the 'customers' and 'consumers' of education. The results of such fragmentation are evidenced by the unclear responses to the surveys reported by Glass and Murray in Chapter 2. A desire by learning development practitioners to counter what some see as the 'commodification' of education reveals awareness of the underlying tensions between academic and managerialist approaches to support for learning (Knight and Trowler, 2001).

▶ Theory, practice and values in learning development

Leading up to the time of the initial gathering of LDHEN at London Metropolitan University in 2003 (where some sixty practitioners met as 'learning developers' for the first time), a range of motivations for using the phrase 'learning development' had begun to coalesce, bringing together theoretical, practice-based and value-oriented approaches. Whichever theoretical stance towards learning one adopts, there is agreement – especially within the dominant constructivist and phenomenological approaches favoured in texts about HE (e.g. Biggs, 2007) – that learning depends upon an array of complex social and psychological factors, and that knowledge or learning cannot simply be transferred like an object from one person to another. For this reason the notion of 'development' was seen as so vital among our group.

Similarly, we were keen to focus on the gerund 'ing' form of the word 'learning', emphasising the practices of all involved, rather than looking simply at 'learners'. The latter emphasis, it seemed to us, was often associated with a 'deficit' or remedial approach, viewing students only in terms of their needs for help or support. We felt that the phrases 'study skills' and 'learner support' both represented a partial approach, maintaining a focus on students without giving corresponding attention to teaching, learning materials and the courses themselves.

A group whose remit is learning development would therefore be – as educational developers had always been – as interested in academic practice generally, and whole institution approaches, as in work with specific learners. Within ALDinHE, we are also motivated by the notion of teachers and students as genuine partners in learning and research, as in the UNESCO World Declaration on Higher Education statement:

> Students must be considered as equal and fundamental partners and stakeholders in their own education with the right to organize themselves as they see fit within the context of their educational institutions, systems and communities. (UNESCO, 2002)

Over several years of postings to the LDHEN list, debates about what we mean by learning development have recurred and been revised (Cash and Hilsdon, 2008). A recent collective attempt to define learning development referred to its focus on student learning as:

working directly with students and in a consultative capacity with other HE staff. The main aim of learning development work is the empowerment of students typically through the enhancement of ... academic practices, such as skills for research; communication; self-awareness; and critical thinking; in order that they may benefit as fully as possible from their experiences of, and life beyond, higher education. (Hilsdon, Ridley and Sinfield, 2008)

The durability of the term is evident, as LDHEN has grown. At the time of writing there were some 480 subscribers, and increasing numbers attend annual LDHEN conferences. Learning development has now become part of the discourse of higher education, as is shown by the growing number of universities using the phrase in job titles and in descriptions of areas of work.

▶ How did we get here?

Until the 1990s, it was rare to find staff in universities who were specifically concerned with learning development. With the expansion in HE came the development of a small number of posts, more common in the ex-polytechnics, and often using short-term or project funding, for supporting 'access students', and promoting 'study skills' or 'learner support'. The model for such work often derived from practice developed in the further education sector and from initiatives to address 'special needs' in learning, such as dyslexia (Wolfendale, 1996). In some of the older universities, however, concerns with how students coped with university life and study problems in particular had resulted in pioneering work in 'learning skills', 'study methods' (Gibbs, 1977; Gibbs and Northedge, 1979) and 'study counselling' (Wheeler, 1984; Peelo, 1994). Many of the ideas promoted by this work, such as the importance of relating students' own experience to their study context, and the central role of language in learning, are now seen as underpinning ideas in the field of learning development.

As we have seen, the evolution of learning development in the UK is linked to the recent, rapid expansion of the HE sector; but has also been conditioned by changes (still in progress) in the way universities are conceptualised. It might seem obvious now to say that learning should be everyone's business in universities, be they lecturers, researchers, undergraduates, administrators or members of any other academic communities. And yet a view persists in some quarters (perhaps more common among staff in the older, more traditional universities) that the business of universities is the production of new knowledge through research, and that teaching is a secondary activity.

This view implies that students should arrive at university already equipped for their learning and assessment tasks, such as to read and interpret complex texts; to argue and think critically, and to write academically. At the very least, so this opinion would have it, they should be able to do these things without much further help beyond the first year of undergraduate study. As Haggis (2006) points out, however, the growing diversity of students makes such an assumption unrealistic. It not only ignores the huge changes that have taken place in universities in recent years, but also misses the point that maintaining a focus on learning, and how it can be supported, is the best way to serve achievement in all fields.

The cultural changes for universities, old and new, are significant. The legacy of practices deriving from an elite model remains a powerful 'informing norm' of HE, creating tensions with aims such as to widen access to those with the 'ability to benefit'. Up to the 1980s it was still the case that less than 10% of UK school leavers were admitted to universities. By 2001 this had risen to 41% (HEFCE, 2001), and by 2008 almost 2 million students were in higher education in the UK (HESA, 2009); but, despite the huge cultural and demographic changes this represented, assumptions about what students should be like and what skills they should bring to university were still shaped by historic ideals: the expectation that they should, for example, already be familiar with independent study activities, and confident in essay writing before coming into HE.

Barnett (2007) points to the great change and uncertainty in all areas of life, especially in culture and in the technologies we use. It is unsurprising therefore that the operation and perceived functions of universities are also shifting, are contested, or remain unclear. To understand better the emergence of learning development, it is worth referring to some of the key factors influencing the recent development of UK universities.

The 1963 Robbins Report on Higher Education marked the beginning of the contemporary period for UK HE. This document drew attention to a lack of coordination and planning in the development of the sector to date, and pointed to the need for expansion based on both social and economic factors. The 1970s saw the development of the polytechnics and a 'binary' approach to higher education, where the universities retained their elite status. A number of new universities, such as those at Warwick, Sussex, East Anglia and Lancaster also appeared in that period, but it was not until the mid-1980s that plans for a move to a unified 'mass' system of higher education took serious shape.

In September 1984, the University Grants Commission (UGC) published 'A Strategy for Higher Education into the 1990s'. This report was a precursor of the Government's 1985/6 Green Paper of the same name. At an early stage in this document, the writers proposed an amendment to the 'famous axiom' of the Robbins Committee that 'courses of higher education should be available for all those who are qualified by ability and attainment to pursue them'. They argued that:

> the Robbins axiom is more appropriately restated as: Courses of higher education should be available for all those who are able to benefit from them and who wish to do so. The principle of access … is concerned with providing places for students from different backgrounds and attempting to compensate for previous inequalities. We would broaden it and include students not only from different social classes, but also from different ethnic groups. Moreover, opportunities for women must be as good as opportunities for men. (University Grants Commission, 1984)

To those in government, this may have been largely driven by the perceived need for the UK to match its economic competitors in terms of HE participation rates, but for many others the importance of education as part of a democratising social agenda was most important. Another key document produced at the outset of the period of expansion was the report *More Means Different* by Sir Christopher Ball, written in May 1990. This was compiled under the auspices of the Royal Society of Arts (RSA) with sponsorship from the Training Agency, NCVQ, BTEC and the company BP. In common with a number of other reports at the time (e.g. PCFC, 1992), Ball also recommended that the UK seek to match its European partners in the proportions of people encouraged to undertake higher education. At the same time, radical changes in the kinds of courses and the modes of assessment, teaching, learning and delivery provided were called for.

More Means Different was one of the first reports to acknowledge, albeit somewhat obliquely, that widening access also means new needs and new conditions for students in HE. The concept of 'value added' is introduced, along with the terms 'capability', 'usefulness' and 'enterprise' in relation to higher education courses. In a key section of the report, under the heading 'Quality and Excellence Redefined', Ball speaks of:

re-interpreting the goals of quality and excellence, not in the old selective and exclusive way, but as the value added by the process and experience of higher education to achieve fitness for purpose. ... Perhaps the finer institutions of the future will not boast of taking the best applicants, but of making the best of their students, whatever their starting point. ... But if quality and excellence are still seen as the exclusive characteristics of the 'best' people then higher education will continue to pursue its high objectives by means of exclusion and rejection. (Ball, 1990)

Elsewhere in *More Means Different* are further indications of a view that new students will bring new 'needs' to be met. On page 39, Ball talks of 'reaching out beyond the traditional pool of student applicants to (among others) lower socio-economic groups and the ethnic minorities' and argues that the new HE institutions will need to become 'more user-friendly' to enable the new kinds of students to succeed.

These dual lines of reasoning continue through various policy documents up to the present (Department for Education and Skills, 2006; DIUS, 2009), illustrating the drives to influence higher education from both commercial and industrial interests (improving UK competitiveness, providing skilled graduates for the workplace) and from political and ethical influences concerned with greater levels of social equality in terms of class, ethnicity, gender and disability. The discourses of 'scholarship' and 'excellence', which had previously been the dominant modes of description of the goals and work of HE (Light and Cox, 2001), have therefore been joined by discourses of 'accountability' in both economic and social terms – i.e. for universities to be agents of social and political change, to serve the UK economy, and to promote social justice in terms of greater equality of opportunity (D'Andrea and Gosling, 2005).

Unsurprisingly therefore, since learning development work is directed largely at the 'new' HE students, its evolution has also been shaped by these calls for 'accountability', largely represented by what we might term, on the one hand, 'skills' issues; and, on the other, those concerned with 'values'. In both cases, however, despite the demands to re-examine the notion of 'quality', the underlying assumptions have been those of 'deficit' models, where students are seen mostly in terms of their needs.

By contrast, a growing number of those adopting a learning development perspective emphasise more holistic approaches, as implied in the 'students as partners in learning' view referred to above. In so doing, we draw upon theoretical work on literacies (Lea and Street, 1998), social identity (Ivanic, 1998), and pedagogy (Lillis, 2001; Meyer and Land, 2006;

Haggis, 2006). Although it would be premature to describe this kind of approach to learning development as well-established, a number of the initiatives described in this book illustrate how values such as partnership and empowerment can support learning in twenty-first-century universities.

▶ Where are we going?

Although debates within our community will continue, my impression is that it was wise at the outset to emphasise 'development' – which, as Land (2004, p. 14) points out, allows for the competing discourses we have identified – rather than, say 'skills' in learning. 'Development' provides a good basis for drawing together a community of practice whose focus is how students experience learning, and which, as we hope to show in this book, best suits the diversity of a twenty-first-century, accessible and democratic university. It is also compatible with an 'academic literacies' approach, which, as we have seen, is a useful underpinning for learning development because it supports students in developing ownership (and critique) of subject-based language and practices.

The UK learning development community has grown through initiatives such as the journal *JLDHE* (*Journal of Learning Development in Higher Education*) and the association ALDinHE. More recently, the association pledged to support the CETL LearnHigher, beyond its HEFCE funding after 2010, enabling continuation of work on learning development resources for the HE sector, many of which are described in this book.

As yet there are no well defined professional development routes for learning developers and employment contracts for learning development staff also remain highly variable across the sector. Academic titles such as 'lecturer' exist in some cases but many are 'academic-related' or 'professional services' staff – and post grades, salaries and promotion prospects are perceived to be lower than for other academics. Furthermore, a good deal of learning development work is still carried out by staff on part-time, temporary and project-based contracts.

It is therefore clear that much is still to do to enhance learning development as a profession and to improve career development opportunities for specialists in this important area of work in HE. In many respects, the emergence of learning development as a field of practice mirrors the development of ED and educational development units a decade or so earlier. Indeed, many learning development practitioners feel most 'at home' working as part of, or alongside, ED units, and within their rather broader framework of functions related to the development of practice, and institutional strategies for teaching and learning.

In working for change, however, as Rust (2009) points out, the key is to effect 'a paradigm shift in the thinking of academics across the sector' – and this will require a greater level of collaboration and joined-up thinking: with academics, with our ED colleagues, and with the growing numbers of staff employed in other 'support' services. It is my view that learning developers are well placed to lead such collaborative ventures, sitting as we so often do in mediating roles between the experience of students, the goals of academics, and the wider ambitions of our HE institutions to retain students and serve their development as citizens and productive members of their communities.

This 'position' of learning developer in the current HE context perhaps helps to heighten practitioners' awareness of the experiential and humanistic factors identified above as underpinning a learning development perspective. The expression of this can be seen in practices which promote the notion of students as adults with full rights of participation in Higher Education (Archer et al., 2003), implying highly participative, literacies-informed learning activities. For example, discussing how to 'speak the language' of the discipline and profession (Hilsdon and Bitzer, 2007); exploring what the terms 'rigorous' and 'scholarly' and 'critical' mean. For learning developers, these values and this view of the purposes of HE mean that we work to do more than 'support' students, or to develop skills – we seek, in addition, to be transformative.

▶ References

Archer, L., Hutchings, M., Leathwood, C. and Ross, A. (2003) 'Widening participation in higher education: implications for policy and practice', in L. Archer, M. Hutchings and A. Ross (eds) Higher Education and Social Class: Issues of Exclusion and Inclusion (London: RoutledgeFalmer).

Ball, C. (1990) More Means Different (London: Royal Society for the Encouragement of Arts, Manufactures and Commerce (RSA)).

Barnett, R. (2007) A Will to Learn: Being a Student in an Age of Uncertainty (London: Society for Research into Higher Education).

BBC (2009) Fall in UK university students. Available at: http://news.bbc.co.uk/1/hi/education/7859034.stm (last accessed 29/3/10).

Biggs, J. (2007) *Teaching for Quality Learning at University* (Buckingham: Open University Press/Society for Research into Higher Education).

Boud, D. (1986) *Implementing Student Self-Assessment*. Green Guide No 5 (Sydney: Higher Education Research and Development Society of Australasia).

Cash, C. and Hilsdon, J. (2008) *Buried Treasures in a Virtual Community Chest*, Society for Research into Higher Education Annual Conference 2008, 9–11 December, Liverpool, UK. Available at www.srhe.ac.uk/conference2008/papers/0292-John-Hilsdon_Caroline-Cash.doc (last accessed 29/3/10).

Cottrell, S. (2001) *Teaching Study Skills and Supporting Learning* (Basingstoke: Palgrave Macmillan).

D'Andrea, V. and Gosling, D. (2001) 'Joining the dots. reconceptualising educational development', *Active Learning* 2 (1), 65–81.

D'Andrea, V. and Gosling, D. (2005) *Improving Teaching and Learning in Higher Education: A Whole Institution Approach* (Buckingham: SRHE/Open University Press).

Department for Education and Skills (2006) *Prosperity for All in the Global Economy – World Class Skills* (the Leitch Report) (London: HMSO).

DIUS (2009) *Higher Ambitions: The Future of Universities in a Knowledge Economy*, Department for Business Innovation and Skills. Available at www.bis.gov.uk/higherambitions (last accessed 6/7/10).

Entwistle, N. and Ramsden, P. (1983) *Understanding Student Learning* (London: Croom Helm).

Gibbs, G. (1977) 'Can students be taught how to study?' *Higher Education Bulletin* 5, 197–218.

Gibbs, G. (1988) *Learning by Doing* (London. Further Education Unit).

Gibbs, G. (1992) *Improving the Quality of Student Learning* (Oxford: Oxford Centre for Staff Development).

Gibbs, G. and Northedge, A. (1979) 'Helping students to understand their own study methods', *British Journal of Guidance and Counselling* 7 (1), 92–100

Gosling, D. (1995) *On Course: Academic Guidance and Learning Development* (London: Educational Development Services, University of East London).

Gosling, D, (2008) *Educational Development in the United Kingdom*, Report to the Heads of Educational Development Group (HEDG) (London: HEDG).

Haggis, T. (2006) 'Pedagogies for diversity: retaining critical challenge amidst fears of "dumbing down"', *Studies in Higher Education* 31 (5), 521–35.

HEFCE (2001) *Supply and Demand in Higher Education* (Bristol: Higher Education Funding Council for England).

HESA (2009) Higher Education Statistics Agency. *View statistics online*. Available at: www.hesa.ac.uk/index.php/component/option,com_datatables/Itemid,121/ (last accessed 29/3/10).

Hilsdon J. (2004) 'Learning Development in Higher Education Network: an emerging community of practice?' *Educational Developments* 5 (3) (Birmingham: SEDA).

Hilsdon, J. and Bitzer, E. (2007) 'To become an asker of questions', *South African Journal of Higher Education* 21 (8).

Hilsdon, J., Ridley, P. and Sinfield, S. (2008) 'Defining learning development', email correspondence, *Learning Development in Higher Education Network*, 24.09.08. Available at: www.jiscmail.ac.uk/learnhigher (last accessed 29/3/10).

Ivanic, R. (1998) *Writing and Identity: The Discoursal Construction of Identity in Academic Writing* (Amsterdam: John Benjamins).

Knapper, A. and Cropley, C. (2000) *Lifelong Learning and Higher Education* (London: Kogan Page).

Knight, P. and Trowler, P. (2001) *Departmental Leadership in Higher Education* (Buckingham: Open University Press/SRHE).

Land, R. (2004) *Educational Development: Discourse Identity and Practice* (Maidenhead: Open University Press).

Lea, M. and Street, B. (1998) 'Student writing in higher education: an academic literacies approach', *Studies in Higher Education* 11 (3), 182–99.

Light, G. and Cox, R. (2001) *Learning and Teaching in Higher Education: The Reflective Practitioner* (London: Paul Chapman).

Lillis, T. (2001) *Student Writing: Access, Regulation and Desire* (London: Routledge).

Mann, S. (2001) 'Alternative perspectives on the student experience: alienation and engagement', *Studies in Higher Education* 26 (1), 7–19.

Meyer, J. H. F. and Land, R. (2006) *Overcoming Barriers to Student Understanding: Threshold Concepts and Troublesome Knowledge* (London: RoutledgeFalmer).

Mroz, A. (2009) 'Get used to life on the edge', *Times Higher Education*, 31 December 2009.

NCIHE (1997) *Higher Education in the Learning Society* (the Dearing Report) (London: National Committee of Inquiry into Higher Education).

PCFC (1992) *Widening Participation in Higher Education* (Leicester: Polytechnics and Colleges Funding Council).

Peelo, M. (1994) *Helping Students with Study Problems* (Buckingham: SRHE/Open University Press).

Rust, C. (2009) 'A Call to Unite in a Common Cause', *Journal of Learning Development in Higher Education JLDinHE* 1. Available at: www.aldinhe.ac.uk/ojs/index.php?journal =jldhe (last accessed 29/3/10).

Simpson, R. (1996) 'Learning development in HE: deficit or difference?' in S. Wolfendale and J. Corbett (eds) *Opening Doors: Learning Support in Higher Education* (London: Cassell).

Smith, D., Wolstencroft, T. and Southern, J. (1989) 'Personal transferable skills and the job demands on graduates', *Journal of European Industrial Training* 13 (8).

Trow, M. (2005) 'Reflections on the transition from elite to mass to universal access: forms and phases of Higher Education in modern societies since WWII', in P. Altbach (ed.) *International Handbook of Higher Education* (Amsterdam: Kluwer).

UNESCO (2002) *The role of student affairs and services in higher education, a practical manual for developing, implementing and assessing student affairs programmes and services – follow-up to the World Conference on Higher Education (Paris, 5-9 October 1998)*. Available at: http://unesdoc.unesco.org/images/0012/001281/128118e.pdf (last accessed 2/3/10).

University Grants Commission (1984) *A Strategy for Higher Education into the 1990s* (London: HMSO).

Wailey, T. (1996) *Supporting Students with Specific Learning Difficulties* (London and New York: Cassell).

Wheeler, M. (1984) *Counselling in Study Methods* (Exeter: University of Exeter).

Wolfendale, S. (1996) 'Learning Support in Higher Education: principles, values, continuities', in S. Wolfendale and J. Corbett (eds) *Opening Doors: Learning Support in Higher Education* (London: Cassell).

Woolard, A. (1995) 'Core skills and the idea of the graduate', *Higher Education Quarterly* 49 (4), 316–25.

2 Learning Development in Higher Education: Community of Practice or Profession?

Linda Murray and Bob Glass

► Summary

This chapter focuses on responses to two recent practitioner surveys about the provision of learning development (LD) in UK universities. We use these to examine the functions and roles of learning developers. We asked what learning developers do and what the future of learning development might be. The responses raise the question of whether 'community of practice' is the best description for this area of work, or whether learning development now represents a new profession within higher education.

► Introduction

We start from the fundamental question: what do learning developers do?

Our answers are based on two data sources: an online survey we conducted in 2009, and self-reported contributions to a database compiled by members of the JISCmail discussion list, LDHEN (Learning Development in Higher Education Network). We received 56 responses to our survey, representing 31 different UK universities. The LDHEN database provided information about a further 24 institutions. We do not claim that our data are fully representative of the sector, but they do provide information from a broad range of institutions, and helped shape our discussion of the following questions:

1 What services are provided by learning developers?
2 Should tutorials with students be the fundamental activity of LD?
3 Do learning developers cross the boundary between generic and discipline-based skills?
4 Do learning developers have a wider remit than working with students?
5 Is LD understood at an institutional level?
6 What are the typical organisational arrangements for LD?
7 What is the nature of employment in LD?
8 How is learning development perceived?
9 What are the typical learning developers' backgrounds and skills?
10 What is the role and purpose of a professional qualification in learning development?

▶ What services are provided by learning developers?

Workshops and one-to-one (1-2-1) tutorials are the most frequently mentioned. The least frequent is booklets and 1-2-1 support by telephone. The potential evolution of LD is indicated in the range of 'other' responses. Amongst those, the most common referred to uses of technology to provide online resources or 1-2-1 sessions; for instance, live chat (such as via Skype, social networks or instant messaging) and podcasts. These were generally portrayed as being at a trial stage.

We also asked about the relative use of provision by students. Overall, the greatest number of students use 1-2-1 face-to-face (F2F) tutorials, followed by workshops, booklets, one-page guides, resources on websites, resources on virtual learning environments (VLEs), group tutorials, 1-2-1 by email and 1-2-1 by telephone, in that order. More students are signing up for 1-2-1 F2F tutorials than for generic study skills workshops.

Although our focus has been on individual work, a great many learning development services are also involved in 'embedding' skills for learning by working with academics and teaching on university programmes. In this sense, as discussed in Chapter 1, the boundaries between LD and educational development remain somewhat blurred (Gosling, 1995).

▶ Should tutorials with students be the central activity of learning development?

1-2-1 tutorials are considered by many practitioners to be central to the work of learning development, although they may be seen as costly and labour-intensive. There is a widely held view that tutorials are inherently more beneficial to students than are workshops. Nonetheless, under the economic conditions facing higher education (HE) in the second decade of the twenty-first century, there will almost certainly be pressures to review resource allocation and the comparative value and cost of these forms of provision.

The importance ascribed to 1-2-1 work could be seen as demonstrating the person-centred values held by many in LD. The real cost-effectiveness of 1-2-1 tutorials and the fairness of any system that seeks to ration this particular resource are questions worthy of further investigation. Arguments for the increasing use of technology are seen in some quarters as a threat to this kind of work. Overall, however, these discussions are more helpfully seen in the light of a whole-institution approach to LD where a focus on learning is everyone's business, and resources for support are not seen as just for stand-alone learning development work. For examples of how these questions are being raised, see especially Chapters 8, 11 and 15 of this book.

▶ Do learning developers cross the boundary between generic and discipline-based skills?

All but one of the institutions in our survey provided some centrally-based advisory/tutoring staff. Of these, approximately one-third also had staff based in academic schools/faculties/departments. Many of our respondents referred to their 'sessions within modules', indicating that embedding of LD within academic programmes is a significant proportion of the work undertaken by learning developers. However, it is also reported that many academic staff seem reluctant to engage in the preparation and delivery of sessions on topics such as 'academic writing' or 'working in teams'. As a consequence, learning developers are often under pressure to provide such sessions alone, with the danger that students may see these as 'remedial' or optional extras. This effect can be reduced if the academic member of staff responsible for the module also attends. Collaborative approaches, where learning developers assist academic staff in preparing the sessions, are reported to work well.

▶ Do learning developers have a wider remit than work with students?

This related question concerns the extent to which LD should include work with academics and other university staff to focus on effective learning. Gibbs encapsulates the question as follows:

> The issue for 'LD' here is whether there are, already, clear signs of what might shift over time in terms of foci of attention and approaches to the whole endeavour. My guess is that, over time, efforts will have to change from working with individual students to working with teachers, courses, degree programmes and the whole institution, in ways that are aligned with other institutional efforts, as part of a broad strategy, and that these efforts will need to be well conceptualised and backed up with convincing empirical evidence of impact. (Gibbs, 2009)

The picture that emerges from our data is one of significant interaction between learning developers and discipline-based academic staff. Over 42% of the respondents had more than five individual one-to-one interactions with such staff per week. A further 23% had up to four interactions per week. Many of these (68%) were of a mostly 'formal' nature involving planning, systematic information exchange and so on. Almost half of the respondents have more than twenty such meetings per term, with a further 30% reporting between six and fifteen. The meetings that were regarded as most important were those with university learning and teaching committees, retention committees and academic writing groups.

The vast majority of such meetings (over 90%) were with academic staff (both formal and informal), followed by meetings with academic-related staff, heads of schools, deans and members of senior management teams. Interestingly over 50% of our respondents had been involved in meetings with senior staff. This indicates that learning developers are engaging with key groups and individuals in their institutions.

Most learning developers (managers aside) spend the majority of their time working directly with students. Whilst this is a critical role, ironically, it can also preclude other institutional interactions, for example, with academic staff or institutional committees. The issue here is a strategic and structural one. Unless institutions are prepared to value and resource LD units appropriately, the opportunities for improved and effective interactions with staff required to fulfil any wider remit will always be limited.

Many learning developers reported that, in their opinion, the logical 'home' of LD is in the institution's academic practice (or similar) unit. With regard to current arrangements, 31% (19 respondents) were already members of an academic practice unit (or the equivalent), and a further 47% had informal meetings with them.

One might expect that, if a broader remit for LD was generally accepted, this might be reflected in staff grades, titles of posts and other organisational arrangements. As Rust (2009) suggests, it would imply convergence of LD with academic practice and educational development activities, and the emergence of specialist LD roles in areas such as curriculum development. In our survey, there were only two instances of such convergence. Thus, it seems that, while learning developers are struggling to promote the institution-wide and developmental aspects of their role, there is much still to be done in this regard.

The 'bottom-up' development of ideas about LD and its community of practice need to be seen alongside the way the work has been funded. LD has often emerged from special initiatives and short-term funding associated with widening participation. For this reason, it is not surprising that there is separation between those in LD and those in other areas of 'support', as well as from educational developers. The result is that, within institutions, a network of more or less connected provision arises, with different groups of staff working with different groups of students. Thus, two-thirds of the respondents indicated that there were other central units providing LD in addition to their own. The most frequently identified 'other' units were ones responsible for supporting disabled and/or dyslexic students and ones providing specific support for the use of English (including support for international students). Of 22 respondents, two referred to units providing maths support and there were single references to the library, a computing service, counselling and 'student support officers employed in departments'. If LD is to develop from a community of practice into a more established profession, the need for recognised qualifications and specialisation will need to be addressed, as has already happened for those working with international students and those working with disabled students. More importantly, perhaps there is a need to address the questions raised by Rust (2009), mentioned above, to encourage joined-up approaches to learning development at the strategic level.

▶ Is learning development understood at an institutional level?

Many who consider themselves to be learning developers are not identified as such by the institutions in which they work. The name of the post varies hugely (35 of 37 respondents used the 'other' category). Some institutions and services still use terminology that betrays a narrower view than 'development', focusing on the need to impart specific skills to students. More optimistically, we found that 'support' was included in only four of the 37 post-names in our survey, suggesting a move away from an assumption of remediation. This is also suggested by the greater use of *learning* rather than *learner* development (Cash and Hilsdon, 2008).

We also looked at whether the names of posts assumed an academic or a non-academic approach to LD. For instance, the use of the term 'lecturer' or 'tutor' implies the former whereas 'adviser' suggests the latter. Within our 37 survey responses, 'advice' or 'adviser' formed part of the post-name in fourteen instances with 'tutor' or 'lecturer' being present less often – nine times. The relevance of this lies in its effect on how the field of LD is perceived in higher education institutions – a topic we return to later in this chapter.

▶ What are the typical organisational arrangements for learning development?

Our respondents described a range of situations, with varying models. Most learning developers are located in a central unit identified as 'providing services for students'. This typically reflects the grouping of all learner support services together. A respondent commented: 'it brings us together with other student facing support services', 'allows us to be a "one-stop shop" and includes colleagues in counselling, disability, dyslexia'. It is not always clear from the name alone which services are co-located in an organisational unit.

The other most commonly identified location is the library (with or without 'learning resources' or 'information services'). The reasons offered by learning developers for this location ranged from 'academic skills and information literacy perhaps', 'availability of space' and 'logical', to the more positive view that 'it helps reduce the stigma associated with the perceptions of students needing support. All students use the library (we hope) ...'. This raises the question of how LD is perceived, which we consider further below.

Organisational location of LD is varied and also subject to lack of stability. Our respondents referred to a host of recent changes. Restructuring and reorganisations were frequent. In some cases, respondents felt they could be more effective if located elsewhere. In a number of cases there was the sense that no identified LD service existed, although LD work was carried out by certain 'support' and academic staff. There are several examples of LD work being located in the counselling service, as LD activities were first developed by someone employed as a counsellor at the time of their inception. From this variety and change in organisational structures at institutional level, we can see that a learning development perspective has evolved to some extent as a 'bottom-up' phenomenon, with organisational arrangements very much dependent on local circumstances.

▶ What is the nature of employment in learning development?

LD services range widely in size – from two to more than six staff. Using the full-time equivalence of the staff team as a measure, the range included 'less than 1'. We were unable to investigate any relationships between the number of staff employed in LD and the policies, or the size, of the institutions. Our data does, however, indicate one aspect of staffing that merits consideration. A high level of dependence on the work of hourly-paid staff and staff on temporary contracts was acknowledged by approximately two-thirds of the respondents. This suggests that the need for an enduring LD function is not yet well established. Viewed positively, this also indicates the new and developing nature of LD, often deriving resources from successful project and research bids by committed professionals. Such flexibility allows for some development of practice to establish the effectiveness of LD. Where this is successful, more significant funding can be justified.

Nonetheless, where a service is reliant on staff employed on an hourly (and maybe term-time only) basis, there can be considerable stresses for all involved in maintaining effective working practices.

▶ How is learning development perceived?

Although LD services seem generally well established and comprise a wide but predictable range of facilities, there seems to be some way to go before a full awareness of what they actually do is reached outside of the learning development community itself. This is despite a considerable expansion in services over the past five years and specific efforts by many learning developers to promote themselves and their services within their institutions.

In relation to their colleagues, learning developers' opinions are divided as to whether knowledge by other staff in their institutions about their services is 'limited' or 'detailed and correct'. Clearly there is an awareness of learning developers and their activities; however, the extent and understanding varies greatly from institution to institution. There might well be many contributory factors to this, not least the historical and cultural backgrounds within individual universities. At the same time, there is no clear pattern or model in existence for the 'outsider' to use as a template or reference for expectations and knowledge of what to expect.

Our survey suggests that some groups are better informed than others about LD services and that the value placed on the services provided by these groups also varies. Learning developers believe that only around 20% of their colleagues have a 'comprehensive and accurate level of knowledge of their services', whilst around 70% had 'some knowledge'. Academic-related staff are the best informed (thirteen 'limited' and seven 'comprehensive'), with academics, middle and senior management staff a little way behind. Learning developers believe that administrative staff know least about the services available, a reasonable outcome given the limited extent of many of their day-to-day interactions with learning developers. Academics and academic-related staff appear to value the services most, with senior and middle management responses showing that services were valued 'by some but not others'. Three key 'errors and limitations' in knowledge were identified, namely that learning developers:

- provide only disability services;
- are proof readers;
- are mainly dyslexia tutors.

Thus, it seems that the 'support' rather than the 'development' approach is still widely assumed, reinforcing a limited view of the contribution that might be made by a comprehensive LD service. These misperceptions also indicate that we cannot yet assume that students will feel no sense of stigma in using the LD service.

Three key 'value drivers' to address these misperceptions were identified in our survey. Two of these were positive feedback from students to academic staff, and the effective promotion of the services and its successes by the LD Unit itself. It appears that learning developers believe that they and their activities are visible to an extent, but that this varies within different institutions and also in varying groups within them. The message is being broadcast but not everyone is interested in tuning in or able to receive it.

Some learning developers indicated that there are misunderstandings regarding their qualifications and abilities. They also believe there is a need for 'a professional approach using qualified practitioners'. Learning developers reported that they are seen by students as fulfilling some of the following roles: *teachers, proof readers, professionals, counsellors, support staff* and *academic-related staff*. The range of roles here suggests the complexity of students' expectations of an LD service.

Learning developers saw both themselves and other learning developers as: *professionals, specialists, teachers, experts, academics,* and as *academic-related support staff.* The recurrently selected descriptors: 'professional', 'teacher' and 'academic-related support staff' suggests a belief amongst respondents that their status is professional and educational, if not always squarely 'academic', although this varies considerably from institution to institution. Several of our respondents also suggest that their aspirations are not currently a reality. The type of employment contracts referred to in the previous section reinforces the fragility of the professional status of learning developers.

▶ What are the typical learning developers' backgrounds and skills?

There is currently no nationally established route into posts of learning developer in higher education (Cash and Hilsdon, 2008). Entering this field at the outset of a career is still rare. The backgrounds of learning developers are varied but usually involve educational or advisory work. Our respondents' experience included eight instances of work in a subject-based academic capacity in higher education and eight of teaching in FE/Access/Adult Literacy and pre tertiary settings. There were five reports of previous work in teaching English as a second language and/or other language teaching. Other work involved careers advice (2) and working in a library (including librarianship) (4). Finally, experience in publishing and as a laboratory technician was reported by two and one respondents respectively. Very few respondents indicated that they had only held one post prior to their current one.

Respondents did feel that their previous post(s) provided useful experience, knowledge and skills. Analysis of this experience does suggest quite specific skills and knowledge pertaining to the role of learning developer which may need to be addressed explicitly when filling, undertaking or developing such a position. According to our respondents, the skills most fundamental to the work of a learning developer are those of communication, teaching and assessment. Many varieties of communication were mentioned, including for instance, 'active' listening and 1-2-1 communication and interaction, as well as 'presenting'. Written communication was, in some cases, specified as that required for authoring resources rather than just those aspects of writing that might be considered the 'content' of a learning developer's work. Teaching skills were also listed – including running seminar groups, lecturing, and delivering workshops. Assessment was also identified as a skill and this probably refers to the ability to diagnose students' learning needs in a variety of settings.

With regard to knowledge, areas that were frequently mentioned were 'HE institutional practices' and 'learning and teaching theory'. Knowledge of access issues and equality legislation and about accessible resources were also listed, often in relation to activities of specialist posts.

▶ What is the role and purpose of a professional qualification in learning development?

Virtually all our respondents felt a postgraduate professional qualification would be useful to the sector, although the strength of this opinion varied with the level of experience. There were also some concerns – that such a course would need to be rigorous and that there was a 'lack of nationally agreed models of good practice'. On the other hand, another comment expressed a fear of 'reducing creativity and real interaction with learners in order to follow certain regimented patterns'. Another concern was that a pre-entry qualification could prove to be a barrier to entry for people who did have relevant experience and skills acquired through related employment and education. The overall preference was for an in-practice arrangement akin to that currently in place for discipline-based staff in HE. At the time of writing, the Association for Learning Development in Higher Education (ALDinHE) is engaged in discussions about the development of opportunities for continuous professional developments (CPD) that are designed to contribute to relevant professional development programmes.

▶ Conclusions

Gibbs (2009) makes the point that LD needs to engage with other 'enhancement' activities in higher education – particularly with curriculum or educational development. Learning developers themselves see these areas as key to interactions within their institutions, but it appears that LD practitioners' views about themselves, and the value of their potential contribution to student learning, do not match those of HE institutions' management, as illustrated in the 'perceptual errors' identified in our survey. That learning developers are highly valued by colleagues who know them and work closely with them in their institutions is beyond question. Our survey suggests, however, that there is still much potential for greater levels of collaboration between learning developers and academics.

We have found that the majority of learning developers are experienced in working at a number of levels in their institutions, and realise the extent and limitations of their institutional environment. As a group, learning developers demonstrate that they take opportunities to develop their services and status within HE institutions wherever possible. Evidence from both of the surveys suggests that this is more likely to find success if supportive structures and funding exist. The evolution of the learning developers' community of practice into a more formally identified profession with, for example, nationally agreed and recognised qualifications, would be the most effective way to build on the success of this work so far.

▶ References

Cash, C. and Hilsdon, J. (2008) *Buried Treasures in a Virtual Community Chest,* Society for Research into Higher Education Annual Conference. Available at: www.srhe.ac.uk/conference2008/papers/0292-John-Hilsdon_Caroline-Cash.doc (last accessed 29/3/10).

Gibbs, G. (2009) 'Developing students as learners – varied phenomena, varied contexts and a developmental trajectory for the whole endeavour', *Journal of Learning Development in Higher Education* 1.

Gosling, D. (1995) *On course: Academic Guidance and Learning Development* (London: Educational Development Services, University of East London).

Rust, C. (2009) 'A Call to Unite in a Common Cause', *Journal of Learning Development in Higher Education* 1, January 2009. Available at: www.aldinhe.ac.uk/ojs/index.php?journal=jldhe (last accessed 29/3/10).

3 Is Learning Development 'Part of the Problem'?

Ann Barlow, John Acroyd and Alyssa Phillips

The writers also wish to acknowledge Combined Studies students at the University of Manchester for their contribution to the authorship of the chapter.

▶ Summary

As learning developers seek to respond to a variety of needs within the current culture of higher education, it can be difficult to maintain a balance between work which aims to develop skills for independent learning and work which meets some of the quality-driven demands of the institution. We argue that engaging in reflective practice can develop our confidence to achieve this balance.

Given that many students have a complex view of the university's role in their personal and professional development, we need to question the nature of our responsibilities and functions as learning developers. This chapter explores some of the philosophical, historical and institutional approaches which have influenced the development of 'the university'. These ideas may form tacit frames which influence ideas and practice. Bringing these factors into conscious awareness will help us in our work to promote self-directed learning within the perceived constraints of requirements such as criterion-referenced assessment.

▶ Introduction

How much individual responsibility should university staff require students to take for their own learning?

We have been exploring this question at the University of Manchester for the past five years, looking at resources and frameworks to support self-directed/independent learning for undergraduate and postgraduate students. We are engaged in research with practitioners (tutors, lecturers, programme directors and learning developers) and students, centred on the identification of resources and practices which enable the development of self-directed learning within the university environment. Through our research and our own practices, we often emphasise the necessity for students to be self-directed learners, and at the same time provide extensive learning development resources to support students in achieving such a state. As practitioners, we often find ourselves performing an uneasy balancing act of providing support for students to meet the requirements of the university's assessment mechanisms, while at the same time encouraging them to be self-directed in their own learning.

Achieving balance in our working practices is becoming more problematic in today's fee- and results-driven universities. Fee-paying parents expect a return for their money in terms of a sound qualification, senior management at universities desire excellent results from the National Student Survey, while employers wish to be satisfied that new graduate recruits are appropriately skilled for meeting the demands of the twenty-first-century workplace. In this environment, there is a risk of learning development being seen as primarily results-driven with a focus on ensuring that students acquire a high-classified degree, and that institutions will be ranked high in student satisfaction and employment tables.

Learning development provides an important service to students and institutions. In addition, learning development can provide an important vehicle for focusing attention on the purposes and practices of student learning. In this chapter, we encourage staff working in learning development to reflect on their role in fostering particular approaches to student learning in their own institutions. Central to this discussion is the consideration of what 'kind' of student learning should be fostered by learning developers: how does this fit with the purposes and realities of the modern university?

One particular challenge facing staff working in learning development is the current prevalence of what is known as 'criterion-referenced assessment', whereby students are increasingly being required to demonstrate that they have met a lengthy series of assessment criteria. This form of assessment raises questions about the kind of learning encouraged. Without a clear understanding of our approaches to learning, there are dangers that learning development will be seen as simply remedial within institutions – a way to ensure students meet criteria, rather than an opportunity for them to develop and foster self-directed approaches to learning.

This chapter also aims to encourage staff working in learning development to reflect on their own practices and, in particular, their own philosophical, historical and institutional reference points for their understandings of approaches to student learning. We have found that, to meet the challenges of criterion-referenced assessment, we need continually to focus our attention on recognising how we frame our own experiences and assumptions of student learning.

▶ Self-directed learning and the reflective practitioner

Self-directed learning places learner autonomy at the centre of the learning experience, and requires staff and students to foster a lifelong approach to learning where students take responsibility for their own learning outcomes. This chapter assumes that staff in learning development *should* encourage an environment of self-directed student learning. For example, the *Learning Guide* at the University of Manchester emphasises three aspects of self-directed learning: that

> independent learners are motivated to learn ... are capable of managing the learning processes effectively ... [and] are able to monitor and reflect critically on how and what they learn. (Wyburd, 2006)

Self-directed learning is not a new concept but lacks an accepted definition (Broad, 2006, p. 119). Various terms describe the process of learners taking responsibility for their own learning, including 'autonomous learning', 'self-directed learning' and 'independent study' (Broad, 2006, p. 119; Wyburd, 2006; and Boud, 1988, p. 17). Self-directed learning is an important aspect of the university experience, with most institutional teaching and learning strategies recognising this approach to student learning. The Dearing Report (1997) also recognised the need for planning more effective support for students, given that they are spending increasing time in independent study (Section 8.13).

Our own practices encourage students to engage with reflective practice (Boud, 1988). For example, in developing frameworks to support first-year students in community placements, we were influenced by

David Kolb's (1984, p. 38) concept of 'experiential learning' and the four-stages cycle of concrete experience. Yet, how reflective are we about our own assumptions towards learning?

Donald Schön advocates reflective practices in order to understand approaches to particular situations. By reflecting upon his or her reaction to a situation, the practitioner engages in continuing professional development. One particular aspect of reflective practice identified by Schön is that of frame analysis. To resolve a problem, the practitioner needs to *frame* that problem using recognised professional expertise. To do this, the practitioner needs to become aware of the *tacit frames* in use. Schön (1983, p. 310) notes that 'when a professional becomes aware of his [*sic*] frame, he also becomes aware of the possibility of alternative ways of framing his practice'.

The difficulty in framing experience, for learning development, is its hybrid nature – it can draw on the practices of several different occupations such as teaching and learning, counselling and librarianship. Our own backgrounds are varied: a philosopher, an historian, and an educator, all engaged in learning development activities. That said, we found common frames of reference for understanding student learning. This became a reference point for our frame analysis: taking us on a journey into the philosophical, historical and institutional assumptions we make about student learning that influence our own practices in encouraging self-directed learning. These philosophical, historical and institutional frames, in particular the rational and the empirical-inductive approaches to learning, provide us with deeper understandings of our practices, and thus a stronger foundation from which to face the challenges present in the modern university.

By adopting a reflective analysis for the learning development profession, practitioners have a theoretical basis from which to encourage a deeper approach to learning, and hopefully avoid the problem of supporting institutions and students purely to 'pass the exam'.

▶ The purposes of a university

Determining this is not an easy task. For example, Matthew Reisz (2008) identifies considerable diversity in what may be expected from university education across the higher education sector in Britain, arguing that this diversity: 'reflects varied histories and public policies that pull in several directions'. Our university mission statements, and visions of their purpose, inform our role in fostering particular approaches to student learning. A number of university mission statements focus on one or all of the following: regional development, encouraging widening participation, engagement of business and employers, and excellence in teaching and learning.

Students are at the centre of the service provided by learning developers. They have provided us with further insights. A group of 100 first-year Combined Studies students were set an online task: *Discuss the origins, purpose and value of a university.*

Three prominent themes emerged. Firstly, there was overwhelming agreement among these students about the financial and employment rewards of a good degree. The majority of postings talked of improving employment prospects:

> For me the primary purpose of coming to university is to gain a degree and ultimately obtain a better job than I could have acquired without further education. I appreciate that there are many other benefits of university, such as gaining independence and furthering your knowledge of a subject you are interested in, but for me these would fall under the 'values' of university category, as these alone would not be enough to tempt most students today to come to university. (Student 1, 2009)

These comments might suggest that students are 'results-driven'. Yet a significant number also emphasised the primary importance of advancing their knowledge of their subjects. One student expressed this as valuing:

> ... an environment where ideas and theories can be shared and cultivated. Both with respects to the discipline the student follows and on a wider socio/political scale. It [the university] does this by introducing the socio/political world to many new, fresh minds in a setting where pro-active behaviour is encouraged. (Student 2, 2009)

Interestingly, both perspectives make some reference to independence and pro-active behaviour, recognising a need for autonomy in study.

The third theme directly links to this notion of learner autonomy. Students discussed the importance of their personal development at university:

> I also believe that university enables students to unlock their full poten-

tial, therefore I agree with ... and ... not only does University provide education but it also enables people to enhance inter-personal skills, such as independence, organisation, and to quote ... 'confidence' (Student 3, 2009)

We also found significant agreement amongst the students as to their perceptions of the purposes and origins of a university. The majority made some reference to the importance of the historical and philosophical foundations. For example, students referred to the medieval universities that emerged out of schools funded by the church, and also the universities of the nineteenth century set up to educate professionals in the new industries created during the industrial revolution. Of most interest for this discussion is the value that this group of students placed on historical foundations:

> I really like the idea of being in a university that has had a lot of students throughout so many years, because even though they were here in the 19th or in the 20th century, they came for the same reason as me: to study and develop their potential, in a place that offered them all they needed to do it. Everything changes with time, but I love the fact that I am sharing something with people who were here a long time ago. (Student 4, 2009)

This group not only knew about the foundations of university education; some also viewed these philosophical and historical foundations as in some way shaping their own approaches to their degree. This is similar to the way our own approaches to learning are framed.

▶ Fundamental approaches to learning in the history of 'the university'

In Britain, the earlier universities of Oxford (recognised in 1167) and Cambridge (1209), together with some Scottish universities established in the fifteenth and sixteenth centuries, were monastic in origin, essentially establishments which promoted learning through discourse, debate and discussion, much along the lines of the ancient Greek philosophers. These universities tended to emphasise the pursuit of knowledge, learning and research for its own sake (Reize, 2008). Critical thinking, along the lines of that of the ancient Greek philosophers, was often the established approach to learning.

Though the process of 'critical thinking' is notoriously resistant to precise definition, it is not in question that this kind of intellectual activity should be embedded in all approaches to student learning. Most learning developers are familiar with the confused look of the undergraduate student who has been told by their lecturer that they needed to be 'more critical' in their essay. If we trace the origins of this intellectual tradition we find ourselves in ancient Athens, considering the ideas originated by Socrates, and perpetuated and developed in recorded form by his student Plato.

For Socrates, truth was elusive, and any proposition claiming the status of it must be subjected to rigorous and relentless questioning to reveal the falsity of that claim; hence his admission that he was ignorant, that he had nothing to teach. This was critical thinking and learning at its most epistemologically barren, its most courageous.

Plato's chief concern was morality or ethics – that we could know ethical truths as certainly as we knew mathematical truths. For Plato, the means of arriving at such truths, at all truth, was 'dialectic', or critical thinking in the form of an interrogative dialogue, with oneself or another. Both Socrates and Plato conceived of knowledge or truth as internal, abstract, the object of purely intellectual inquiry. Indeed, the road to truth was that which led away from the world of sensory perception, into the intelligible realm of the mind (Cornford, 1962, p. 74). Learning was, for them, a looking within. The emphasis here was on the close relationship between the teacher and the student, the critical dialogue they engaged with and the intellectual knowledge that could be revealed from within the student through questioning. There is a degree of autonomy for the learner here in searching for the truths within.

Plato's student Aristotle, the third of the great ancient Greek philosophers, believed that the chief object of philosophical inquiry was not the inner world, but instead the empirical world of concrete facts, reality as seen, heard and felt. Although he observed the contents of the natural world systematically, his prime means of arriving at conclusions remained rational analysis through questioning and inquiry.

This reliance on intellectual contemplation was rejected by later figures such as the sixteenth century British philosopher Francis Bacon (Bacon, 2000). He argued that reason must be placed after, not before, the facts, and proceed by inductive inference from them. The proper exercise of reason in scientific inquiry involved extrapolation from accumulated empirical data to generalised conclusions, rather than the spinning of metaphysical webs into which the facts must be fitted

('Rationalists, like spiders, spin webs from themselves'; Bacon, 2000, p. 79). At around the same time, the need for practical experimentation over theoretical speculation was also emphasised by the Italian astronomer and physicist Galileo (Becker, 1959, pp. 20–1).

So, and very broadly speaking, the Western intellectual tradition has bequeathed to us two conceptions of knowledge or truth, and two methods of attaining it – the purely rational, and the empirical-inductive.

The Enlightenment of the eighteenth century had a profound influence on British universities, with empiricist assumptions, influencing the learning encouraged, alongside the older rationalist tradition. Learning in British universities became more formalised. This was reflected in the introduction of lectures, although there was a continued emphasis on the relationship between the student and teacher (Perkins, 1972). Even if students were bent on taking up places in elite professions outside of the university, subject matter still included the teaching of logic and rhetoric, ensuring the survival of the older rationalist tradition. This rationalist approach to learning was emphasised by Isaac Watts (1798, 'The Improvement of Mind, or a Supplement to the Art of Logic'). This text bears a remarkable resemblance to current study skills manuals in terms of its anticipated audience. Watts noted in his introduction. 'I have endeavoured to eschew the mistakes we are exposed to in our conception, judgement and reasoning ... I have also laid down many general and particular rules how to escape error and attain truth.' He also asserts that, 'if the ... scholar and the gentleman would but transcribe such rules into their understanding; and practice them upon all occasions, there would be much more truth and knowledge to be found among men ...' (Watts, 1798, p. 3).

During this period, there was also increasing emphasis on the university as a place of teaching, as opposed to being purely a protector/defender of knowledge: 'a University ... is a place of **teaching** universal **knowledge**' (Newman, 1982).

The latter half of the nineteenth century saw real change in the definition of the purpose of the university, as well as the expansion of university education. The development of a national system of education led to increased demand for higher education opportunities, particularly in industrial areas of the country. But longstanding universities were not prepared to engage with the potential for research that was emerging through the industrial revolution (McNay, 2005).

It was becoming clear that, in England, the four universities of

Oxford, Cambridge, London and Durham were too conservative or hidebound by restrictive statutes to respond readily to modern circumstances. (Robertson and Lees, 2007, p. 10)

As the goal of educating members of the professions became more prevalent, universities became the vehicles for delivering elite professional knowledge while at the same time establishing that the individual was well-versed in the required knowledge. The latter, of course, is achieved by means of rigorous assessment, and this increasingly came to involve formal frameworks such as criterion-referenced assessment. However, universities continued to embed the philosophical approaches to critical thinking and learning discussed earlier.

The changing role of the university in Britain was illustrated in the 'Two Cultures' exchange (1959–62) between F. R. Leavis and C. P. Snow (Strohl, 2006, p. 134). Snow argued that an urgent problem in higher education was the breakdown of meaningful communication between the cultures of the humanities and the sciences. This breakdown in communication was preventing progressive change as neither group alone was able to respond adequately to world problems such as poverty. Leavis (1962) responded with a particular view of the modern university – his 'liberal humanist' notion of higher education that:

> at its most basic level is a belief in the value of knowledge without immediate application; in other words it is a faith in the intrinsic value of a university education to produce reflective, responsible citizens free from political, military, bureaucratic or market demands in a modern industrial society. (Strohl, 2006, p. 134)

These arguments about the role of the university are still debated by students today. In recent years, we have seen the mass expansion of higher education, underpinned by the UK government's emphasis on the importance of higher education to provide skills for the 'knowledge economy' (BIS, 2009). Specialism of knowledge has replaced Newman's unifying ideal of education. Specific frameworks for criterion-referenced assessment, including 'key skills', are in common use, with the aim of ensuring that graduates are equipped for the challenges of the modern economy.

► The challenge of criterion-referenced assessment for learning developers

There are clear potential benefits to teacher and student of approaches emphasising learning outcomes and criterion-referenced assessment. The formulation of pre-specified learning outcomes encourages clarity of pedagogic purpose, and provides a general framework for the coherent delivery of a course. Criterion-referencing indicates to the student precisely what he or she is required to do, and tends to produce a high level of what is known as 'validity' in assessment – that is, it provides students with the opportunity to demonstrate, clearly and specifically, that they have learnt what they can reasonably be expected to have learnt during a course; and provides teachers with the opportunity to assess students' knowledge and understanding of the curriculum as delivered (Brown and Knight, 1994, p. 17).

Perhaps more important is that, as higher education becomes less the preserve of the few and more a process for equipping increasing numbers of the population for vocational roles in a society, criterion-referenced assessment seems an effective means of ensuring that the highly specific knowledge, understanding and skills required by sophisticated workforces are being developed, as well as the equally vital generic or transferable skills called for by Dearing (1996, 1997).

According to the former Secretary of State for the Department of Universities, Innovations and Skills, John Denham (2008), universities have an important role in developing one in particular of these key skills: the ability to think critically. However, there is the potential for conflict between criticality and forms of assessment where too much prescription may discourage a questioning approach. Our concern is to avoid assessment becoming an overly formulaic exercise in meeting a series of rigidly defined expectations.

Similarly, as we have argued above, there is a potential danger for learning developers in supporting students to meet such assessment requirements. Without the breadth of perspective afforded by a reflective and philosophical framework, learning developers, and learning development provision, may adopt a purely instrumental role. If the goal is simply to ensure that students meet pre-specified learning outcomes and pass the exam, a key dimension of learning development may be overlooked: that of preparing students for independence and the achievement of their full potential through lifelong learning.

▶ Conclusion

There is an onus on universities to create new knowledge and, as Dearing (1997) expressed it, to 'sustain a culture which demands disciplined thinking, encourages curiosity, challenges existing ideas and generates new ones'. If learning developers are to subscribe to the latter approach, there has to be careful management of the response to the student whose main concern is 'passing the exam'. Both staff and student may be tempted to identify the means of meeting the necessary criteria and to lose sight of the wider and more abstract goal of university education and self-directed learning.

By developing an understanding of the philosophical and historical foundations of higher education, together with a critical engagement with the current institutional structures within which we work as learning developers, we are more able to recognise the tacit frames which underpin our responses to student learning. In consequence, we will enhance our capacity to be reflective practitioners and become more able to rise to the challenges facing learning developers in the rapidly changing higher education culture of the twenty-first century.

▶ Further Sources

Further information about our research and implementation of frameworks for self-directed learning can be accessed at:
www.learnhigher.ac.uk/learningareas/independentlearning/home.htm

A resource pack detailing the frameworks used for community placements can be found at:
www.learnhigher.ac.uk/learningareas/independentlearning/resourcepage.htm

University of Manchester strategic documents referred to can be viewed at:
www.manchester.ac.uk/aboutus/facts/vision
and www.humanities.manchester.ac.uk/tandl/resources/strategydocs/

All URLs last accessed 29/3/10.

▶ References

Bacon, F. (2000) *The New Organon*, ed. Lisa Jardine and Michael Silverthorne (Cambridge: Cambridge University Press).

Becker, C. L. (1932 and 1959) *The Heavenly City of the Eighteenth-Century Philosophers* (New Haven and London: Yale University Press; issued as a Yale Paperback in 1959)

BIS (2009) *Higher Ambitions* (London: Department of Business, Innovation and Skills).

Boud, D. (ed.) (1988) *Developing Student Autonomy in Learning* (London and New York: Kogan Page Nichols).

Broad J. (2006) 'Interpretations of independent learning in further education', *Journal of Further and Higher Education* 30 (2), 119–43.

Brown, S. and Knight, P. (1994) *Assessing Learners in Higher Education* (London: Kogan Page).

Cornford, F. M. (1962) *Before and After Socrates* (Cambridge: Cambridge University Press).

Dearing, R. (1996) *Review of Qualifications for 16-19 Year Olds* (London: HMSO for the Central Office of Information).

Dearing, R. (1997) *Higher Education in the Learning Society,* Report of the National Committee of Inquiry into Higher Education (London: HMSO for the Central Office of Information).

Denham, J. (2008) *Investing in Our Future.* Speech given 29 February 2008. Summary available at: www.publications.parliament.uk/pa/cm200809/cmselect/cmdius/170/17004.htm (last accessed 29/3/10).

Denman, B. D. (2005) 'What is a University in the 21st century?', *Higher Education Management and Policy* 17 (2), 9–28.

Freidson, E. (1994) *Professionalism Reborn: Theory, Prophecy, and Policy* (Cambridge: Polity Press).

Kolb, D. (1984) *Experiential Learning: Experience as the Source of Learning and Development* (Englewood Cliffs, NJ: Prentice Hall).

Leavis, F. R. (1962) *Two Cultures? The Significance of C. P. Snow* (London: Chatto & Windus).

Lock, J. (1964) *An Essay Concerning Human Understanding*, abridged and edited with an introduction by A. D. Woozley (London: Collins).

McNay, I. (2005) 'Higher education communities: divided they fail?' *Perspectives: Policy and Practice in Higher Education* 9 (2), 39–44.

Newman, J. H. (1982) *The Idea of a University*, new edition, ed. Martin J. Svaglic (Notre Dame, IN: University of Notre Dame Press).

Perkin, H. (1984) 'The historical perspective', in B. R. Clarke (ed.) *Perspectives on Higher Education: Eight Disciplinary and Comparative Views* (Berkeley: University of California Press).

Perkins, J. A. (1972) 'Organization and functions of the University', *Journal of Higher Education* 43 (9), 679–91

Plato (1956) *Protagoras and Meno,* translated by W. K. C. Guthrie (Harmondsworth: Penguin Books).

Reisz, M. (2008) 'Diversity Challenge', *The Times Higher Education*, 17 January 2008. Available at: www.timeshighereducation.co.uk/story.asp?sectioncode= 26andstorycode=400160 (last accessed 27/3/10).

Robertson, A. B. and Lees, C. (2007) 'Owens College and the Victoria University, 1851–1903' and 'The Victoria University of Manchester 1903–39', in Brian Pullan (ed.) *A Portrait of the University of Manchester* (London: Third Millennium).

Schön, D. A. (1983) *The Reflective Practitioner: How Professionals Think in Action* (London: Temple Smith).

Strohl, Nicholas M. (2006) 'The postmodern university revisited: reframing higher education debates from the "two cultures" to postmodernity', *London Review of Education* 4 (2), 133–48.

Watts, I. D. (1798) *The Improvement of Mind or a Supplement to the Art of Logic in Two Parts*.

Welch, A. R. (1997) 'The peripatetic professor: the internationalization of the academic profession', *Higher Education* 34, 323–45.

Wyburd, J. (2006) *University Language Centre, The Learning Guide.* Available at: www.learnhigher.ac.uk/learningareas/independentlearning/backgroundandbriefings.htm (last accessed 29/03/10).

4 Raising the Student Voice: Learning Development as Socio-political Practice

Sandra Sinfield, Debbie Holley, Tom Burns, Kate Hoskins, Peter O'Neill and Katherine Harrington

▶ Summary

This chapter examines learning development, not as a department or a unit simply designed to fix ailing students, but as an ethos, embodied in emancipatory practice and designed to create positive spaces for students within higher education situations, which can exclude many students. We show how three Centres for Excellence in Teaching and Learning worked together to support the student voice and action in ways which have now become embedded in our institutional practice. Among the examples which lend themselves to replication elsewhere is the experience of our annual student conference, led by students, for students.

▶ Introduction

In this chapter, we explore how we have created a sharing academic community with a learning development ethos. We focus on the efforts of one post-1992 institution where the Learning Development Centre and three Centres for Excellence in Teaching and Learning (CETLs) worked with students to create emancipatory spaces and creative resources. Our proposition is that learning development should not be a department in isolation designed to 'fix' ailing students, but should be embodied in practice that puts the students at the centre of the work

– such that they 'reach their own accommodation with discourses of belonging, identity and power' (Medhurst, in Munt, 2000, p. 11, quoted in Burns and Sinfield, 2004, p. 31).

Drawing on Foucault's understanding of discourse and power and Bourdieu's concept of habitus, we argue that traditional academic discourses of knowledge and truth remain hostile and alien to non-traditional students and that certain knowledge is *not* the 'value-free, decontextualised, neutral and apolitical' construct it is thought to be (Morrice, 2009, p. 8). And, as Leathwood and Read (2009, p. 146) have pointed out, having high numbers of non-traditional students in universities is 'not sufficient to enable them to feel like they "belong"'. It is in this charged and contested atmosphere that learning development is situated – and should itself be contested.

▶ Learning development: emancipatory practice and its socio-political context

The move to widen participation in higher education (HE) has been accompanied by a dwindling unit of resource and the introduction of student tuition fees and student loans (Bennett, 2002). However, rather than acknowledge the struggles faced by non-traditional students (Leathwood and O'Connell, 2003), debate tends to focus on the 'crisis in education' (Lillis, 2001) and the lowering of standards. Many now argue that New Labour's drive to increase participation in some form of higher education contributed to the creation of a two-tier system, where non-traditional students predominantly populated vocationally orientated courses at post-1992 universities (Thomas, 2001). Indeed, according to a speech in the House of Lords, 'There are Mickey Mouse students for whom Mickey Mouse degrees are quite appropriate' (Starkey, 2003). At this time of widening participation, non-traditional students may find themselves occupying a dichotomous position: needed in HE to meet government targets – but still not wanted by 'the academy'.

Learning development itself occupies a similarly dichotomous position in the academy – needed to boost retention figures, but still seen as a remedial backwater … Whilst, typically, learning development practitioners work 'for' and with the student to de-mystify alien academic forms and processes, this is contested and contentious terrain. As Morrice (2009, p. 9) points out, 'there are multiple literacies and what counts as literacy varies depending on context, culture, cultural group and social class'. Literacies can be seen as 'rooted in conceptions of knowledge, identity and being' (Morrice, 2009, p. 9), and learning development in practice does not reduce or regulate students' access to myriad forms of knowledge, but rather, reminds students that:

> knowledge emerges only through invention and re-inventions, through the restless, impatient, continuing, hopeful inquiry human beings pursue in the world, with the world, and with each other. (Freire, 1996, p. 53)

As such, we argue for learning development to be allowed to be understood as a set of socio-political or emancipatory practices designed to empower students, from a range of diverse contexts, for 'action' (Freire, 1977). And what we have created are spaces in which that action can take place, for:

> Literacy is primarily something people do; it is an activity, located in the space between thought and text. Literacy does not just reside in people's heads as a set of skills to be learned, and it does not just reside on paper, captured as texts to be analysed. Like all human activity, literacy is essentially social, and it is located in the interaction between people. (Barton and Hamilton, 1998, p. 3, cited by Lisa Clughen at the LDHEN Symposium, April 2009)

▶ Creating spaces for emancipatory practice: the role of the CETLs

What we have attempted in our university is to create spaces for powerful action by our students, facilitated by our Learning Development Unit (LDU) and variously and together our three CETLS: LearnHigher, Write Now and RLO (Re-usable Learning Objects).

As described in the Introduction to this book, LearnHigher developed resources and engaged in practice-led research to inform the effective development and use of learning resources. The Write Now CETL aimed to enrich student learning and writing through a variety of evidence-based pedagogical initiatives. Write Now was a collaboration between London Metropolitan, Liverpool Hope and Aston Universities. At London Metropolitan, one of the major initiatives of Write Now was the new Writing Centre, which continues to work with academic staff across the university on 'Writing in the Disciplines' initiatives and runs a peer mentoring in academic writing programme for students. The overarching concept of the RLO-CETL was to develop a learning resource community where lecturers and learning facilitators could reuse and repurpose learning objects. A strength of RLO was its collegiality where the learner-centred design, implementation, embedding, evaluation and reuse of high-quality multimedia RLOs were important goals (Boyle, 2008). The Learning Development Unit (LDU) at London Metropolitan University works with staff and students across the university, producing resources, courses, drop-in advice clinics and activities embedded within discipline teaching to support both staff teaching and student learning – the LearnHigher connection at our university sprang from our LDU.

▶ Student spaces – student voices

At our institution, LearnHigher utilised capital funding to create high-quality social learning and workshop spaces and a dedicated teaching and learning room for student teaching and staff development. We worked with students and recent graduates of our own multimedia programmes to produce our interactive resources (see also Chapter 15 where our Desk, NoteMaker, and Preventing Plagiarism resources are discussed in more detail). The LDU website for staff and students was re-designed by the multimedia graduate who also built the Learn-Higher space in Second Life (look near the London Metropolitan University islands) – with elements designed by our Computing students.

LearnHigher at London Metropolitan engaged students in real and meaningful ways. We worked with our students in our research projects: our Literature Reviews on Notemaking and Academic Reading were produced by one of our students, the latter as an interactive wiki accompanied by a reflective blog (inspired by Write Now's Evolving Essay project). The use of virtual and collegiate academic spaces, the reflexive wiki (http://litreview.pbworks.com/) and open forum blog (http://onlinelitreview.blogspot.com/) enabled the student writer to engage the wider academic community in a range of questions about the decisions that need to be taken when undertaking such a review, for example, breaking down the topic into specific research areas, deciding on the scope of the topic and on the range of literature that must be read (thus academic reading *per se* was explored, as were the educational policies that might have had a tangential impact on student reading in HE). Nearer the end of the writing process, decisions were made about the logical sequencing of arguments. Rather than offering a model review, or even a series of models, a real literature review was constructed in real time. Participating academics and students raised interesting questions and collegiate dialogue was demonstrated alongside the writing process. The reflective blog revealed the thoughts and feelings of someone engaged in the process of writing a literature review – the frustrations and struggles alongside those moments of epiphany or insight … and all were easily available and echoed academic realities for the majority.

▶ Write Now

Rather than duplicating existing provision, the Write Now CETL (www.writenow.ac.uk) decided that its major student-facing service at the University Writing Centre would be a peer mentoring in academic writing programme for students. Given our high proportion of non-traditional and international students, and those with English as an additional language, we anticipated that this would be an interesting context in which to assess the effectiveness of peer tutorials in UK higher education. Over the first three years of the scheme, we held 2,300 one-to-one hour-long tutorials, open to all students (undergraduate and postgraduate). At the time of writing, we are engaged in ongoing research into the effectiveness of the scheme, drawing on student and mentor feedback, and, more recently, also audio recordings of actual tutorials, in addition to an ambitious quantitative study of the relationship between tutorial participation and student achievement.

Writing Centre tutorials are non-directive and collaborative in nature, as students are encouraged to grapple with the issues that are truly vexing – or exciting – them. Andrea Lunsford has offered a careful interrogation of what we might mean by collaboration in a Writing Centre context (1991). She points out that studies are unanimous in their demonstration that collaboration tends to be associated with excellence and she maintains that practitioners should insist on real collaboration as opposed to surface collaboration, and that they must not shirk the radical challenges that this might pose (1991, p. 9). For collaboration to be real rather than surface, we argue that there must surely be an attempt to reduce as far as possible the hierarchies inherent in the traditional university, and the peer relationship of

Writing Centre tutorials aims to do just that. Collaboration often helps less confident students to cut through questions, theories and doubts and enables them to actually *do* something and to make progress. Perhaps contrary to the expectations of the more cynical, students do not in fact seem to want others to do their work for them, and an effective tutorial, rather than taking ownership away from students, empowers them. Unlike traditional transmissive teaching, peer tutoring offers an opportunity for the student's ideas and voice to take centre stage, and most students seem to welcome this and understand its benefits.

This collaborative ethos extends beyond the Writing Centre tutorials. Writing Mentors are given numerous other responsibilities and have been involved in CETL research, conference presentations (including the CETL *Get Ahead* conference discussed below) and publications. For example, Lynn Reynolds, a Psychology undergraduate, carried out 'The Evolving Essay Project'. Frustrated with being given model essays, she wanted to create her own model essay which would reveal rather than conceal the writing process that lay behind it. Her wiki and blog, which received attention from all over the world, can be found at http://evolvingessay.pbworks.com and she published her account of this project in a chapter co-authored with Write Now staff in a volume on staff–student partnerships in higher education (Harrington et al., 2010). Similarly, Sara Canizzaro, another Writing Mentor, went to the University of Goettingen in Germany where she taught two workshops as part of a research collaboration on the experience of students writing in two language traditions in an era of internationalisation in higher education. This was followed up by online tutorials in which London Metropolitan student Writing Mentors carried out internet writing tutorials with Goettingen students. We hope that we have created an environment where non-hierarchical collaboration is the norm rather than the exception.

▶ Reusable Learning Objects

The RLO-CETL (www.rlo-cetl.ac.uk) awarded student bursaries throughout the five years of the CETL. This enabled students to work with us on the initial and ongoing design process. The outcome of this initiative has been very positive, in that this policy has facilitated successful dissemination of our output, making our learning objects accessible for students. Involving a wider team does require a heavier time investment, for it tends to take longer to consult about project processes and procedures; however, this is far outweighed by the quality of materials.

One issue identified through our evaluation was that of freeing the student voice, and enabling our student ambassadors to speak confidently and clearly to articulate their viewpoint. Rowland (2000) discusses the concept of an 'ideal speech community' where a learner cannot be empowered until conditions are created in which each is free to communicate sincerely and honestly, undistorted by the influences of power. Tenni et al. (2003, p. 5), talking about the researcher as autobiographer, suggest that a willingness 'to see, confront and discover oneself in one's practice and to learn from this is at the core of this work and central to the creation of good data'. This proved to be excellent advice, as two student ambassadors, working with the RLO-CETL, were extremely vocal and critical about the role of the tutors on the project.

The resulting student work speaks for itself – the first three learning objects to be designed by the team were 'referencing a book', 'referencing a journal' and 'referencing a website' (all three can be found within LearnHigher's Preventing Plagiarism course: http://learning.londonmet.ac.uk/TLTC/learnhigher/Plagiarism/ – also see Chapter 15 of this book). Each of these was created under a creative commons licence, enabling free use, reuse and repurposing within the academic community. These learning objects have been strategically used and rolled out across the whole of our Business School, to over 5,000 first year students within the first three years (Bradley and Boyle, 2004).

▶ *Get Ahead*: promoting student success with a conference by and for students

One of our most ambitious collaborations was the conference for and mainly by students: *Get Ahead: achieving success at university* (http://www.youtube.com/user/adm111#p/u). This is now an annual event and is designed to bring students from diverse backgrounds together to celebrate learning and teaching. Our reflections on the conference were themselves presented at the Student CETL Network conference in Plymouth, in July 2008 (now the Student Learning and Teaching Network, http://studentlandtnetwork.ning.com/), and were designed to illustrate how learning development at its best harnesses student energy and motivation in active and emancipatory ways – and shifts learning development and support dramatically away from a 'remedial' backwater.

Our conference is an event for students, organised by students and supported by students. A recent alumnus took the lead role in organising *Get Ahead* and contributed to the presentation at the Student CETL Network Conference; his reflections on this are below. The conference offered academic presentations on various aspects of writing, reading and note-making, and also on how technology, such as mobile phones, can be used to support study. LDU, CETL and Student Services staff facilitated the event; and many of the sessions were delivered by students themselves. Where students felt that they lacked the confidence to present, we trained them in successful presentation strategies and helped them to develop and deliver dynamic and engaging sessions. Our *Get Ahead* conference directly impacts upon the students who attend on the day. Further, the conference demonstrates to subject academics and to senior management that we can create dynamic and innovative spaces for supporting students – and that so much of benefit to students is achieved when they are actively involved rather than side-lined or silenced.

A by-product of our conference was the production of a simple conference planning resource – in the form of a laminated A3 'poster' (see Figure 4.1) – that we had designed for others to use if planning a conference of their own. And indeed over the last several years we have had many enquiries from student advocates at other institutions with respect to how best to run their own conference – whilst within our own institution, faculties are now experimenting with the student conference as a high profile and energetic way of involving students in a dynamic institution. As our student organiser, Andy Mitchell, said: 'This was a really positive experience which demonstrates what students can achieve if they are given the opportunity – and how positive it is for staff and students to collaborate actively.'

▶ Conclusion

Learning development sits in a contested space in terms of its location within 'remedial' policies of some institutions; but it can embody the very best of emancipatory practice. In this chapter, we have argued that learning development should constitute an ethos or approach to teaching and learning – one that acknowledges the socio-economic realities

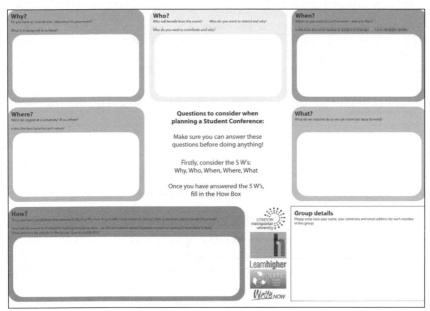

Figure 4.1 Conference planning resource – available free from
http://learning.londonmet.ac.uk/TLTC/learnhigher/Dissemination/activity.html

of our students and the power inequities of HE (Foucault, 1988). We argue for collegiate practice and for creating emancipatory spaces for our students. As an example of a more embracing and student-centred approach which can easily be adopted by other institutions, we have outlined our own student-facing conference, with students working together, facilitated by us, to put on a conference run by students, for students and enjoyed by all. For us, this has included involving students in research, mentoring, resource devising and development. Our students have worked with us and with and for each other, and thus become part of our community of practice.

▶ References

Barton, D. and Hamilton, M. (1998) *Local Literacies: A Study of Reading and Writing in One Community* (London: Routledge).

Bennett, R. (2002) 'Lecturers' attitudes to new teaching methods', *International Journal of Management Education* 2 (1), 42–58.

Bourdieu, P. (1977) *Reproduction in Education, Society and Culture* (London: Sage).

Boyle, T. (2008) 'The design and development of learning objects for pedagogical impact' in I. Lockyer, S. Bennett, S. Agostinho and B. Harper (eds) *The Handbook of Research* on *Learning Design and Learning Objects: Issues, Applications and Technologies* (Hershey, PA: Information Science Reference).

Bradley, C. and Boyle, T (2004) 'Students' Use of Learning Objects', *Interactive Multimedia Electronic Journal of Computer-Enhanced Learning* 6 (2). Winston-Salem, NC: Wake Forest University. Available at: http://imej.wfu.edu/articles/2004/2/01/index.asp (last accessed 29/3/10).

Burns, T. and Sinfield, S. (2004) *Teaching, Learning and Study Skills: A Guide for Tutors* (London: Sage).

Clughen, L (2009) *Things to Do in Social Learning Spaces.* 'The "Writers' Groups in the Disciplines" (WGiD) Project at Nottingham Trent and London Met Universities', LDHEN Symposium.

Evans, M. (2004) *Killing Thinking: The Death of the Universities* (London: Continuum).

Foucault, M. (1988) *History of Sexuality*, Vol. 3: *The Care of the Self* (Harmondsworth: Penguin).

Freire, P. (1977) *The Pedagogy of the Oppressed* (Harmondsworth: Penguin).

Friere, P. (1996) *Pedagogy of Hope*, 3rd edition (London: Penguin).

Goodyear, P. (2006) 'Technology and the articulation of vocational and academic interests: reflections on time, space and e-learning', *Studies in Continuing Education* 28 (2), 83–9.

Harrington, K., O'Neill, P. and Reynolds, L. (2010) 'Using wikis and blogs to support writing development: the online evolving essay project', in S. Little (ed.) *Developing Staff–Student Partnerships in Higher Education* (London: Continuum).

HEFCE (Higher Education Funding Council for England). Available at: http://www.hefce.ac.uk/Learning/TInits/cetl/ (last accessed 29/3/10).

Holley, D., Andrew, D., Cook, J., Celik, C. and Mitchell, A. (2006) 'Elements of expectancy: incorporating the student voice in the online design process'. *Networked Learning* 2006, 10–12 April, Lancaster University.

Lea, M. and Street, B. (1998) 'Student writing in Higher Education: an academic literacies approach', *Studies in Higher Education* 23 (2),157–72.

Leathwood, C. and O'Connell, P. (2003) '"It's a struggle": the construction of the "new student" in Higher Education', *Journal of Education Policy* 18 (2), 597–615.

Leathwood, C. and Read, B. (2009) *Gender and the Changing Face of Higher Education: A Feminised Future?* (Maidenhead: Open University Press).

Lefebvre, H. (1991) *The Production of Space*, trans. D. Nicholson-Smith (Oxford: Blackwell).

Lillis, T. (2001) *Student Writing, Access, Regulation, Desire* (London: Routledge).

Loader, B. (1998) *Cyberspace Divide: Equality, Agency and Policy in the Information Society* (London and New York: Routledge).

Lunsford, A. (1991) 'Collaboration, control, and the idea of a writing century', in C. Murphy and J. Law (eds) *Landmark Essays on Writing Centers*, vol. 9 (London: Routledge, 1995).

Medhurst, A. (2000) 'If anywhere: class identifications and cultural studies academics', in S. Munt (ed.) *Cultural Studies and the Working Class* (London: Cassell).

Molotch, H. (1993) 'The space of Lefebvre', *Theory and Society* 22, 887–95.

Morrice, L. (2009) 'The Global in the Local: issues of difference (mis)recognition and inequity in higher education'. Paper presented at the ESRC seminar series: *Imagining the University of the Future*

Munt, S (ed.) (2000) *Cultural Studies and the Working Class* (London: Cassell).

OECD (2000) *Schooling for Tomorrow: Learning to Bridge the Digital Divide* (Paris: OECD).

O'Neill, P., Harrington, K. and Bakhshi, S. (2009) 'Training peer tutors in writing: a pragmatic, research-based approach'. *Zeitschrift Schreiben*. Available at: www.zeitschrift-schreiben.eu/cgi-bin/joolma/index.php?option=com_frontpage&Itemid=29   (last accessed 29/3/10).

Peters, M. and May, T. (2004) 'Universities, regional policy and the knowledge economy', *Policy Futures in Education* 2 (4), 263–77.

Rowland, S. (2000) *The Enquiring University Teacher* (Buckingham: SRHE and Open University Press).

Satterthwaite, J. (2004) 'Learning in the clouds: what can be learned about the unknowable?' in J. Satterthwaite et al., *Educational Countercultures: Confrontations, Images, Vision* (Stoke on Trent: Trentham Books).

Sinfield, S., Burns, T. and Holley, D. (2004) 'Outsiders looking in or insiders looking out? Widening participation in a post-1992 university', in J. Satterthwaite, E. Atkinson and W. Martin (eds) *The Disciplining of Education: New Languages of Power and Resistance* (Stoke on Trent: Trentham Books).

Starkey, D. (2003) *Taking the Mick.* Available at: www.guardian.co.uk/politics/2003/jan/15/education.highereducation (last accessed 28/3/10).

Tenni, C., Smyth, A. and Boucher, C. (2003) 'The researcher as autobiographer: analysing data written about oneself', *The Qualitative Report* 8, 1.

Thomas, L. (2001) 'Power, assumptions and prescriptions: a critique of widening participation policy-making', *Higher Education Policy* 14, 361–76.

Section B

Supporting Students in Transition

5 A Personal Development Planning Perspective on Supporting Student Transition into Higher Education

Christine Keenan

▶ **Summary**

This chapter examines how personal development planning (PDP) approaches can be used to support students in making a strong and effective transition into higher education (HE). As a term, 'personal development planning' defies or evades precise definition, but is used here to encompass a range of developmental approaches that directly involve students in their social, personal and academic integration into higher education (Keenan, 2008). An exploration of three specific interventions to ease student transition to HE will focus on three of the key questions associated with PDP:

- How to engage students?
- How to engage staff?
- Does 'it' work?

▶ **Introduction**

There is no consensus on the precise definition of PDP. In 1997, the Dearing Report (NCIHE, 1997, 9.17) called for a broader concept of student learning to include skills around communication, numeracy, information technology and learning how to learn.

The Quality Assurance Agency (QAA, 2001) offers a dual perspective, suggesting an institutional responsibility to provide:

a structured and supported process undertaken by an individual to reflect upon their own learning, performance and/or achievement and to plan for their personal, educational and career development.

That enables students to:

- become more effective, independent and confident self-directed learners;
- understand how they are learning and relate their learning to a wider context;
- improve their general skills for study and career management;
- articulate personal goals and evaluate progress towards their achievement;
- and encourage a positive attitude to learning throughout life.

Recently published reports, for example, the Higher Ambitions Report (BIS, 2009), emphasise the importance of student engagement through indicators such as attendance, progression, retention numbers and satisfaction scales, with the potential threat of financial sanctions for underperformance at institutional or indeed course level. Also, student satisfaction with PDP is one of the factors assessed in the influential National Student Survey (NSS). The importance of institutional commitment to providing a structured and supported process that students can engage with therefore cannot be underestimated. However, the difficulty of convincing staff and students to engage with PDP practices remains and the lack of a clear definition makes it difficult to quantify results in order to answer the question 'Does it work?'

For a fuller exploration of the background and development of PDP in HE, see Buckley (2008). This chapter focuses on the role of PDP in the early stages of the student HE journey. It demonstrates that the early introduction of PDP approaches helps students develop self-awareness particularly in the context of a new learning environment. This encourages them to make a conscious engagement with their learning and broader university experience. With reference to the works of Chickering and Gamson (1987) and Yorke and Knight (2004), this chapter describes how effective pre-induction introduction to learning resources, and an imaginative curriculum in the transition phase, can enthuse, inspire and engage students leading to greatly improved retention in the first year.

Firstly, discussion about a *pre-induction* resource, 'Stepping Stones 2HE', provides an example of how to empower and engage students to develop a strong sense of their learner identity. Secondly, there is an example of students *building their own* PDP unit. The third and final example shows how an academic practice unit has been designed to *sustain* the development of learning and academic skills throughout the first year. Adopting a PDP approach promotes self-awareness and engagement in learning. This leads to improved student satisfaction and retention (providing a way of measuring impact for the institution), and offers reassurance to staff that the investment of time is beneficial to all.

▶ Transition support

From a learning developer's point of view, there are significant advantages to be had if students are convinced of the benefits of learning to learn, self-awareness, and taking ownership and responsibility for personal development. Staff are more likely to be proactive in this area if they are convinced of the benefits to students and do not simply see it as an intrusion into an already packed curriculum. Some academic staff take a view that PDP is irrelevant to their subject (HEFCE, 2003). Others perceive that it is important to incorporate broader concepts of learning to learn, self-awareness and reflection, into the formal and informal curriculum because these are critical skills not simply for employability but also for life. Students who see value in the accumulation of strong personal skills such as leadership and volunteering will often also be proactive participants in the life of the university, equipping themselves to take control of their own futures. Others, particularly in the health and social care professions, will need to develop reflective practice as an integral feature of their professional identity.

The emphasis of this chapter is on:

- how transition resources can incorporate features of PDP to help boost confidence and start students on the road to taking a positive attitude towards a rich engagement with their learning;
- how to involve students in ownership of their personal development curriculum in the first term;
- how a dedicated first year Academic Practice Module can incorpo-

rate a variety of PDP notions such as learning to learn and employ-ability and can enthuse and stimulate interest through generic study skills and discipline-specific scholarship.

It is useful and interesting to consider the role of PDP in the transition phase as a scaffolding of the development of these metacognitive skills, during and beyond the transition experience.

▶ Stepping Stones 2HE: an example of building PDP 'learning to learn' approaches during transition

Stepping Stones 2HE (Steps) is a set of online pre-induction resources, first developed at Bournemouth University in 2002 in response to students' negative feedback about their transition and induction experiences. Students did not like the passive nature of induction, and wanted to be more proactive – getting down to learning and getting on with work more quickly (Keenan, 2005, 2009a). Steps aims to encourage students to engage with HE by providing a meaningful, purposeful, and relevant introduction to university life.

Chickering and Gamson (1987) cite institutional contact as one of their seven principles for good practice in undergraduate education. Steps takes the principle further by looking at relationship development as an enhancement of student/institution contact during the transition phase. Firstly, the relationship between the student and the institution is addressed by the provision of generic information about what it will be like at university – study, learning, what to expect (particularly in the first week or two, the settling-in period), and news about the wider university. Secondly, it aims to develop a strong relationship between the student and their learning by the provision of introductory learning activities and resources, which will be developed in a social collaborative sense during induction week. Thirdly, the resource provides a link (through the 'About You' survey discussed below) between the individual student and a real person at the university, whom they will be working with when they arrive. The survey provides an opportunity for students to reflect on their previous learning experiences, their expectations about starting at university, and their expectations of the university, and offers a 'safe space opportunity' to ask any burning questions they may have.

My research with students at Bournemouth also indicates that they want the university to facilitate ways for them to get to know each other and make friends. This links to Chickering and Gamson's second principle: encouraging cooperation among students. The provision of pre-induction learning resources allows students to prepare independently prior to arrival, but this personal learning is then integrated and shared collaboratively during induction, significantly increasing bonding and group cohesion, and creating a firm basis for the social and academic integration called for by Harvey et al. (2006).

Additionally, students are provided with information about learning to learn, with the benefit that they are already developing a sense of understanding and purpose. The provision of pre-induction learning resources meets a number of student-centred needs. For example, new students will often ask for a reading list. My research with students revealed that this request was a proxy for the desire to get a flavour of what they would be doing on the course and getting down to work as quickly as possible (Keenan, 2005, 2009a). Steps provides students with a sense of purpose, providing a real and practical introduction to study, setting the scene for what Yorke and Knight (2004) refer to as 'understanding' in their USEM (Understanding, Skills, Efficacy beliefs, Metacognition) model. Students begin to take control over their own learning, beginning the shift from perceiving learning as retention of knowledge, to one of understanding, application and communication of knowledge as well.

Steps includes subject-specific learning activities which provide an introduction to study. Some basic guidance is provided on how to approach the activities, and useful information sources are suggested to help students make a start. This fulfils Chickering and Gamson's third principle: encouraging active learning. All the learning activities are designed to promote active engagement, while the shared collaborative stage during induction week facilitates active social learning in order to produce required outputs: typically, jointly produced posters or group presentations. Working together in groups towards a common goal in this way, not only provides a purposeful, meaningful and relevant start to academic work, but also has the effect of underpinning what Yorke and Knight (2004) refer to as the 'development of skilful practices' in their USEM model.

Linking pre-induction learning activities to collaborative work during the induction phase also provides students with the opportunity for an introduction to assessment and feedback. Students give poster presentations, or group presentations: high quality work is produced, which students can rightly take pride in. In this example, staff can give feedback immediately, setting the scene for the future. Chickering and Gamson cite giving prompt feedback as a further principle of good practice. In the induction period, this works particularly well to close the preparation, doing, evaluation, and feedback cycle, and we usually combine it with a social event or celebration of achievements at the end of the first week.

Chickering and Gamson further claim that students need support in developing effective time management and this is explored within the learning resources. Students are able to control the preparation time they put in before arrival, but clear guidance is given about how much work should be done so that they do not feel overwhelmed. It is also essential to provide appropriate learning spaces (rooms, computer labs), timetabled for students' exclusive use during induction week, to enable collaborative working. This can be clearly linked in to the idea of deadlines, and an explanation of the institution's coursework hand-in regulations.

Working together provides opportunities for getting to know each other and friendship development so essential for helping students to settle in, integrate, and feel part of the university. During transition, students often feel disorientated and look to their new friends and peers for a whole range of psychological and social support. Disposition, personality and individual qualities will have a huge effect on how students respond to their new environment and, as Yorke and Knight suggest, will have a huge impact on their future employability. The provision of fully integrated pre-induction and induction resources that build on a principle of strong and effective social and academic integration can therefore be seen as a key personal development need at the transition phase. This can then help the development of strong efficacy beliefs that will sustain the student during the first term, and into the remainder of the first year. Yorke and Knight (2004) also comment on the lasting importance of classroom experiences on a student's self-concept and learning identity, clearly supporting the notion that a PDP approach during the transition phase can have positive and lasting effects. This reinforces a further principle of good practice outlined by Chickering and Gamson – that good practice communicates high expectations. The provision of well designed, meaningful and relevant pre-induction resources, closely aligned with induction activities, gives a clear message to the student that engagement with academic study is a serious expectation of the institution; the cycle of preparation, collaborative activity, assessment, and feedback gives students a feel for how it happens in a relatively informal and safe environment, building on high levels of motivation and enthusiasm and getting students off to a good start.

In setting and having high expectations, it is important that students feel safe and understand what is expected of them. An explanation is provided to the effect that the students can think of their learning as a stream. 'Stepping Stones' are provided by the institution by way of lectures, seminars, provision of resources, kit, etc. However, learning takes place in the way that students construct their learning bridges between the stepping stones. Through Steps, students develop insights into 'learning to learn' through a practical introduction to independent learning, but crucially, they are also provided with some safeguards and advice about what to do if they should fall off a stepping stone into the water, and how to seek help or support should they need it. This relates closely to Yorke and Knight's final notion of metacognition, the thinking, planning, reflection and self-awareness that are essential in engaging with our own learning.

The Steps resource includes an 'About You' survey, in which students are invited to reflect on their previous learning and learning preferences. They are also asked to provide their expectations of themselves in coming to university, as well as their expectations of the university. This not only gives some very useful insights, particularly as they are articulated just prior to the student starting at university, but also demonstrates respect and value of student talent and ways of learning, the final of Chickering and Gamson's principles, and critically also shows that we are interested in the student as a unique and individual person. One school at Bournemouth University, with a well-established personal tutorial system, amended the About You survey to provide the basis for the first personal tutorial meeting. In the pre-induction resources, students are given information about the purpose of personal tutorials, and guidance on how to prepare for meetings with personal tutors and how to get the most benefit from the meetings. The survey questions were adjusted for this and explanation was given to the students about the purpose of the survey. The benefit was more knowledge about each other prior to the first meeting, leading to a sense that there was already a strong basis to work from. The shared information which informed that first personal tutorial meant that students felt they were already known and treated as individuals. Building mutual respect and developing a good understanding of student expectations enables learning developers to get a better sense of working with new students, particularly in developing mutual understandings of each other's expectations. Student expectations evolve rapidly during the course of the first year, but gaining insight into what each other's expectations are helps avoid any unnecessary misunderstandings right from the start.

▶ Involving students in designing the PDP curriculum

I asked a new group of first year technology students at Bournemouth University to bring copies of job advertisements (not simply jobs they might aspire to themselves, but a broad range) to our first seminar together (Keenan, 2009b). In the seminar groups, we worked closely together to deconstruct the advertisements in order to identify requirements, for example, subject knowledge, personal qualities or attributes and general skills required. These were clustered into themes such as communication, interpersonal skills, team working, leadership, etc. Using these themes, we constructed the curriculum together for the rest of the term and together we identified who would lead the sessions. For example, the Students' Union were invited to lead a session on leadership and volunteering. For the assessment, students were asked to provide a critical reflective commentary on PDP; they could think up their own essay title, but any argument they made had to be based on evidence, and they had to provide at least four correctly cited references (Keenan, 2009b).

▶ Scholarly PDP

My final example describes how academic staff, learning developers, learning technologists and students collaborated to develop an Academic Practice Unit (APU) within the curriculum.

The rationale for the APU came from a desire to provide an overarching study skills unit that provided consistency across the first year in the School of Applied Sciences at Bournemouth. A primary issue to be addressed was how to engage first year students in learning to learn when they did not perceive such a unit to be an essential or integral part of their programme. As the engagement issue was deemed to be pivotal, a student-centred approach was essential in order to demonstrate to students that engagement with APU was indeed significant to their broader studies. The design team were also aware of the need to engage academic staff in the process, and to counter the view that a generic unit across the whole first year of about 340 students would lower the quality of the overall student experience.

The APU therefore had to be designed to be generic to give purpose and relevance to the whole first year cohort within the School, yet also tailored to provide context to different academic groups.

Working together, the design team built an online learning environment within the university virtual learning environment (VLE), combining e-lectures (using Echo360® lecture capture – see www.echo360.com [last accessed 26/7/10]) and PowerPoint® presentations with hotlinks to support the e-lectures. Following an initial face-to-face lecture introducing the unit, lectures are subsequently uploaded to the VLE on a weekly basis over two semesters. The online lectures reflect stages of the academic cycle and include assignment preparation, academic writing, using feedback, and group-working. Each week, students access the workspace to find the e-lecture and supplementary learning materials. Students have the choice of either a high bandwidth option where they access the e-lecture video, or a lower bandwidth option of audio and PowerPoint. In addition, they are set a task for the week, to be submitted through the VLE workspace. Discipline identity comes through a scholarship lecture. Every academic within the school provides a face-to-face scholarship lecture outlining their research; the lectures are uploaded to the APU workspace and supplemented with pdf versions of published work. Supplementary information also guides students in their reading of the publications to help them develop an idea of academic writing as communication, and they get a sense of how referencing works. The unit leader reports that enthusiastic feedback from students has been 'amazing'.

Students are involved in the ongoing evolution of the APU, mainly through active and real-time feedback. Feedback from students takes a variety of forms – for example, the unit has a bulletin board and any issues can be raised and dealt with in real time, so feedback is seen to have a purpose. Any ongoing issues become evident through discussion threads. Student representatives also provide feedback at course monitoring level. Feedback from second and third year student focus groups about their experience of the APU in the first year has enabled the course team to modify and improve the unit.

The APU also addresses a central aspect of learning development that students often find difficult when they arrive at university, which is to do with academic writing. Often, students do not understand what is expected and the lack of formative and developmental feedback means that they are unable to practise this skill in a

safe and phased way. In this APU, there are three key pieces of formative assessment. In the first term, students undertake a referencing exercise. In the second, they are asked to produce a reflective
piece of work drawing on a full mix of content from the APU unit;
this has to include references to academic sources and must be fully
referenced. The third assessment is an e-portfolio comprising ten
completed tasks covering the range of academic skills developed
through the e-lectures, and five summaries of the academic scholarship lectures. Students are provided with templates and fully
instructed on how to submit their work. In partnership with learning technologists, a system has been designed to develop a new
version of an e-portfolio within the grade centre of the VLE (entitled
Blackboard). This allows more flexibility in providing important
developmental assessment. Students upload their work and are
able to refine their attempts following formative feedback from
tutors. In terms of staff time, this is viable because the pieces are
very short and very focused. Second year students report that,
although they found the tasks difficult at the time, they were invaluable in developing their confidence and giving them a sense of
discipline to meet regular deadlines; they also learned how to use
feedback provided by tutors to help them develop their all-impor-
tant academic skills. The levels of interaction are helpful in a
number of ways: the students benefit from regular contact with
tutors, and tutors can monitor levels of engagement and identify
students who may be falling behind.

▶ Conclusion

The introduction to this chapter identified three key questions
around the notion of PDP: how to engage students, how to engage
staff, and how we know it works. Learning developers seek to
develop student-centred approaches that understand how students
learn and how they make use of learning resources in order to gain
an understanding of how learning develops and takes shape within
our students. This is clearly all wrapped up with a myriad of
notions: of student identity, communities of learning, learning
approaches and more. This chapter described a range of interventions developed on the basis of research with students and in partnership with students, which aim to ease transition into and
through the first year in a structured and supported way. We know

that, where the interventions have been introduced, student retention definitely improves in the first term, as students are helped to negotiate their transition into the life-world of the institution. The set of resources, the examples of curriculum design, and engagement of students in the process, reflect established principles of good practice, as identified by Chickering and Gamson, and by Yorke and Knight. The outcomes demonstrate that confidence is built, and group identity is strengthened, with the obvious benefits of enhanced peer support and friendship development. This provides a clear example of how a range of PDP ideas and concepts can be applied to issues surrounding student transition and induction to university, and demonstrates how institutional approaches can be adjusted to support and facilitate social and academic integration.

▶ References

BIS – Department for Business Innovation and Skills (2009) *Higher Ambitions: The Future of Universities in a Knowledge Economy* (London: BIS). Available at: www.bis.gov.uk/Policies/higher-education/shape-and-structure/higher-ambitions (last accessed 29/3/10).

Buckley, C. (2008) *PDP: From Introduction to the Present*. Available at: www.learnhigher.ac.uk/learningareas/pdp/introduction.htm (last accessed 29/3/10).

Chickering, A. and Gamson, Z. (1987) 'Seven principles of good practice in undergraduate education', *AAHE Bulletin* 39, 3–7.

Harvey, L. and Drew, S. with Smith, M. (2006) *The First-Year Experience* (York: Higher Education Academy). Available at: www.heacademy.ac.uk/assets/york/documents/ourwork/research/literature_reviews/first_year_experience_full_report.pdf (last accessed 28/3/10).

HEFCE (Higher Education Funding Council for England) (2003) *How Much Does Higher Education Enhance the Employability of Graduates?* Available at: www.hefce.ac.uk/pubs/RDreports/2003/rd13_03/ (last accessed 29/3/10).

Keenan, C. (2005) *Stepping Stones 2HE: Students Working to Bridge the Transition Gap*. Conference Presentation at the SEEC Annual Conference.

Keenan, C. (2008) 'Stepping Stones 2HE: a model for student retention', in G. Crosling, L. Thomas and M. Heagney (eds) *Student Retention Programs in Higher Education* (London: Routledge).

Keenan, C. (2009a) 'Stepping Stones 2HE: Students Active in Transition to HE', in *Induction and Disabled Learners* (Action on Access).

Keenan, C. (2009b) 'Stepping Stones 2HE: fresh thinking for introducing PDP to freshers', in *Enhancing Student Centred Learning* (IISLT Subject Centre. Threshold Press).

Knight, P. T. and Yorke, M. (2003) 'Employability and good learning in higher education', *Teaching in Higher Education* 8 (1), 3–16.

NCIHE (1997) *Higher Education in the Learning Society* (Norwich: HMSO).

QAA (2001) *Guidelines for HE Progress Files*. Available from: www.qaa.ac.uk/academicinfrastructure/progressfiles/guidelines/progfile2001.asp (last accessed 29/3/10).

Yorke, M. and Knight, P. T. (2004) *Embedding Employability into the Curriculum* (York: Higher Education Academy).

6 Learning Developers Supporting Early Student Transition

Ed Foster, Sarah Lawther and Jane McNeil

▶ Summary

Research into student transition provides learning developers with a valuable set of perspectives when considering how to support higher education students, particularly in the first year of study. This chapter shows how one institution has used both theory and research to develop its approach to student transition in that year. Firstly, we briefly review theory which aims to explain student transition. Secondly, we summarise research conducted at Nottingham Trent University (NTU) to explore the differences between students' prior learning experiences and those of their first year at university. Finally, we consider the nature and impact of actions that learning developers have taken at NTU to support student transition in the first year.

▶ Introduction

Although student transition has been widely researched in the US since the mid-1970s (for example, Tinto, 1975), interest in the subject came later to the UK. This interest grew significantly through the 2000s in parallel with the early growth of the learning development (LD) community.

Student transition theories provide learning developers with useful models and fruitful areas to research in order to better structure learning development interventions. Johnston (2010, p. 4) suggests that student transition has two facets. Firstly it is the 'individual student experience of change involved in joining the university'. Secondly, student transition reflects the 'programmes of academic and other activities which the university provides to support and enhance student transition'. Johnston's second claim is very similar to Hilsdon, Ridley and Sinfield's (2008) view of learning development (LD) as the provision of a range of approaches and interventions to help students enhance their academic practices in order to 'benefit as fully as possible from higher education'.

In this chapter we will concentrate primarily upon three areas:

- A brief overview of student transition theory, drawing particularly upon UK research.
- Research conducted at Nottingham Trent University into the student experience of change. We will primarily focus upon students' prior learning experiences and their expectations of learning in higher education (HE) as they move from post-16 education into HE. We believe it is vital that learning developers are aware of students' prior learning experiences because, to help students learn effectively at university, we need to understand what they have already experienced. Failing to appreciate their prior learning may result in development of interventions requiring skills, attitudes or autonomy that many new students simply do not possess.
- Exploring how learning developers at Nottingham Trent University have worked with academic colleagues to implement and embed a range of interventions to support and enhance the early stages of student transition. We will use NTU's Welcome Week as an example of good practice.

The combination of research-informed resource development and staff development has placed student transition high on the agenda at NTU. Learning developers are influencing the university's strategic planning in this very important area.

▶ Theories of student transition

As students progress to each new level in their education, they need to adapt to new forms of pedagogy. Theoretically, each preceding stage prepares students for the one to come; primary education lays the foundations for secondary, secondary for post-16 and so on. The transition from post-16 to higher education is particularly challenging, as many students will also be living independently for the first time and higher education places higher expectations of learner autonomy on individual students. The changes faced by new students in higher education are therefore not just about greater knowledge or more complex forms of assessment, but also about living and managing one's own life. Cook and Rushton (2008, p. 16) suggest that transition takes place in a number of areas as students progress through higher education: subject content; maturation; independent living (or a changed relationship whilst still living at home); motivation; and taking responsibility.

Tinto's (1987) transition theory suggests that student transition is about coping and persisting in a new environment. He argues that there are three distinct phases: separation – in which students finds themselves moving away from traditional sources of support and guidance; transition – in which they are unclear about who to follow; and incorporation – when they understand the rules and can operate in the new environment. Very importantly, Tinto suggests that students need to make transitions into both the academic and the social environments. Percy (2002) argues, from a psychoanalytic perspective, that students need to feel emotionally confident in their new environment in order to take risks and engage in new forms of learning.

Purnell's model (Purnell and Foster, 2008) takes a similar stance to that of Tinto, reflecting on the journey students make in order to successfully participate in learning within the new institutional context. This model develops work by Nicholson (1990) and suggests four stages in the transition process: preparation, encounter, adjustment and stabilisation. The first stage, preparation, is characterised by the student projecting forward to what life in the new environment will be like and starting to plan for it. This stage is based on the students' prior learning, cultural capital and information from institutional publicity. However, in this stage students may have done very little thinking about what learning will actually be like once they reach university. The second stage, encounter, is the point at the start of the year in which the student first enters the institution and is embroiled within the hurly burly of student life, starting with Freshers Week. Purnell suggests that this is a relatively short period (perhaps 4–6 weeks) and is dominated by questions such as 'Will I cope?' and 'Will I make friends?' Purnell considers that the third stage, adjustment, may take students the remainder of the first year to work through and is influenced by a number of factors: social relationships and belonging, the quality of learning, teaching, assessment and feedback on progress. In the final stage, stabilisation, students engage with the curriculum and learning opportunities provided therein.

Purnell's model suggests that transition is largely over by the end of the first semester/year. Whilst this may be true for some students, it is not the case for all. Hardy, Hand and Bryson (2009) found that by the end of the first year students were still uncertain about their role and ambiguous about how hard they were expected to work at university. Cook and Leckey (1999) found that students were continuing to use inappropriate learning strategies developed in post-16 education late in their first year. Hill (2004) found that second and final year students would sometimes make writing mistakes in areas they appeared to have mastered in the first year. This was partly due to time pressures, but also because in later years tutors did not always pick up on these mistakes and students had not internalised the importance of taking control of their own work.

If learning development is about helping students to develop the skills, attitudes and confidences necessary to benefit from higher education, then due consideration needs to be given to supporting students through these stages.

▶ Students' experience of change

In this section, we concentrate on students' prior learning experiences and their expectations about what learning at university will be like. We believe that these two sets of factors form the foundations from which students subsequently engage in learning. We will illustrate some of the problems and misapprehensions that students have about learning at university.

The student data used in this chapter comes from two sources. Firstly, learning developers conducted two sets of 100, one-to-one interviews with first year students at NTU during Welcome Week in October 2007 and 2008. The 200 students interviewed broadly represented the University's academic school structure, although, due to the relatively small number interviewed, we were unable to accurately balance other demographic features such as gender, age etc. The second data source is a survey of first year students conducted between March and May 2009 for the HERE Project (Higher Education: Retention and Engagement). The HERE Project is run jointly by learning developers at NTU, and the universities of Bournemouth and Bradford, as part of the national 'What Works? Student Retention &

Success' programme. For the sake of brevity, we will concentrate on the NTU data, although broadly similar findings were reported at all three partner institutions; 656 first year students responded to the survey at NTU and 370 gave us permission to subsequently follow their progress through university.

In the Welcome Week interviews, students indicated that they had experienced many of the practices common in higher education, for example extended academic writing, managing multiple deadlines, and note-making in class (Foster, Bell and Salzano, 2008). However, there were a number of important differences that indicated that, while students may have believed that they were well prepared for higher education, some important foundations were missing. Jessen and Elander (2009) found that students had overestimated how transferable their learning in post-16 education would be to university. They were overconfident in their ability to understand what was expected of them in higher education, and, when tested, were surprised at how different the expectations actually were. This overconfidence may, in turn, partially explain some reluctance to engage with aspects of learning development such as skills modules.

We discuss two areas of difference below:

* Learning independently
* Different feedback paradigms

Learning independently

Learning how to learn independently is one of the most important intended outcomes for a programme (NCIHE, 1997) but the structure of higher education is often largely predicated on the assumption that students *already* possess many of the skills and motivations to learn in this way. Our experience suggests that, whilst much of the subtlety expected in later years is not required in the first year, from the very outset students are expected to learn in a much more autonomous manner than they have previously encountered. First year lessons are largely designed on the assumption that students have prepared by reading ahead, are self-motivated to attend, and have the skills to make effective notes in the classroom. Similarly, many first year assignments are designed so that students create an extended piece of writing by marshalling a number of arguments together. Crucially, our research shows that students have had only a limited experience of these practices.

In the 2007 Welcome Week survey, 94% of students stated that they had managed multiple coursework deadlines prior to coming to university, but many reported support from their teachers in doing so, for example, being allowed to draft smaller sections rather than being asked to submit completed work. In the same survey, students reported that they had made notes in the classroom during prior studies. However, tutors often pointed out the important parts, and so students had not independently practised how to prioritise information and develop decision-making skills crucial to drafting good notes.

Different feedback paradigms

The Welcome Week surveys strongly suggest that 'feedback' means different things in the two sectors. In post-16 education, feedback is often formative, providing guidance to help the student improve a particular piece of coursework. In higher education, coursework feedback is normally summative and focused on the next piece(s) of work, not improving the one at hand. Making best use of feedback at university requires a much more sophisticated set of learning skills and far greater planning.

Students entering the first year had experience of producing extended pieces of writing before coming to university, although they appeared to have done so in a very different manner. For example, in the 2007 Welcome Week survey, 95% of respondents stated that they had completed at least one piece of academic writing of over 1,000 words in post-16 education, 90% of them had received feedback on drafts whilst doing so. In the 2008 survey, students were asked how often they could submit drafts. The majority (50 respondents) stated 'once' or 'twice', but a minority (10 respondents) were able to submit drafts an unlimited number of times. In some instances, students were expected to submit smaller sections of work, such as the introduction, for feedback. Students could ask their tutor to review drafts, but, in the majority of instances (69%), this conversation was primarily instigated by the tutor or the responsibility was shared. Student comments about the feedback process included: *'They would write down what needed changing and then they would talk it through with you.'*

Ultimately, if higher education is to create self-reflective learners capable of independent learning, then students must, at some point, assume responsibility for learning from feedback and become capable of self-assessment. However, our findings suggest that it is a mistake to assume that students are experienced and capable of doing so at the point they enter university. This deficit may also partly explain why satisfaction with feedback at university consistently scores almost 10% lower than other factors in the UK National Student Satisfaction Survey (Fearn, 2008).

If we expect students to learn independently and engage with feedback in higher education there are a range of issues that need tackling. Staff need to actively promote the value of independent learning, they need to teach students how to learn from feedback, and programme teams need to consider options such as changing the practice of feedback over the first year, for example, offering formative feedback on early assignments or exploring other models such as feedback on exemplars or peer review.

Expectations about learning at university

When asked what will be different about studying at university (2008 survey), students commonly identified that they would be expected to do more independent learning, and were likely to have fewer contact hours. For example 'Less spoon feeding, more independent work' or 'more relaxed, they won't chase after you, more independent learning'. However, responses were very brief, offering minimal evidence of much understanding, 5% of respondents even thought that they would receive more one-to-one support. When asked about writing, for example, students understood that they would be writing longer pieces of work, but, even when pressed by the interviewers, only one recognised that they would not receive formative feedback or that deadlines would be inflexible, stating: 'there won't be any re-submission of work'.

This lack of knowledge at the point of entry may not be a problem as long as it is effectively addressed during the first year. However, the 2009 National Student Forum reported that, often, initial advice and guidance from the higher education sector was poor at explaining what the learning experience ahead would be like. One student stated:

I needed more detail on how I would be taught and the course content. And also the learning support that would be available. What are the expectations around essay writing for example? It's a big cultural shift. (NSF, 2008, p. 12)

When the HERE Project surveyed first year students later in their first year (between March and May), 48% of respondents reported that no one had explained the differences between learning at university and post-16 education. In December 2009, when their progression was reviewed, those students to whom the differences were not explained were more likely to be repeating part of the year, to have failed or withdrawn, or to have been required to make good failed modules.

Overall, our findings suggest that students enter higher education relatively unaware of the differences between their prior and new ways of learning. Many lecturers are teaching as if students have actually understood these differences and seem to assume that students are already well prepared for higher learning.

▶ How learning developers are helping to improve the experience of early student transitions

Learning developers at NTU have been central to bringing student transition into the mainstream learning and teaching discourse. The focus of our work has been to raise staff awareness about the differences between students' prior experiences of learning and to contrast these with staff expectations about how students are likely to learn in the first year. This has led to changes in practice across the university. This section provides examples of how our student transition research, resource development, and staff development activities, have helped to ease students' transition into higher education, and, as a practical example, shows how the Welcome Week at NTU draws all these principles together.

Student transition research at Nottingham Trent University
We are continuing our research into early student experiences and expectations of higher education. Students are surveyed about a wide range of issues, including personal priorities whilst at university, their experience of induction, their understandings of learning at university, and, most recently, what they think being a student actually means. These findings feed into staff development events, development of learning resources and, ultimately, university policy.

Resource development
Developing learning resources has been a core function of the learning

development team at NTU for some time. We have developed, and worked with colleagues to embed, a wide range of academic skills resources. These include the academic writing resources that were developed for LearnHigher, and a wide range of learning resources designed to help course teams improve student induction, such as workshops on the differences between post-16 and higher education, icebreakers, and guides identifying key issues to cover during induction. Our most recent work has been to develop video resources explaining to students how they are expected to engage with different forms of learning at university and a series of resources showcasing best induction practice from academic programmes at the University. Staff reactions to the materials provided are extremely positive.

> Students comment that they have been able to gain much insight into the expectations and issues related to being a student in HE. (Education Lecturer, NTU)

Staff development

We also provide a range of staff development activities to help promote a better transition experience, including bespoke workshops, briefings and meetings with academic colleagues. The response has been extremely positive. Most recently, learning developers have organised a shadowing scheme for teaching staff. Our lecturers have the opportunity to spend a day with teachers in a local post-16 college to find out what kind of learning experience our future students will have. In return, our hosts are offered the opportunity to spend a day with lecturers here. In this way, we hope to extend the dialogue between the two educational sectors and use this enhanced knowledge to improve the transition experience for students.

▶ Case study – Welcome Week

For most UK students, the first week at university is known as Freshers Week. For many, evenings of alcohol and partying are followed the next morning by large lectures on 'inspirational topics' such as health and safety, and module options (Foster et al., 2009). From an administrative perspective this is, of course, very practical. Large lectures are a time-efficient way to communicate to large numbers of students but, if students are out partying, there is a risk that they may be too tired to fully comprehend complex messages or engage with intellectually challenging tasks. This approach does little to help students engage with the course and university:

> when you feel lost and bewildered, the last thing you want is long lectures. (Edward, 2001)

In 2005, learning developers at NTU created (and continue to deliver) Welcome Week to address this issue. There are two main objectives for Welcome Week: firstly, to increase the range of opportunities for all students to develop supportive friendships, and secondly, to improve the quality of student induction.

Welcome Week offers a range of opportunities to develop mutually supportive friendships through activities such as reading groups, theatre trips, outdoor activities and a range of recreational sports (Foster et al., 2009). Although, since the implementation of Welcome Week, all student feedback has improved, those living in university halls continue to have a higher level of overall satisfaction. We have therefore placed particular focus on trying to meet the needs of those students living outside university halls. These tend to be more mature, local and international students. The University provides targeted social activities for them, to help them develop friendships and support structures, and we have seen a steady improvement in student feedback amongst these groups.

Of equal importance is the fact that Welcome Week provides an institutional focus on new student induction programmes. Each year, student satisfaction with induction is measured and improvements are made. We have not yet fully broken out of the single week (as proposed by Cook and Rushton, 2008), but have a far greater variety of activity contained within it. In 2005, we surveyed a sample of 65 undergraduate induction programmes. Across all programmes, new students spent 62% of their time in some form of lecture. In 2009, we reviewed a slightly different sample of 64 programmes and found that students only spent 39% of their time attending lectures. The proportion of time dedicated to workshops, independent learning tasks, and small projects had grown significantly.

The impact of Welcome Week has been very positive. Previously, student feedback scores on their induction experience were very low (the second lowest in a survey of 20 issues). However, in 2009, over

80% of all responses about the experience were 'good' or 'excellent'. Individual feedback is overwhelmingly positive:

> Welcome Week really helped me settle in. I didn't come directly from school and had doubts about whether I'd fit in. Welcome Week was so well organized that I was able to get on with making friends and feeling I belonged. (Welcome Week student, 2006)

Moreover, early student retention improved significantly. In 2004, the year before Welcome Week began, 132 students had withdrawn by Christmas. In 2005, over the same period, early withdrawals were reduced to 85. Despite increasing numbers of students in subsequent years, early withdrawals have remained low.

▶ Conclusion

Learning development is about helping students to develop the skills and confidence to succeed in higher education. It is therefore essential that learning developers operate in a manner that students can engage with. We argue that student transition theory and research can provide an important additional framework to help learning developers achieve this focus. In particular, we suggest that it is vital to pay attention to the prior learning experiences of first year students and the disjunction between post-16 and the first year of higher education. It is essential that first year students are effectively introduced to the differences between the two sectors. Moreover, they also require support to develop the attributes necessary to engage with the more autonomous learning expected in higher education. Learning developers can play an important role in supporting this process. The understanding and insights which learning developers gain from supporting students, teaching a particular academic skill, or developing learning resources, are precisely those required to help students start to engage in learning at university.

▶ References

Cook, A. and Leckey, J. (1999) 'Do expectations meet reality? A survey of changes in first year student opinion', *Journal of Further and Higher Education* 23, 157–71.

Cook, A. and Rushton, B. (2008) *Student Transition: Practices and Policies to Promote Retention* (Birmingham: Staff and Educational Development Association).

Edward, N. (2001) 'Evaluation of a constructivist approach to student induction in relation to students' learning styles', European Journal of Engineering Education 26 (4), 429–40.

Fearn, H. (2008) 'Overall satisfaction falls, but small places win big smiles' [online], Times Higher Education. Available at: www.timeshighereducation.co.uk/story.asp?sectioncode=26&storycode=407758 (last accessed 29/3/10).

Foster, E., Bell, R. and Salzano, S. (2008) '"What's a Journal?" – Research into the Prior Learning Experiences of Students Entering Higher Education', 3rd Annual European First Year Experience Conference, University of Wolverhampton, 7–9 May 2008.

Foster, E., Lees, M., O'Neill, W. and Lawther, S. (2009) 'More than "Getting Smashed with Randomers" – Improving Student Induction'. European First Year Experience Conference, University of Groningen.

Hardy, C., Hand, L. and Bryson, C. (2009) 'Settled in well socially, but just getting by academically: Social and academic transition to university at the end of the first year'. European First Year Experience Conference, University of Groningen.

Hill, P. (2004) 'Am I Been a Pedant When I Say That accepting Students Different Litreracy Practice's Will Effect There Prospects?' In: Writing Development in Higher Education Conference Proceedings, Sheffield Hallam University, 11–12 May.

Hilsdon, J., Ridley, P. and Sinfield, S. (2008) 'Defining LD', email correspondence, Learning Development in Higher Education Network, 24 September 2008. Available at: www.jiscmail.ac.uk/learnhigher (last accessed 29/3/10).

Jessen, A. and Elander, J. (2009) 'Development and evaluation of an intervention to improve further education students' understanding of higher education assessment criteria: three studies', Journal of Further and Higher Education 33 (4), 359–80.

Johnston, B. (2010) The First Year at University (Glasgow: McGraw-Hill).

NCIHE (National Committee of Inquiry into Higher Education) (1997) Higher Education in the Learning Society (London: HMSO).

NSF (National Student Forum) (2008) Annual Report 2008 (London: NSF). Available at: http://nationalstudentforum.com/NSF_annual_report_2008.pdf (last accessed 26/7/10).

Nicholson, N. (1990) 'The transition cycle: causes, outcomes, processes and forms', in S. Fisher and C. Cooper (eds) On the Move: The Psychology of Change (Chichester: John Wiley & Sons, 1990).

Percy, A. (2002) 'Student induction: the psychology of transition', in P. Frame (ed.) Student Induction in Practice, SEDA Special 113 (Birmingham: Staff and Educational Development Association).

Purnell, S. and Foster, E. (2008) 'Transition and engagement', in L. Hand and C. Bryson (eds) Student Engagement, SEDA Special 22 (Birmingham: Staff and Educational Development Association).

Tinto, V. (1987) Leaving College: Rethinking the Causes and Cures of Student Attrition (London: University of Chicago Press).

Tinto, V. (1975) 'Dropout from Higher Education: a theoretical synthesis of recent research', Review of Educational Research 45, 89–125.

7 The Case for One-to-One Academic Advice for Students

Judy Turner

▶ Summary

Economic constraints have led to a reduction in one-to-one academic support at universities across the UK with a related increase in the expectation that students will work independently using electronic resources to develop their academic skills. This is not always helpful for all. Using case studies, this chapter illustrates transitional difficulties faced by four students in engaging with academic studies and provides evidence for the significant contribution that timely one-to-one support from professional academic advisers can make to student success and retention, and how it can enhance the use of online resources and generic workshops.

▶ Introduction

The National Audit Office (NAO, 2007) reports that one common reason for students to withdraw from a course is that they do not have appropriate study skills or are not ready to be independent learners. The Quality Assurance Agency (2004) also proposes that universities should focus on meeting learners' needs.

For many universities there are three generic mechanisms by which students may develop their academic skills.

1 The most readily available and cost-effective resources are online materials for students designed to support them to become independent learners. For example, there is likely to be information on how to write essays, which students are encouraged to access.

2   There may also be generic workshops on academic skills: these are more costly to provide.

3   The most intensive and expensive provision is, however, one-to-one individual academic support sessions. The present financial constraints upon universities are resulting in senior management at some universities reducing the provision of these individual sessions and an increased expectation that students will use online resources when they need to acquire or develop the appropriate study skills for university.

As we have seen in the preceding chapters of this book, the academic demands of studying for a degree are particularly apparent at transitional stages: starting at HE, moving from the first to the second year, and becoming an independent researcher when working for a dissertation. Many students are able to work independently and develop academically at the required rate. These students will successfully engage with the use of online resources in conjunction with support and advice from peers and tutors, to produce coursework which communicates their understanding and ideas effectively and appropriately. For other students, who lack the necessary skills or have not become independent learners, this challenge may be insurmountable (NAO, 2007). Students who lack independent learning strategies or have low self-esteem often abandon their studies when apparently unachievable, academic challenges arise (Harrison, 2006).

This chapter argues that one-to-one academic support, provided by a professional team of learning developers, is an essential supplement to online resources and generic workshops for some students. Case studies will illustrate the use of appropriate and well-timed academic support for students with a range of difficulties and prior experiences. The chapter demonstrates how generic academic tutorials can make a significant contribution to successful transitions in academic development and to student retention.

▶ Case study 1: Alleviating the baggage of a history of academic failure for a mature learner

Amira is a mature Law student nearing the end of her first year. She had successfully completed an access course before starting her degree but the legacy of poor results at school led her to feel unworthy of her place at university. She felt alienated from the students on her course, whom she perceived to be much more able. She reported that despite working hard she was unable to do all the reading necessary and was getting poor marks, which she saw as further evidence of her lack of ability. She no longer spent quality time with her family and felt that her whole life had become a disaster. She could not see how to resolve these difficulties and believed that she could not cope with the challenges of a degree. She came to ask the Study Advice Service for advice on the leaving process.

The first session focused on practical time-management techniques. Her study hours were erratic. She continued to manage the housework and spend time with her family as she had before starting her degree. Studying was viewed by her family and herself as a spare time activity which she fitted around these commitments: she normally studied late at night after the house became quieter but found that she was anxious and short-tempered in the day as she was tired and worried about her deadlines and lack of time to read. She came to believe that studying was not a worthwhile activity. Family members frequently interrupted her when she was working and as a consequence she felt that her first priority should be the care of her family, and that studying was a luxury.

As the discussion continued, Amira became more analytical as she had time and space to consider her problem objectively. She was able to see that her right to study had been earned through hard work on the access course and that it would eventually contribute to the well-being of her family. Once this breakthrough had been made she began to identify solutions to some of her practical difficulties.

- She identified her best time of day for working and realised that she would be more productive if she got up before her family and worked early in the morning rather than trying to work in the evening.
- She identified difficulty with finishing the tasks she set herself for her study periods. This resulted in a feeling that she had not achieved much when studying and an associated panic that she would not be able to complete work for the deadline. She realised that her anxiety was impacting on her ability to work effectively. The Study Adviser suggested breaking work into small achievable chunks and practising matching small tasks to short study periods.
- She realised that one of the biggest difficulties she would have to deal with was the feeling that family needs were more important than her studies. She decided that she would find times when her family would be the focus of her attention and, in exchange, would

establish times when she could work without interruption. She also realised that she could delegate some of the household chores.

- In discussion with the adviser, she began to see the value of being a mature student and how her experience and viewpoint would contribute in the classroom.

Amira left the session feeling much more positive about continuing with her studies.

The second session was used to check on Amira's progress and encourage her new-found sense that studying for her degree was a worthwhile objective and that she could allow herself to maximise her chances of success. The session was also used to work through a range of study techniques that would result in her working more effectively in the time available.

When Amira first came to see the Study Adviser she believed that she had tried all possible approaches to studying and was failing because she was not adequate to the task. After a single thirty-minute one-to-one session, she realised that the extreme measure of leaving university was not necessary and that she could increase her success and enjoyment of studying by developing her time-management skills and by studying more effectively. The second session gave time to further adapt and develop these new strategies and ensure that she had the resources and confidence to be an adaptable and creative independent learner.

▶ Case study 2: Enhancing a post-graduate student's writing skills at PhD level

Tom was a PhD student. His first degree in science had not helped him develop the written communication skills he was going to need now in writing his Archaeology thesis. His supervisor referred him to the Study Advisers because, while he recognised that Tom had great ideas, he thought he must be dyslexic as his written communication was so poor. For a variety of reasons, the supervisor was unable to help Tom to develop his academic writing. The supervisor micromanaged at a sentence level, adding commas and commenting on the choice of words and grammar, rather than focusing on the overall content or the analytical thinking that was taking place. Tom was demoralised and had been unable to hear any of the positive comments that were made on the ideas behind the writing. Consequently, he began to feel that his research was a complete failure as he felt he had failed to capture the interest of his supervisor.

During the first session, it became apparent that Tom was not likely to have dyslexia. The Study Adviser did a brief screening session and also noticed that Tom had written acceptable Methods and Results sections. It soon became clear, however, that he did not have a basic understanding of writing as a means of communication. An examination of his writing showed that he needed to learn to:

- plan and structure his thesis;
- organise ideas into chapters and paragraphs;
- learn to write logically without omitting steps in the argument;
- back up his arguments with appropriate academic evidence, and interpret and explain this evidence.

This process of developing his writing took considerable time, during which his ability to communicate, first orally and then in writing, was developed.

Tom came to realise that not only did he have innovative and exciting research which would make a significant contribution to Archaeology but he could communicate these ideas effectively in writing, with the additional bonus that the writing process helped him to understand his ideas more fully.

Tom continued to see the Study Adviser regularly for a year. During that time his writing gradually became more confident and he successfully completed his thesis. The change in his confidence was apparent as he began to socialise with other postgraduates in his department and was able to network at conferences. Towards the end of the year he was able to teach a first year seminar with enthusiasm and assurance.

▶ Case study 3: Discovering a specific learning difficulty

Liam was a 20-year-old second year Classics student who came to the Study Advisers after receiving critical feedback from his tutor on the grammar, spelling and sentence structures in his essays – for example, 'The English in this essay is so very poor that it is hard to work out what is going on.' There were also other comments suggesting that he had misunderstood concepts and ideas. His marks were in the 40s and low 50s and he was finding it difficult to engage with his course as he felt discouraged and inadequate.

An examination of his coursework showed that his work was poorly structured and unfocused. He wrote in long rambling sentences which lapsed into incoherence, adopting a pseudo-academic jargon of poly-syllabic words. He had not mastered the use of academic evidence to substantiate his arguments. Despite this it was possible to detect the presence of several good ideas. An examination of his spelling and sentences and of his educational history suggested that he might have a specific learning difficulty so Liam was encouraged to refer himself for an educational assessment.

Liam was assessed by an educational psychologist and found to have dyslexia and to be very bright. He had problems with short-term memory, which appears to be an underlying cause of difficulties with writing coherently (e.g. Kintsch and Rawson, 2007), particularly under time pressure in exams. Liam had always underachieved in exams and previous difficulties with spelling, reading and neatness at school were attributed by his teachers to carelessness. This judgement had had a significant negative impact on the development of his self-esteem.

While the finding of dyslexia did not have a direct effect upon the way in which Liam developed his writing skills in subsequent sessions with the Study Adviser, it had an immediate and very positive effect upon his self-confidence. He learnt for the first time that he had high intellectual ability. The Study Adviser was able to point out Liam's clear thinking and good ideas. He stopped feeling that his analysis was wrong and 'stupid' and started to believe that his academic interpretations of the texts could be acceptable. Eventually, after more positive feedback from tutors and a mark in the mid-60s for his next essay he came to see that he might indeed even be original and creative.

He persevered in finding ways to communicate his ideas in language acceptable to his tutors. The Study Adviser showed him how to:

- break sentences down into single ideas;
- use uncomplicated communication and use words precisely;
- organise his argument through the use of paragraphs;
- structure the essay around a well communicated thesis.

Most importantly, Liam came to understand that the purpose of writing coursework is to communicate rather than to impress. His essay marks improved rapidly as his writing style and communication developed and tutors started to comment on his originality and interesting interpretations. He continued to seek support regularly throughout the year working with the Study Adviser on specific issues that helped him develop into an independent learner. In his final year his average mark was in the high 60s and the change in his self-esteem was so evident that he gained a graduate job at only the second interview.

▶ Case study 4: From an international perspective

Keya was an international student with a 2.1 in History from a European university, now studying for an MA in International Relations. She came to see the Study Advisers at the suggestion of her tutor because she was getting marks in the low 40s and markers were commenting on her lack of analytical thinking, failure to use academic evidence to support her arguments, and lack of appropriate referencing. She was disappointed with her low marks as she was considered to be an excellent student in her own country and she could not understand what was going wrong. She was both despondent about her prospects of passing the course and angry at the institution which was 'causing her to fail'. She was considering leaving and would be asking for her fees to be reimbursed.

During the first session the Study Adviser discussed sections of an essay with Keya and asked her to explain what she believed the essay to be about. It was clear from this discussion that Keya had spent appropriate amounts of time on background reading. Grammatical and vocabulary errors were minimal and the main theory and appropriate evidence had been included.

It became clear that the low mark resulted from two aspects of poor academic practice. Firstly, the writing lacked an underlying argument except to the extent that it regurgitated the opinions given in a lecture on the topic by her tutor. Secondly, the writing made some use of academic evidence but this use was erratic and many statements were made without the appropriate references; it was unclear which sections were her own ideas and which were taken from her academic reading. The result was confusing as it was not possible to see how the evidence was contributing to establishing a thesis and the student was at risk of being accused of plagiarism.

The Study Adviser explained UK academic expectations underlying the process of essay writing, particularly in presenting an argument based on academic evidence from a wide variety of sources yet containing the author's own analytical and independent conclusions and interpretations of the evidence. Keya was surprised by these expectations and explained that in her culture it was inappropriate to disagree with a tutor's ideas and that the purpose of essay writing was to clearly state the facts that had been taught by the tutor in lectures. The session focused on:

- the absence of academic 'truths' in her discipline;
- using academic evidence to support arguments;
- referencing and avoiding plagiarism, and what this means in the UK;
- organising ideas into paragraphs containing a single point related to the question;
- developing a point of view, which forms the thesis;
- critical thinking and interpreting the evidence;
- guidance on how to use online resources on academic writing, referencing and proof reading.

She had difficulties thinking about what her own beliefs were in relation to the essay question but made some progress during the session and seemed to have understood the major re-conceptualisation of her essay-writing technique. She appeared able to understand the concepts behind the adviser's explanation of the appropriate critical thinking, and ideas for how to implement this. She attended two more sessions to learn how to put these new ideas into practice effectively. For her next essay she achieved a pass mark in the mid-50s and positive comments from the tutor on her progress. After three sessions, she was able to engage with the new learning process and was enthusiastic about her new-found ability to produce her own ideas about current issues in her academic field.

▶ Why offer one-to-one sessions?

The opportunity to form a relationship with an expert member of the academic community is especially important for many students but particularly for those who lack confidence in their academic abilities. For Amira, Tom and Liam, a lack of academic confidence was leading to failure and imminent withdrawal from university but these students felt unable to approach their tutors or lecturers for support. The one-to-one session with an academic adviser provides an opportunity to identify the individual's strengths and find straightforward, practical solutions to difficulties. Progress can be easily monitored and study techniques refined to build the learner's confidence. This is an efficient and highly effective method of helping these students to engage successfully with their academic discipline.

Like Keya, students who are achieving poor marks may lack an understanding of which aspect of their approach to study is the problem. Without such an understanding, students are unlikely to be able to effectively apply appropriate online learning development materials. A generic workshop on essay writing, for example, is unlikely to result in sufficient insight for some students to make progress. The most successful intervention for students with more complex problems is an individually tailored session incorporating guidance on using appropriate online materials. Liam believed that his thinking was flawed and that he was, therefore, unable to be a Classicist. Without a closer examination of his writing in a one-to-one session, it would not have been possible to determine that his main difficulty was with written communication rather than with academic and critical thinking.

An individual session is particularly effective for helping the student to transform their understanding and achieve major re-conceptualisations or 'threshold concepts' (Meyer and Land, 2003). Discussion enables the learning adviser to demonstrate ideas and methods to the student in a way that allows the student to engage with, develop and personalise them. 'Eureka' moments vary between individuals but *do* produce a major change in their study methods. For example, Keya's academic progress hinged upon her grasping the concept that it was acceptable, and necessary, to criticise academic ideas, coming to understand that this is appropriate academic practice in the UK and for her subject discipline (Street and Lee, 2006). For Liam, the new concept was to understand that writing is intended to communicate clearly rather than to impress. In both these cases, progress was only made after the students had made the transition into a transformed understanding of their individual working methods.

Academic advisers are often intermediaries between the feedback from tutors and the student's development. Tom interpreted his supervisor's feedback as meaning that he was an incompetent researcher not capable of working at PhD level. Keya did not understand what her tutor meant when she wrote 'reference?' or 'evidence' in the margin. While many students have been found to ignore feedback (REAP, 2007), others are simply unable to interpret or implement the suggestions given (Higgins, Hartley and Skelton, 2001). For some, personalised explanations of these difficult, fundamental concepts can result in greater changes in their understanding.

Students generally require two one-to-one sessions. The first session models a metacognitive method of approaching academic development by focusing the student upon the learning process itself. This self-awareness leads to better learning (Bransford et al., 1999). Students often come to the second session having tried a variety of new approaches to their work. The second session is used to refine study practices still further, using successes from the previous session and rectifying misunderstandings. With the support of the academic adviser, the student begins to develop alternative ways of thinking or working. These alternatives are practised and the results examined, adapted and developed as appropriate. The resultant success with coursework leads to increased confidence and the student is enabled to make progress towards being an independent learner with much more awareness of their learning processes.

Perhaps one of the most indispensable contributions of one-to-one sessions is to the knowledge base and understanding of the academic adviser. Regular contact with students enables the academic adviser to keep up to date with the rapidly changing needs of the student population, and with changes in teaching methodologies being adopted and adapted across the university. The academic adviser also has regular opportunities to try a range of approaches to learning and receives feedback from the students on their efficacy. This understanding of the learning process is then used to refine and develop the online resources and generic workshops.

▶ Conclusions

There are special properties of one-to-one sessions which make them an essential addition to online resources or generic academic advice for some students. One-to-one learning is an effective and efficient method for students who are struggling to adapt and develop their learning practices. It is also of great value for students whose previous educational background, lack of confidence or assumptions about the UK education system provide barriers to developing independent learning strategies. These students often have the ability to succeed in their courses, and it only takes a few tailored sessions to help them to see where their current practices need to adapt or change. It is important that the one-to-one session is given by someone with the academic expertise to provide the student with appropriately adapted tools for their learning development. Students need to feel confident in the support, and academics in the university need to feel that the service provided will be helpful and appropriate. Individual one-to-one Study Advice sessions are available at many universities but this academic development resource may dwindle in the current economic climate if unsupported by academics and administrators.

▶ References

Bransford, J. D., Brown, A. L. and Cocking, R. R. (eds) (1999) *How People Learn: Brain, Mind, Experience and School* (Washington DC: National Academy Press).

Harrison, N. (2006) 'The impact of negative experiences, dissatisfaction and attachment on first year undergraduate withdrawal', *Journal of Further and Higher Education* 30, 377–91.

Higgins, R., Hartley, P. and Skelton, A. (2001) 'Getting the message across: the problem of communicating assessment feedback', *Teaching in Higher Education* 6, 269–74.

Kintsch, W. and Rawson, K. A. (2007) 'Comprehension', in M. J. Snowling and C. Hulme (eds) *The Science of Reading: A Handbook* (Oxford: Blackwell).

Meyer, J. H. F. and Land, R. (2003) 'Threshold concepts and troublesome knowledge: link ages to ways of thinking and practising within the disciplines', Occasional Report, ETL Project. Available at: www.etl.tla.ed.ac.uk//docs/ETLreport4.pdf (last accessed 29/8/09).

NAO (National Audit Office) (2007) *Staying the Course: The Retention of Students in Higher Education* (London: The Stationery Office). Available at: www.nao.org.uk/publications/0607/Student_retention_in_higher_ed.aspx (last accessed 26/7/10).

Quality Assurance Agency (2004) *Enhancement Themes 2003–2004: Responding to Student Needs in Scottish Higher Education*. National Conference, Glasgow.

REAP (2007) 'Re-Engineering Assessment Practices in Scottish Higher Education'. Available at: www.reap.ac.uk/ (last accessed 29/3/10).

Street, B. and Lea, M. (2006) 'The Academic Literacies Model: Theories and Applications'. Available at: www3.unisul.br/paginas/ensino/pos/linguagem/cd/English/22i.pdf (last accessed 3/9/09).

8 The Assignment Success Programme

Martin Sedgley

▶ Summary

This chapter discusses the design and impact of 'Assignment Success', a discipline-specific, academic writing programme which has proved very popular with our international MSc students. Attendance on the optional pilot was over eight times higher than at previous generic workshops, and overall student feedback was very positive.

Its success was strongly influenced by a collaborative teaching approach. As the School of Management's learning developer, I co-presented the workshops with an academic tutor, using writing examples and exercises related directly to her modular assignments.

▶ Introduction: Cultural collisions

In 2007/08, the international contingent of the UK student population was 15%. At postgraduate level, this figure rose to 66% (UKCISA, 2009). Business and administrative studies proves the most popular discipline for international students, and, at the University of Bradford School of Management, 95% of our 2008/09 taught postgraduate population were international.

Mass education has to adapt to greater diversity (Lillis and Turner, 2001). International students bring different understandings of learning that have been constructed through contextual reading and writing in their previous educational cultures (Lea and Street, 2006). They arrive initially excited about the prospect of higher-level education, which they hope will build on their existing knowledge. But, in the midst of what is probably their first, major life transition, they soon find themselves struggling to understand new academic expectations.

By the end of the first semester, confusion has often escalated into bewilderment at disappointing grade assessments. International students experience such 'failures' as particularly shocking in their stark contrast to previous academic achievements, which had seemed to reflect hard work and intellectual ability that UK higher education (HE) now apparently doesn't recognise (Lea and Street, 2000). After the excited anticipation of just a few weeks earlier, they now sense themselves sliding down a cultural chasm, not sure where they are going wrong. An early process of acculturation seems crucial to students' grasping the new UK academic expectations soon enough to develop appropriate learning strategies for matching them accurately (Bloxham and West, 2007; Lea and Stierer, 2000).

Assignment Success focuses on academic writing issues that our tutors report as most commonly problematical. These are: engaging with the question; essay structure; referencing; and critical analysis. In response, I developed a programme of workshops covering these topics in collaboration with an academic tutor, Dr Anna Zueva, utilising exemplars from previous students' high-grade essays. These came from two module subjects, International Business Environment and Cross-cultural Management, which we hoped our current international students could relate to reasonably easily.

In these two respects, i.e. discourse acculturation within a subject discipline, Assignment Success engages with elements of both the socialisation and academic literacies approaches to academic writing (Lea and Street, 2000). So the first section of this chapter further explores these theoretical foundations.

The next section describes and evaluates the Assignment Success Programme. The evaluation refers to year-on-year attendance data, students' quantitative workshop ratings, and qualitative feedback from students and staff on perceived value.

Finally, I reflect on how a multi-disciplinary group of staff within the School of Management intend to build on Assignment Success and related developments in future. The discussion of our experience and future plans will be of interest to other HE tutors exploring similarly collaborative development of subject-specific writing programmes.

▶ Theoretical foundations: models of learning development and writing support

Educators recognise cultural collisions as potential opportunities for learning (Bridges, 1980; Jarvis, 1987). It is at these points of transition, where new ideas challenge existing 'knowledge', that possibilities for learning arise. However, Jarvis cautions that too great or too small a disjuncture may well lead to meaninglessness rather then newly constructed and understood meanings. Catt and Gregory (2006, 26) emphasise the 'important distinction between productive struggle and hopeless floundering'. The early stages of HE massification in the 1990s saw the widespread emergence of remedial workshops for students identified as lacking in key academic skills necessary for successful transition. Based on a deficit model, skills development courses became commonplace, focused on concepts such as essay writing, time management, and exam preparation, and these still constitute a significant element of support at most UK universities (Wingate, 2006).

More recently, this study skills approach has been criticised because *any* student potentially faces huge challenges during transition into HE (Street, 2004; Lea and Stierer, 2000). This seems particularly true of essay writing, which Winter (2003) describes as presenting students with great difficulty in terms of comprehending the required conventions. Western HE discourse is by no means as transparent as has sometimes been assumed by institutional staff, and international students in particular often make assumptions about effective study strategies that do not correspond with tutors' notions of deep learning (Bloxham and West, 2007; Lillis and Turner, 2001; Norton et al., 1996). Tutors' expectations are often tacit in nature, and difficult to explain to those on the periphery of the learning community, not yet versed in the language of that discourse (O'Donovan et al., 2008; Price, 2005). Students encounter challenging differences between their existing, 'everyday' understandings of business management, for example, and the new rigour of studying this as an academic subject (Lea and Stierer, 2000).

Growing recognition among academic researchers that many students were experiencing these kinds of struggles contributed to the development of the socialisation model of HE academic writing support. This perspective attributes a role to tutors of orientating students to a new learning culture and enabling them to interpret the requirements of academic tasks (O'Donovan et al., 2008; Street, 2004). Drawing on social psychology and constructivist education approaches, this model acknowledges that institutions and even subject disciplines apply their own particular discourses to construct knowledge in different ways (Creme and Lea, 2008; Lea and Street, 2000; Lillis and Turner, 2001). Writing, among other aspects of learning, is understood to be a social practice situated in a particular context. Whilst still essentially a skills-based approach, this approach recognises writing as a learning process developing through practice and feedback within that academic setting.

However, there are some criticisms of the socialisation model, notably in its representation of the academy as one culture. It is argued that students often need to change language practices from one academic setting to another – the institution's conventions cannot be learned generically at one point and simply transferred to other disciplinary settings (Bloxham and West, 2007; Creme and Lea, 2008; Street, 2004). More fundamentally even, there is a danger of students divorcing the idea of successful study from subject knowledge by trying to identify a discrete 'toolkit' for passing assignments without the need for deep engagement in the actual course of study (Cottrell, 2001; Wingate, 2006). This critique derives from the theoretical perspectives of a third model of writing development, the academic literacies approach. There is less pedagogical application of this model to date, but the principle of embedding academic writing development into the curriculum, for example, is being explored in specific initiatives (Blake, 2009; O'Doherty, 2009).

In piloting Assignment Success, I hoped to draw on elements of both skills and literacies approaches, responding instinctively to the idea of a multi-faceted approach to supporting an increasingly diverse body of students.

As a learning developer, I frequently hear students expressing a need for fast acculturation into the new academic system. A colleague likened this demand to the educational equivalent of the 'survival' level of Maslow's Hierarchy of Needs (1970). Although independent learning may be our ultimate western educational objective, this can loom like a mountain shrouded in mist, and many international students will simply not find their own way. I see a clear responsibility for staff, as the experienced guides, to help students gain confidence and then maintain momentum on the steep learning curve of Semester 1. So a socialisation approach involving workshops that aim to quickly enable students' understanding of new academic writing expectations seems particularly important in this respect.

Whilst there is an institutional assumption that generic writing workshops will induct students into a seemingly unified discourse, a variety of academic writing approaches may actually be required by tutors from different disciplines. The academic literacies approach has generated increasing support among researchers for the idea of integrating writing skills *within* academic programmes (Cottrell, 2001; Gibbs, 1994; Wingate, 2006). In this pilot Assignment Success programme, we were exploring the value of targeting students' understanding of how best to meet the writing requirements within a particular management discipline.

As a common example of good practice, both skills and literacies approaches seem to agree on the real value of utilising previous assignment exemplars to help students develop their capacity to participate more fully. These can include detailed, constructive commentaries from the tutors on the strengths and weaknesses of past assignments, demonstrating not only *what* 'good' work looks like, but also *why* the academic authority considers it to be good (Bloxham and West, 2007; Price, 2005; Rust et al., 2005). When combined with interactive exercises, such as students making their own evaluations of the exemplars, opportunities are provided for participation that is key to students developing a practical understanding of the institution's assessment criteria (Ivanic et al., 2000). Assignment Success incorporates several examples of working with students' past assignments to facilitate current students' access to the discourse and, most importantly, the tacit subtleties of assessment.

▶ Programme background and outline

Assignment Success started in the second week of Semester 1, so that students had a week to experience their modules' lecture/tutorial structure and style of delivery. The weekly, one-hour workshops were then scheduled into a free slot in the timetable. They were promoted via student email lists, notice-boards and the school website. Many tutors also encouraged students' attendance through lecture announcements.

The academic tutor and I agreed on the following topics as being crucial for the students' evolving understanding of modules' academic requirements. We also recognised a sequential progression to these stages:

* Week 2: Engaging with the assignment title
* Week 3: Developing a clear, planned structure
* Week 4: Referencing – why and how
* Week 5: Critical analysis
* Week 6: Peer review

▶ Programme activities

Week 2: Engaging with the question

For this first workshop, we recognised that many academic tutors speak of a good essay introduction signalling the student's understanding of an assignment question's key concepts and implications. Using an essay extract such as the introduction can work effectively within workshop time constraints, easing the reading challenges for international students still adjusting to using a second language. A sample of six introductions from previous students' assignments provided the focus of study. The tutor rated the quality of these on a 1–10 scale, and the samples chosen ranged from 0 to 9 After a general presentation about the functions of a 'good' essay introduction, we distributed one of the samples to each of six class groups. They were asked to rate their introduction on the 1–10 scale against the criteria which had just been presented. Group feedback was then compared with Anna's own detailed analyses of each introduction.

Week 3: Essay structure

Mindful again of the time limits, but still keen to try interactive exercises, we ran an 'essay jigsaw' activity in this second workshop. A hard-copy of an assignment had been cut up into paragraph sections. These were distributed among the class, one section to each group, along with the question title. Each group had to summarise a single thesis statement for their paragraph and guess roughly where this might be placed in the overall essay structure. After group discussion and feedback, this was compared with a visual overview of the structured argument developed through the actual essay paragraphs.

Week 4: Referencing

In the face of students' initial panic about using an alien referencing system, it is tempting to teach the mechanics of the necessary style, refer students to the institutional guideline resources, and hope the job's done. However, recent research indicates the complexity of students' misunderstandings about principles of authorship. We were conscious of needing to address not so much *how* but rather *why* and *when* to reference (Neville, 2009b).

We took an extract of an exemplar assignment and removed the citations from the text. This was distributed to all class members, who were asked to identify where they would expect to see citations and why. The tutor then talked through the original text, with annotated commentary explaining the need for a citation at each point. A full list of references was supplied, so that Harvard referencing style was illustrated simply by demonstration.

Week 5: Critical analysis

Clearly, a one-hour workshop on critical analysis can only be an introduction to such a complex issue. We gave the students an extract from a distinction-level essay and asked them to identify the particular junctures at which they believed the writer was demonstrating critical thinking, and what was characteristic of the writing at these points. Their *critical analyses* of the essay were then compared with the tutor's detailed commentary on the critical elements that had elevated this assignment to such a high grade.

Week 6: Peer review

The potential value of peer feedback has been well documented (O'Donovan et al., 2008; Rust et al., 2005). We decided to include a final workshop in the Assignment Success series on peer review, partly to also explore our students' perceptions of the process.

By this stage of Semester 1, students needed to have prepared assignment drafts for imminent deadlines within some subject modules. They were asked to bring an extract from one of these to the peer review session. In small groups, they chose one extract to read. They then offered feedback to the student writer, using a set of evaluative criteria taken from Cottrell (2005, p. 190).

► Programme evaluation

Attendance at Assignment Success increased dramatically, being eight times higher than at five generic workshops with similar topics in the previous year.

The significant increases in attendance on this optional programme demonstrate that we are developing an academic acculturation process that students find helpful and credible. This persuaded us to begin a process of consolidating the more successful elements of the programme for the following year, and to explore opportunities for widening its dissemination through the School curriculum. We intend to register attendance at future workshops, so that a comparison may be drawn between the academic performance of students attending and not attending the programme. If this is then continued over a two- or three-year period, we may be able to identify a trend in terms of the contribution of such a programme to students' academic success.

Of more immediate value, therefore, are data received from student feedback. A simple questionnaire survey, using open questions for free response, was conducted with MSc participants on the Assignment Success Programme; 62 responses were obtained. For the purposes of this chapter, responses have been interpretively collated within the main categories of three survey questions: *usefulness of workshops*; *most useful workshop(s)*; *aspects for improvement*.

In what ways were the workshops useful for you?
Feedback overall indicated a perceived value to the programme as an induction into some elements of the prevailing academic discourse. Participants' comments were typically of the following nature:

> The workshops should be made compulsory for all international students.
>
> Very useful.
>
> Clarified points that were not clear from lectures.
>
> Clearly explained.
>
> I was able to learn a lot of things I had no idea about.

Specifically, 14 responses highlighted benefits relating to improved knowledge of academic expectations at the School.

A further 15 mentioned the value of learning particular study techniques for writing the module assignment appropriately. Specific skills were also singled out – 13 responses mentioning 'critical analysis', and 8 responses mentioning 'referencing'.

Which workshops did you find most useful?
The most useful workshops were: Critical Analysis – highlighted by 22 students; and Referencing – highlighted by 20 students. Overall average ratings for their usefulness were, on the questionnaire's 1–5 scale, 4.3 and 4.25 respectively.

How can workshops be improved?
The main criticisms of the Assignment Success Programme were logistical. The surprisingly large numbers attending by the third week necessitated moving to a lecture theatre with raked seating, which still

became fully packed. Student interactions were inevitably compromised, particularly for the smaller group-working exercises. The limited time of one hour was the other factor most mentioned.

▶ Recommendations for future provision

Clearly, there are practical challenges arising from the success of the programme in attracting and maintaining large attendances. In the future, we aim to run longer workshops of up to two hours to allow for more interaction, hopefully in smaller groups, as the timetable permits.

Critical analysis and referencing have been highlighted by many students as the most baffling barriers to our academic discourse. For many HE students, critical analysis requires something of a quantum jump in their understanding, without which their learning cannot progress. The idea that meaning is contested at all is new to many international students, requiring a sudden tolerance of ambiguity that can be quite disorientating (Lillis and Turner, 2001; Northedge, 2003; Shahabudin, 2009). We plan to run extra workshops in this area in future, with more emphasis on practical exercises, culminating in peer review focused on the quality of analysis.

Although vested mainly in a socialisation approach, the pilot programme of Assignment Success has already stimulated debate among the participating tutors about their own literacy practice. A larger group of tutors from three different subject disciplines are now planning a more coordinated approach to teaching critical thinking skills within, and between, their modules. These discussions are already encouraging us to question our shared and differing understandings of what critical analysis means, and how tutors can best induct students into the particular interpretations of their own disciplines through tutorials that progressively deepen understanding. I believe this is one way of responding to the academic literacies' argument that what really constitutes 'good' writing depends as much on the epistemology of disciplines (or even individual tutors) as it does on students' deficits (Bloxham and West, 2007; Lea and Street, 2000; Lillis and Turner, 2001).

However, this is a significant challenge for tutors, with major implications for resources, as well as the logistics of timetabling and syllabus management (Shahabudin, 2009). There is a tricky balancing act in developing new initiatives that place such significant demands on staff and class time. I was fortunate to have the opportunity to work with an academic who has an enthusiastic belief in the value of teaching academic writing in the context of subject disciplines, fostered partly by earlier experience of postgraduate writing clinics in US universities. This attitude was a key factor in the successful implementation of the project.

► Conclusion

There is a great willingness among many tutors in our School to explore how best to enable international students' success. We believe a collaborative approach involving academics and learning developers supports students' understanding of the disciplinary discourses. Our School is unusual in having its own Effective Learning Service, which is valued by academics who actively promote the service to students through their classes and personal tutoring. This shared, localised focus on contextual student support is a key factor, I believe, in the positive experience that so many students report from their time here.

Developments emerging from Assignment Success will provide the 'scaffolding frameworks' (Shahabudin, 2009, p. 20) that can help international Master's students move from a passive acceptance of directive teaching to a more active engagement in independent study. Hopefully they are inspired not only to reach a new peak in their postgraduate learning, but to also enjoy the climb on the way.

This is fertile ground from which collaborative programmes such as Assignment Success can grow and spread across disciplines. It needs to be tilled slowly and carefully, with respect for the experience that all faculty participants bring to the process. By harnessing the goodwill and cooperative relationships that exist among so many staff we may find ourselves gradually embracing more of the understanding of writing as a contextualised social practice (Lea and Stierer, 2000; Wingate, 2006). We also need to better understand the complex academic challenges facing international students, so that we can develop teaching practices that welcome them more easily into the learning community here. There is much scope here for in-depth qualitative research into the postgraduate students' transitional experience.

► References:

Blake, R. (2009) 'Embedding report writing workshops into an undergraduate Environmental

Science module through a subject specialist and learning developer partnership'. Unpublished paper delivered at: *Learning Development Higher Educational Network (LDHEN) Conference*. Bournemouth University, 6–7 April 2009.

Bloxham, S. and West, A. (2007) 'Learning to write in higher education: students' perception of an intervention in developing understanding of assessment criteria', *Teaching in Higher Education* 12 (1), 77–89.

Bridges, W. (1980) *Transitions: Making Sense of Life's Changes* (Cambridge, MA: Perseus).

Catt, R. and Gregory, G. (2006) 'The point of writing: Is student writing in higher education developed or merely assessed? in L. Ganobcsik-Williams (ed.) *Teaching Academic Writing in UK Higher Education: Theories, Practices and Models* (Basingstoke: Palgrave Macmillan).

Cottrell, S. (2001) *Teaching Study Skills and Supporting Learning* (Basingstoke: Palgrave Macmillan).

Cottrell, S. (2005) *Critical Thinking Skills: Developing Effective Analysis and Argument* (Basingstoke: Palgrave Macmillan).

Creme, P. and Lea, M. R. (2008) *Writing at University: A guide for students* (Maidenhead: McGraw Hill).

Gibbs, G. (1994) *Improving Student Learning – through Assessment and Evaluation* (Oxford: Oxford Centre for Staff Development).

Ivanic, R., Clark, R. and Rimmershaw, R. (2000) 'What am I supposed to make of this? The messages conveyed to students by tutors' written comments', in M. R. Lea and B. Stierer (eds) *Student Writing in Higher Education: New Contexts* (Buckingham: Open University Press).

Jarvis, P. (1987) *Adult Learning in the Social Context* (London: Croom Helm).

Lea, M. R. and Stierer, B. (eds) (2000) *Student Writing in Higher Education: New Contexts* (Buckingham: Open University Press).

Lea, M. R. and Street, B. V. (2000) 'Student writing and staff feedback in higher education: an academic literacies approach', in M. R. Lea and B. Stierer (eds) *Student Writing in Higher Education: New Contexts* (Buckingham: Open University Press).

Lea, M. R. and Street, B. V. (2006) 'The "Academic Literacies" Model: Theory and Applications', *Theory into Practice* 45 (4), 368–77.

Lillis, T. and Turner, J. (2001) 'Student writing in higher education: contemporary confusion, traditional concerns', *Teaching in Higher Education* 6 (1), 57-68.

Maslow, A. (1970) *Motivation and Personality* (New York: Harper & Row).

Neville, C. (2007) *The Complete Guide to Referencing and Avoiding Plagiarism* (Maidenhead: Open University Press).

Neville, C. (2009a) *How to Improve your Assignment Results* (Maidenhead: Open University Press).

Neville, C. (2009b) *Student Perceptions of Referencing* (Bradford: LearnHigher).

Northedge, A. (2003) 'Rethinking Teaching in the Context of Diversity', *Teaching in Higher Education* 8 (1), 17–32.

Norton, L., Dickins, T. and McLaughlin-Cook, N. (1996) 'Coursework assessment: what tutors are really looking for?' in G. Gibbs (ed.) *Improving Student Learning: Using Research to Improve Student Learning* (Oxford: Oxford Brookes University).

O'Doherty, M. (2009) 'I'm not here to teach students how to write!' Unpublished paper delivered at Conference: *Bridging the Gap: Transitions in Students' Writing*, Liverpool Hope University

O'Donovan, B., Price, M. and Rust, C. (2008) 'Developing student understanding of assessment standards: a nested hierarchy of approaches', *Teaching in Higher Education* 13 (2), 205–17.

Price, M. (2005) 'Assessment standards: the role of communities of practice and scholarship of assessment', *Assessment and Evaluation in Higher Education* 30 (3), 215–30.

Price, M., O'Donovan, B. and Rust, C. (2007) 'Putting a social-constructivist assessment process model into practice: building the feedback loop into the assessment process through peer review', *Innovations in Education and Teaching International* 44 (2), 143–52.

Rust, C., O'Donovan, B. and Price, M. (2005) 'A social constructivist assessment process model: how the research literature shows us this could be best practice', *Assessment and Evaluation in Higher Education* 30 (3), 231–40.

Shahabudin, K. (2009) *Investigating Effective Resources to Enhance Student Learning: An Overview of LearnHigher Research, 2005–2008* (Reading: LearnHigher).

Street, B. (2004) 'Academic literacies and the "new orders": implications for research and practice in student writing in higher education', *Learning and Teaching in the Social Sciences* 1 (9), 9–20.

UKCISA (UK Council for International Student Affairs) (2009) *Higher Education Statistics*. Available at: www.ukcisa.org.uk/about/statistics_he.php (last accessed 29/3/10).

Wingate, U. (2006) 'Doing away with "study skills"', *Teaching in Higher Education* 11 (4), 457–69.

Winter, R. (2003) 'Contextualising the patchwork text: addressing problems of coursework assessment in higher education', *Innovations in Education and Teaching International* 40 (2), 112–22.

9 Enabling Transitions through Inclusive Practice

Val Chapman

▶ **Summary**

This chapter focuses on the need for inclusive practice from a student life cycle perspective. It offers a rationale for inclusive learning and teaching, focusing mainly on disability, and addresses the underpinning philosophy, legislative requirements, and definitions of inclusion. Strategies that enable disabled students to progress successfully through key transition points in higher education (HE) are described, and these are supplemented by key questions to illustrate the important inclusion issues. The chapter also highlights our well regarded web-based resource that helps staff to further develop their inclusive practice.

▶ **Introduction**

Why inclusion?

There are strong business, economic and political cases for enhancing the recruitment, retention and achievement of disabled students. There are also powerful ethical and moral imperatives that require us, as sentient, civilised human beings, to treat each other with dignity and respect, whatever our social background, ability, age, ethnicity, sexual orientation, gender, faith or religion. Each one of us has multiple identities, each possessing a range of characteristics giving us our own unique profile; however, some characteristics may be more meaningful in some contexts than in others. For example, one's sexual orientation is of significance when looking for a partner, but may be largely irrelevant in other aspects of life; a dyslexic student reinforces this point:

in a world where I don't have to read or write, I'm regarded as really bright, I'm the leader of the pack. It's only when I have to communicate using text that I become disabled.

It is an important point to bear in mind that the predominant features of our identity can change in relation to the context – and so can the consequent discrimination. Different factors are in play at different stages of the disabled student's life, and the issues affecting the student on entry to HE may well be quite different from those affecting them when embarking on a work placement, for example, or when entering their final year.

▶ Models of inclusion

There are a number of models of inclusion. The responsibilities that are currently enshrined in EU and UK law, and that universities must address, seek to safeguard traditionally disadvantaged groups from discrimination. Collectively, these responsibilities offer a broad framework for inclusion, though from a perspective of compliance rather than good practice. The legislation covering the six diversity strands requires universities to:

* take active steps to eliminate discrimination;
* actively promote equality of opportunity between different groups;
* identify specific equality goals;
* demonstrate that fair treatment is in place;
* celebrate diversity;
* consult appropriately; and
* remove any residual barriers that limit full participation or equality.

It is claimed that the social model of disability (Oliver, 1990) underpins the Disability Discrimination Act (DDA). This model is one that perceives disabling factors to be located not within the individual (the medical model), but in the attitudes of others, in inaccessible environments, in policies that are rooted in assumptions and stereotypical thinking, and in discriminatory practices. In other words, it is not the impairment that results in a wheelchair user not being able to enrol on a course, but the absence of a ramp into the building where it is taught; it is not the visual impairment that prevents a person from registering for a course independently, but the failure of the university to offer accessible online forms.

Of course, the social model does not have to be restricted to disabled people. It can apply to all groups of students who have particular requirements, whether these relate to the need to pray at regular intervals throughout the day, the need to arrive late due to carer responsibilities, or the need to take an exam over a longer period of time because of ill health. Many disabled people report that the social model has not met their expectations, preferring the emergent 'civil rights' model of disability (Vanhala and Kelemen, 2008), which demands changes to policies and practices to enable their fullest participation in society, employment and education as their entitlement rather than as a dispensation that is frequently reliant on goodwill.

A philosophy that is gaining increasing acceptance in HE is one that recognises that disabled students should not be treated as a separate category with distinct and totally different needs, but rather that: 'they fall within a continuum of learner differences and share similar challenges and difficulties that all students face in higher education' (Healey et al., 2006, p. 9). 'Universal Design' (Connell et al., 1997) is a relatively new paradigm that is clearly aligned with this philosophy; it is an approach to the design of products, services and environments which ensures that they are usable by as many people as possible, regardless of age, ability or circumstance.

▶ Defining inclusion

So what is inclusive learning and teaching? Let us debunk some of the associated myths by stating clearly what it is not.

- Inclusive learning and teaching is not 'rocket science'; it is about thinking ahead, putting oneself in the student's shoes; it is about adopting a flexible mindset that results in practice that easily accommodates a range of needs.
- It does not mean converting every resource into Braille in anticipation that a blind student might enrol on the course – this is neither practical nor necessary. It is also important to note that not all blind people are Braille users; many prefer information in electronic format that can be read by a screen reader.
- It does not require academic staff to become expert in all impairments or other diversity issues; it does, however, require teaching staff to be 'expert' in their own subject and to think of a range of ways in which course outcomes can be achieved and demonstrated.

- It does not have to cost a fortune: it may take a little time to build up a broad range of resources in a variety of formats, but this approach benefits all students and makes the teaching and learning more creative and rewarding for everyone concerned.
- It is not bolted onto practice as an afterthought. Inclusive practice should be factored in at the course development and design stages and should be automatically considered when reviewing courses and policies.
- It does not mean treating everyone the same: just as the experience of parenthood varies enormously from person to person (and for the individual over the course of time), the experience of disability is highly individualised and is often variable. One simply cannot make assumptions about what someone's preferred learning style or particular requirements might be. Equity is not achieved through equal treatment, and careful dialogue with the disabled individual is necessary to determine what will work best for them in any given learning situation.

▶ Transition points

As with all students, there are a number of defining moments in the disabled student's life which can empower or demoralise, make or break. The following are highlighted in this chapter:

- Pre-entry/admission;
- Enrolment, registration and induction;
- First term/semester;
- Year-to-year progression;
- Assessment and final year dissertation;
- Progression to employment/postgraduate study.

▶ Pre-entry/admission

The Quality Assurance Agency's (UK) Draft Code of Practice (CoP) (QAA, Sept. 2008, p. 9) states that:

> The institution's publicity, programme details and general information should be accessible and should describe the opportunities for disabled students to participate.

This information should also make clear which learning outcomes are absolutely core to the programme of study and constitute competence standards that apply equally to all students and may not be adjusted.

Competence standards are defined by the DDA, Part 4 (HMSO, 2005: section 28S) as 'an academic, medical or other standard applied by or on behalf of a higher education institution for the purpose of determining whether or not a person has a particular level of competence or ability'. Though competence standards cannot justify direct discrimination, they may justify less favourable treatment of a disabled person where the standard is genuine, is applied equally to all people, and provided its application is proportionate to the intended aim. However,

> any such requirement or condition only amounts to a competence standard if its purpose is to demonstrate a particular level of a relevant competence or ability. Hence, a requirement that a person has a particular level of knowledge of a subject is likely to be a competence standard. (CoP 5.73)

This aspect of the legislation is particularly relevant in relation to admissions criteria. For example, the ability to play a musical instrument to a specified level is likely to be a competence standard for entry onto a music degree programme; whereas the requirement to have 'a high level of physical fitness' is unlikely to be a competence standard for a theory-based course in choreography (because it is not 'relevant' to the nature of the course).

It is critical that universities examine their course entry and assessment criteria to ensure that they have genuine competence standards in place and that they are not discriminating against disabled people. Higher education institutions (HEIs) need to ensure that their application and selection processes are fair and within the law. Additionally, they need to take care that their progression and transfer arrangements do not discriminate against disabled students, and these should align with the duties outlined in the institution's Disability Equality Action Plan (now required of all HEIs).

To illustrate: a blind woman applied to do a Higher National Diploma (HND) in Equine Studies which included coaching both horse and rider in dressage, and stable management. Although it was anticipated that she would be able to complete some parts of the course and was a competent rider herself, she could not undertake core aspects of the course which involved visual analysis of the horses' and riders' performance, nor could she identify and respond promptly to health and safety issues involved in stable management and the supervision of riding. The course team discussed the possibility of making a reasonable adjustment by having other students act as the applicant's 'eyes'. This led to a discussion about whose knowledge and understanding would be tested in the coaching situation, the 'observer's' or the disabled student's? Their main concern focused on whether or not the student would achieve the core learning outcomes relating to health and safety that constituted genuine competence standards. In not accepting this applicant, the institution felt that it was likely to have substantial reason to justify its decision.

Three key questions
1   Are criteria for admission fair, transparent, relevant to the requirements of the programme (including any professional requirements) and has it been ascertained that they do not unjustifiably disadvantage or debar applicants with disabilities?
2   Are applicants encouraged to disclose their impairment, within appropriate levels of confidentiality, so that the institution (both central services and the course team) can make the necessary anticipatory arrangements and/or reasonable adjustments?
3   Does your university's admissions process allow reasonable adjustments to enable applications from disabled students to be given equal consideration, including the offer of appropriate support for applicants attending interviews?

▶ Enrolment, registration and induction

In order for an education provider or employer to discriminate against a disabled person, they 'must have known or reasonably have known' about a person's disability. However, in order for them to say that they did not know about a student's disability, they must have taken 'reasonable steps' to find out about it through, for example, asking on an application form. If the applicant chooses not to divulge their disability despite the invitation to do so by the prospective university (or on the relevant application form), they will not be able to make a claim for discrimination under the DDA.

Students who disclose their disability have the right to this information being kept confidential. Such information is regarded as 'personally sensitive' under the Data Protection Act (DPA) and may not be passed on to others without permission. Institutions should have a policy outlining which members of staff will be told about the student's disability; typically, this might include the disability officer, the personal tutor, the exams officer and/or individual tutors.

If the student expresses a preference for limiting disclosure to just the centralised disability service, the University still has a duty to make reasonable adjustments, though this may be less comprehensive and/or appropriate if teaching staff are not informed. For example, staff may not provide the student with copies of handouts in advance of the lecture if there appears to be no valid reason for doing so.

Pre-course publicity and marketing materials should encourage disclosure, explaining that this is in the best interests of the student in terms of their gaining access to the fullest and most appropriate range of reasonable adjustments. With the safety of the applicant and/or those with whom they will engage in mind (for example, a degree in Sports Studies with an outdoor education component that includes rock climbing), some courses will need to ask direct questions about disability and health; however, no assumptions should be made about a person's lack of ability to undertake a course due to their impairment; each case should be reviewed on its own merits and individual risk assessments should be carried out by the relevant department in conjunction with the disability officer. If a student fails to divulge information that could potentially result in harm to themselves or others, and the university finds out the truth later, the student may be removed from the course.

Three key questions

4   Do admissions staff know what to do in the event of someone disclosing a disability? Who to contact, and how to maintain appropriate levels of confidentiality?
5   Do the enrolment procedures and induction events take into account the access requirements of disabled students, or orientation training to meet specific requirements, for example, of visually impaired students?
6   Is it made clear which aspects of the curriculum are essential to the identified learning outcomes (competence standards) and which can be modified, for example, the need to undertake field trips?

▶ First term/semester

There is much research (for example, Davies and Elias, 2003; Yorke,

1999) that shows student dropout is at its peak within the first semester. The transition to higher education can be difficult for many students, especially if they are living away from home for the first time and have to take on the tasks of shopping, cleaning, cooking, and managing finances. These challenges are often exacerbated for those disabled students who must take responsibility (possibly for the first time) for negotiating their own support for these domestic activities, as well as for their learning support. Clear and effective strategies, and named contacts who can ease transition, will help to improve rates of initial retention and ongoing success for these students.

At school or college level, students need to be supported to develop the confidence, skills and knowledge to apply to HE (Rose, 2006). In order to make the transition as smooth as possible, those with responsibility for providing support for disabled pupils should be prepared to liaise with the central services of the universities, with the permission of the student, to give information about the nature and levels of support previously provided. Teaching staff should note that adjustments to learning and teaching practices should be based on a consideration of the particular needs of the individual disabled student and not on the nature of their impairment.

Three key questions

7 How are staff notified of the particular learning and/or assessment requirements of disabled students on their courses?

8 In using more Socratic teaching and learning methods that require a high level of interactive communication skills, and that differ from those used in school or from other cultural norms, do teaching staff make it clear what they actually require from students for successful engagement?

9 How do teaching staff help disabled students and/or those who have been studying HE in a Further Education college to integrate with others on their course?

▶ **Year-to-year progression**

A wide range of factors such as the curriculum itself, pedagogical styles, assessment procedures, financial circumstances, employment and/or carer/domestic responsibilities may all enhance or inhibit student retention and success. Within modular programmes, it is often the case that, just as the disabled student achieves a suitable working environment in which their tutors know of, and are able to meet, their particular learning and assessment requirements, they must embark on a new module and have to 'educate' their new tutors from scratch again. Departments should develop effective recording and reporting procedures so that, where necessary, notes about adjustments to practice are passed on to new tutors. Clear and documented communication between the student, the tutors, the administration office and the centralised disability service are crucial to this process.

Three key questions

10 Is a range of assessment modes used throughout the course and are adjustments to assessments for disabled students organised effectively and in good time?
11 Is anonymous marking used?
12 Where particular students are unable to participate, are alternative arrangements made?

▶ Assessment and final year dissertation

Waterfield and West (2006, pp. 30–4) advocate a philosophy of assessment in higher education that aligns with 'universal design'. They champion a broad-spectrum solution to assessment that benefits everyone, not just disabled people, through clarifying the conceptual distinctions between three common approaches currently in use in HE in the UK: the 'contingent approach' (Waterfield and West, 2006), featuring modified assessment provision, which is often the result of negotiation between the exam office and the centralised disability service with no consultation with academic staff; the 'alternative approach', which aims to match the impairment to the assessment method (some students will always need such adjustments even when the anticipatory adjustments have been made); and the 'inclusive approach', through which academic staff allow for the assessment of the learning outcomes in a variety of different ways, and this is made available to *all* students.

Many dyslexic students studying practical or creative subjects, such as Computing or Fine Art, may well succeed in gaining good grades for their work in the earlier stages of their degree programme; however, they often fare less well in completing their dissertation, Courses need to give careful consideration to what they are assessing. Are marks awarded mainly for knowledge and understanding of the subject, or is the ability to write a critical learning outcome as well? If not, then the assessment mode should be flexible enough to allow students to demonstrate their learning in a variety of ways – to use a travel anal ogy, if the intended outcome is simply to arrive in Rome, then the mode of transport and the route and time taken for the journey are irrelevant.

Three key questions

13 Do staff use formative assessment and provide early opportunities for students to check they are on the right track – that they understand the level, register and demands of the course, including how to avoid plagiarism?

14 Are learning outcomes written in such a way that a range of assessment methods can be used to check knowledge and understanding?

15 Is the assessment regime flexible enough to allow some choice for students to accommodate any challenges associated with their impairment?

▶ Progression to employment/postgraduate study

Research (Archer et al., 2003) has shown that students from non-traditional backgrounds can face obstacles not only in accessing higher education and achieving successful progression, but also in successful transition into the labour market and postgraduate education. In general, the findings of Tunnah et al. (Disabilities Task Group, 2008) challenged some of the previous assumptions about disabled graduates in the labour market. They found that, overall, there was substantial parity between disabled and non-disabled graduates obtaining employment; however, disabled graduates as a whole continued to be more likely to be unemployed (9%) than non-disabled graduates (6.3%); and of those in employment, 54.9% of non-disabled graduates were recorded as working full-time as compared with only 48.9% of disabled graduates. Notably, disabled graduates (9.7%) were more likely than their non-disabled peers (8.2%) to be found in part time and voluntary work. These reported trends indicate a continuation of the pattern from the 2003 survey, so there is every indication that this tendency will continue unless active steps are taken to intercede and enhance disabled students' employability so that more equitable employment rates are achieved (reports for these and subsequent years are available at www.agcas.org.uk/ agcas_ resources/17-What-Happens-Next-A-Report-on-the-First-Destinations-of-Disabled-Graduates (last accessed 5 July 2010).

Three key questions

16 Are students clear about their rights and obligations in relation to disclosure in applying for jobs?

17 Are students aware of their entitlements in relation to reasonable adjustments in the workplace and initiatives that support this, such as the Access to Work Scheme?

18 Have the disabled students been given access to comprehensive information about the competence standards that they would have to meet in professions for which they are academically qualified, and on the implications for disabled students regarding their entry to those professions?

▶ Conclusions

There is much anecdotal evidence to suggest that one of the unanticipated outcomes of the DDA is the deployment of more sophisticated and covert approaches to discrimination in education and particularly in employment (Chapman, 2009). This view appears to be supported by the data; however, such discrimination does not appear to be uniformly applied. Deal (2003, p. 906) describes evidence of a hierarchy of impairments, a view supported by Leacy and Tunnah (2009, p. 26). They report that graduates with non-visible disabilities continue to perform better than graduates with more visible/apparent impairments, except for graduates with mental health difficulties, who are least likely to be employed (Jones et al., 2006, p. 434). So we have yet to achieve a fair playing field and we find discriminatory attitudes to disabled people, even by disabled people themselves within the subcategories of impairment. In order to help address this ongoing discrimination, the Learning for All partner of LearnHigher focused on research and the further development of a web-based resource (http://scips.worc.ac.uk) to help teaching staff develop inclusive learning and teaching practices. The continued high level of usage of this resource internationally, suggests that teaching staff are indeed committed to the principles of inclusion, and that they appreciate some support in its practice.

▶ References

Archer, L., Hutchings, M. and Ross, A. (2003) *Higher Education and Social Class: Issues of Exclusion and Inclusion* (London: Routledge Falmer).

Chapman, V. (2009) 'Employability and disability', *Teaching Learning and Assessment*, Leeds Metropolitan University, April. Available at: www.leedsmet.ac.uk/alt/publications.htm (last accessed 29/3/10).

Connell, B. R. et al. (1997) *The Principles of Universal Design*, NC State University, Center for Universal Design. Available at: www.design.ncsu.edu/cud/about_ud/udprinciples.htm (last accessed 29/3/10).

Davies, R. and Elias, P. (2003) *Dropping Out: A Study of Early Leavers from Higher Education* (London: DfE).

Deal, M. (2003) 'Disabled people's attitudes toward other impairment groups: a hierarchy of impairments', *Disability and Society* 18 (7), pp. 897–910. Available at: http://web.ebscohost.com/ehost/pdf?vid=3&hid=12&sid=1f858254-ec72-4f4c-97ba-57c93368f959%40SRCSM2 (last accessed: 11/01/10).

Department for Education and Skills (2002) *Providing Work Placement for Disabled Students*, DFES publications. Available at: www.lifelonglearning.co.uk/placements/index.htm (last accessed 29/3/10).

Disabilities Task Group (2006) 'What Happens Next? A Report on the First Destinations of 2004 Graduates with Disabilities', Association of Graduate Careers Advisory Services (AGCAS) Disabilities Task Group. Available at: www.agcas.org.uk/agcas_resources/17-What-Happens-Next A Report-on-the-First-Destinations-of-Disabled-Graduates (last accessed 29/3/10).

Healey, M., Fuller, M., Bradley, A. and Hall, T. (2006) 'Listening to students: the experiences of disabled students of learning at university', in M. Adams and S. Brown (eds) *Towards Inclusive Learning in Higher Education: Developing Curricula for Disabled Students* (London: RoutledgeFalmer).

HMSO (2005) 'Disability and Discrimination Act' (Chapter 13), HMSO, London. Available at: www.opsi.gov.uk/acts/acts2005/pdf/ukpga_20050013_en.pdf (last accessed 14/10/10).

Jones, M., Latreille, P. L. and Sloane, P. J. (2006) 'Disability, gender and the British labour market', *Oxford Economic Papers* 58 (3), July, 407–49. Available from: http://oep.oxford-journals.org/cgi/reprint/58/3/407. (last accessed 18/02/10).

Leacy, A. and Tunnah, E. (2009) *What Happens Next? A Report on the First Destinations of 2008 Disabled Graduates*, AGCAS. Available from: www.agcas.org.uk/agcas_resources/17 (last accessed 29/3/10).

Oliver, M. (1990) 'The individual and social models of disability', *Joint Workshop of the Living Options Group and the Research Unit of the Royal College of Physicians*. Available from: www.leeds.ac.uk/disability-studies/archiveuk/Oliver/in%20soc%20dis.pdf (last accessed 11/01/10).

QAA (2008) *The Framework for Higher Education Qualifications in England, Wales and Northern Ireland*, Quality Assurance Agency for Higher Education, August. Available from: www.qaa.ac.uk/academicinfrastructure/FHEQ/EWNI08/FHEQ08.pdf (last accessed: 18/02/10).

Rose, C. (2006) 'Do you have a disability – yes or no? Or is there a better way of asking?', *Guidance on Disability Disclosure and Respecting Confidentiality* (London: Learning ans Skills Development Agency).

Waterfield, J. and West, B. (2006) *Inclusive Assessment in Higher Education: A Resource for Change*, University of Plymouth; the published outcome of the Staff–Student Partnership for Assessment Change and Evaluation Project (SPACE). Available from: www.plymouth.ac.uk/pages/view.asp?page=10494 (last accessed 29/3/10).

Vanhala, L. and Kelemen, R. D. (2008) 'The Shift to the Rights Model of Disability in the EU and Canada'. Paper presented at the annual meeting of the Law and Society Association, Hilton Bonaventure, Montreal, Quebec, Canada, 27 May 2008. Available from: www.allacademic.commeta/p_mla_apa_research_citation/2/3/6/1/9/p236190_index.html (last accessed 29/3/10).

Yorke, M. (1999) *Leaving Early: Undergraduate Non-completion in Higher Education* (London: Falmer).

Section C

Developing Effective Academic Practice

10 Building Student Confidence in Mathematics and Numeracy

Mundeep Gill and Martin Greenhow

▶ **Summary**

This chapter demonstrates how we can build students' confidence in mathematics and numeracy, starting with a brief review of key issues that students face and examples of strategies and resources that have been used in response.
   The following questions arise:

- How can we identify and access 'at-risk' students?
- How can we make effective provision for such students?
- How can we get students to engage with such provision?
- How can we measure, however imprecisely, the efficacy of such provision?

Using Brunel University as a case study, we advocate a blended use of resources, including: diagnostic tests, confidence logs, existing and bespoke computer-aided learning (CAL), 'topic of the week' tutorials, one-to-one drop-ins, the Maths Café and computer aided assessments (CAA). Student feedback demonstrates their popularity, whilst subsequent examination performance provides a measure of their (joint) effect.
   We then focus on our Mathletics CAA system. Our experience demonstrates that correctly implemented CAA benefits students not only by building confidence via repeated practice but also by filling knowledge and expertise gaps in rather elementary mathematics that lecturers generally, but sometimes erroneously, take for granted. In our view, learning developers need to introduce and integrate this type of support as well as more traditional resources.

▶ Introduction

The decrease in the numbers of students taking Mathematics post-16 has led many UK universities to change their entrance requirements. Students can now undertake even highly quantitative degree courses, such as Economics and Physics, without completing an AS-level or A-level in Mathematics. For students with Mathematics A-level, not only has there been a steady decline in the grades (Smith, 2004) but the quality of the students is also questioned; students can now achieve a relatively good grade and yet still be unprepared for the mathematics covered in their degrees (Hawkes and Savage, 2000). Lecturers must tailor content and delivery to student cohorts with diverse mathematical backgrounds, while at the same time meeting the mathematical needs of the course as a whole. Other issues, such as students entering higher education (HE) via non-traditional routes and those with mathematics anxiety, have been discussed at length in a previously published literature review (see Gill, 2007).

It is therefore important to help students not only to bridge any skills gaps but also to build their mathematical confidence. This should encourage students to engage with the material and motivate them to overcome their difficulties and hence to progress (Moxley et al., 2001).

▶ Resources and mechanisms

Whilst a wide range of resources and mechanisms can be used to help students, time, and hence cost, greatly influences what can be offered to them. One well-established mechanism is 'pre-degree' courses such as summer schools or foundation programmes (see Gill, 2007, for an overview). These are successful but expensive. Although they help some students to bridge knowledge gaps and build confidence, they do not meet the mathematical needs of the whole student population.

Trying to support this wider population, the Higher Education Funding Council for England (HEFCE) have funded the development of freely-available resources ranging from generic resources, such as mathcentre (mathcentre, 2009) and Mathematics Hyper-Tutorials (McDonald, 2009) that can be used across disciplines, to more subject-specific resources such as the Metal Project (Metal, 2009) and HELM (HELM, 2009). However, simply telling students that these resources are available and expecting them to embrace them in their own learning is not realistic. Many students do not possess the study and/or manipulative skills to build up new skills independently, regardless of the sophistication of the resources. Moreover, lecturers and teaching staff do not usually have the time to provide students with extra support. Hence some universities have introduced Mathematics Support Centres (Pell and Croft, 2008), which range from large-scale centres, such as Loughborough University's Mathematics Learning Support Centre (2009) and Coventry University's centre (Coventry University, 2009), to smaller-scale support services, such as at Brunel University, described below.

▶ Support at Brunel

At Brunel University, a Maths Support Tutor was appointed to help embed widely available resources in undergraduate courses for a range of departments and to give extra support to students who needed to overcome underlying mathematical difficulties/issues of confidence before they could access the material taught in regular lectures. Support included one-to-one sessions, drop-ins and the maintenance of a web portal (LearnHigher, 2009), which directs students to online resources. We here discuss the weekly workshops and the Maths Café; both were aimed at those reading degrees other than mathematics (here termed 'non-mathematicians') to help them bridge the gap between GCSE and undergraduate mathematics and to help build confidence.

Weekly workshops

Weekly two-hour workshops are scheduled during term time. Since they are available to all non-mathematicians, they are generic. However, the last part of each session gives students the opportunity to apply the skills they have learnt to discipline-specific questions.

The workshop room only has seating space for 30 students, but when there is a high demand repeat workshops are advertised. Workshops are run as small group sessions to encourage students' active involvement (Griffiths, 2003; Cannon and Newble, 2000). Sessions are designed to give students ample opportunity to ask questions, and to help them identify and overcome any misconceptions (Biggs, 2003).

Whilst much preparatory work is put into designing and delivering the workshops, there is still a need to be flexible with the material covered since the student cohort attending the session is not known until the workshop takes place. To get an idea of students' level of understanding of the workshop topic(s), confidence logs are used (Figure 10.1 shows a typical log). Students are asked to complete a log when they arrive at the workshop. The log asks students to rate their confidence with each of the skills that will be covered in the session. This helps the tutor to get a better understanding of the level of students' competence with the topic area at the start of the session. Since students are asked to complete the same log at the end of the session, it also enables the tutor to assess whether the small group workshop has helped students build confidence. Students themselves can use this as an opportunity to assess which skills they are now confident with and which still need further development.

Confidence Log	Confidence Level					
	Very Confident	Confident	Some Confidence	Little Confidence	No Confidence	No Knowledge
• Applying the rules of indices						
• Expanding bracketed expressions (e.g. 3ac(5ab+2c))						
• Multiplying together two bracketed terms (e.g. (x+7)(x–4))						
• Factorisation of algebraic expressions (e.g. $5x^2-15x$)						

Figure 10.1 Confidence log
An example taken from the workshop Algebra 1.

Once students have completed the 'after' log at the end of the workshop, students and tutor discuss which areas of weakness remain and require further help. At this point students are given extra resources, and directed to online resources. The confidence log also monitors whether the structure of the workshop and material covered has helped students develop skills and confidence. Figure 10.2 shows aggregated results for the 2007/8 academic year.

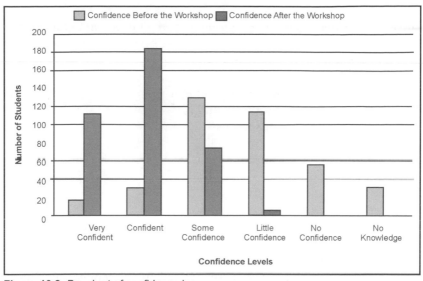

Figure 10.2 Bar chart of confidence logs
The results from all confidence logs that were completed for the weekly workshops in 2007/8.

Figure 10.2 shows that, for many students, initial confidence in the skills being covered is low. A small percentage of students (8%) did not even have any previous knowledge of some of the skills. Only 13% of students stated initially that they were either very confident or confident. Although the workshops were aimed at non-mathematicians, of the students who declared their previous grades, 21% had previously completed an AS-level or A-Level in Mathematics. Their objective in attending the sessions was mainly for revision.

The striking feature of Figure 10.2 is the shift from the low end of the confidence scale at the start of the session to the higher level of confidence at the end of the session. By the end of the workshops, 78% of students felt they were very confident or confident with the skills that were covered. This shows a very positive change in attitude, which encourages them to engage with and overcome the mathematical difficulties they are having in their lectures.

The use of confidence logs in the small group workshops has shown that this environment can build confidence with mathematics and fill knowledge gaps. These logs can be adapted and used in other situations; they can also be given to students to use independently to identify their own areas of weakness and hence seek out further support.

Maths Café

Since 2007/8 we have successfully run a Maths Café during the Easter revision period. This is a two-week event (again aimed at non-mathematicians) where students

- can receive one-to-one support on a drop-in basis;
- collect paper-based resources; and
- have access to online resources.

Approximately £5000 was used to pay for

- initial planning and advertising;
- tutors to provide the one-to-one support;
- paper-based resources printed in bulk (mainly from mathcentre, see mathcentre, 2009);
- light refreshments provided throughout each day;
- data collection and analysis, reporting and dissemination (internally and externally).

One of the main reasons for the Café was to meet the demand for one-to-one sessions prior to the examination period; this required two tutors permanently on duty.

We felt it was important to get an understanding of the types of problems students were having. It was hoped that information collected could lead to developing an integrated approach to supporting students from the different courses across the university. We collected data on the students' gender, level of study, course, and the mathematical topic/skill they needed help with.

This event attracted similar numbers of student visits in its first two years (325 in 2008/9 and 352 in 2007/8). Although absolute numbers of students attending are important, it is equally important that the target groups are making use of this extra revision resource. Table 10.1 summarises data from the Maths Café for the two years.

The Maths Café is clearly appealing to the target groups of students from the Foundation Level and from Level 1 who are studying quantitative modules but did not undertake any post-16 mathematics qualifications. Feedback collected from the students indicates a high satisfaction rate, with 63% of students in 2008/9 (and 98% in 2007/8) finding the support given very useful or useful.

Considering the time of year, we expected a positive impact on students' examination marks, ideally moving them from a fail to a pass

Table 10.1 Students attending the Maths Café

Academic Year	2007/8	2008/9
Percentage male attending	74%	67%
Modal GCSE grade	B	B
Percentage of students who had **not** completed an AS/A-Level in Mathematics	61%/65%	74%/78%
Percentage of students from:		
Foundation Level	34%	33%
Level 1	56%	61%

in their quantitative methods modules. However, it is difficult to deter-mine this impact since the Café was an optional resource for students and was not designed and set up in a way in which control groups could be used (or identified). The first year the Café took place (2007/8), 55% of students who were enrolled on a Level 1 quantitative methods module attended to get help with a final piece of coursework and to prepare for the end of year examination. Hence the exam results for the academic year 2007/8 for this module have been compared with results from the previous two years to determine any impact. From the analysis it was found that students from 2007/8 had done worse than the cohort of the previous two years. It is difficult to establish if there were any confounding influences acting, such as a change in teaching or admissions policy (Gill and Greenhow, 2008). In our opinion, these students knew they were poorly prepared for their assessments and therefore sought help in the Café. Clearly it is not known if students would have done worse if this extra support had not been provided. Overall, based on the number of students attending the Café and the positive feedback received, this was a positive initiative that helped many students 'bridge the gap'.

▶ CAA as a confidence-building tool

All of the above resources act in a mainly responsive mode; students themselves need to take the initiative to access materials and support. Even the highly popular Maths Café did not reach all the students who needed it. To some extent, this is a vicious circle; weak students often do not seek the help they need and hence become weaker. For many, especially the weaker students, assessment drives learning and hence regular testing may provide a proactive, rather than responsive, way to keep students on task, sharpen their skills and ultimately build their confidence. CAA provides at least a partial solution to achieving these goals within reasonable staffing constraints. An extensive review of how CAA can be implemented across a range of disciplines in higher education can be found in Sim et al. (2004), whilst the advantages of providing timely feedback, testing large groups and allowing students to repeat questions are highlighted by Bull and McKenna (2004) and Brown et al. (1997).

The special nature of CAA within mathematics (broadly interpreted to include topics with substantial mathematical content) requires some preliminary comment. Many basic mathematical techniques and skills lend themselves to objective testing, and hence may be implemented in a sufficiently rich CAA system. What sets mathematics apart is that accuracy and technical mastery of the basics is absolutely necessary before students can aspire to understand concepts fully or to use their mathematics meaningfully in their own discipline. CAA can help secure these basics but we fully acknowledge that higher-level skills such as mathematical modelling, proof, devising solution strategies and interpreting results are largely inaccessible to objective questioning. (These more aspirational module goals are better assessed by more synoptic tasks and a human marker.) In short, CAA tests necessary, but not sufficient, skills for a typical mathematics module. Nevertheless, putting the basics in place for the majority of students would be a substantial achievement in itself. Consequently syllabuses were changed to include some (typically 20%–30%) of the module mark as a suite of CAA tests covering the basics (typically between 5 and 10) spread throughout the academic year. The continuously-available tests were not invigilated, so that group work was implicitly sanctioned (even encouraged), and up to five attempts (with new questions, see below) were allowed. Students' best ever mark counted towards their module assessment. The rest of the assessment was from a traditional unseen written exam, typically comprising more synoptic questions, and the module could only be passed as a whole if the exam mark was 40% or more, regardless of the overall mark. This rule therefore neatly sidesteps any real advantage that could be gained by cheating on the CAA tests, for example by aliasing (getting a friend to take the test).

CAA for elementary mathematics dates from at least the early 1990s with systems such as CALM (2001). Today, highly sophisticated systems like STACK (Sangwin and Grove, 2006) and the commercial package MapleTA® allow free-form mathematical input. These systems are, however, not that user-friendly and the student training required precludes them from general use beyond Level 1 mathematics undergraduates (where the required questions may need such a powerful system). At Brunel University, we use Mathletics, described by Greenhow (2008), based on an extended form of Question Mark Perception (see QuestionMark, 2009). A strength of Mathletics is that its development over a number of years has resulted in extensive coverage of mathematical topics ranging from those at GCSE to those needed for the second year at university – see Greenhow (2008) for a list or Greenhow (2009) for downloads.

More elementary questions, especially those on numeracy, form part of the diagnostic, formative and summative tests taken by roughly 500 students from our Foundations of IT and Foundations of Engineering programmes, and from Design and Technology, Economics, Mathematical Sciences, Mechanical Engineering and Education. This assessment service is central to the way we have embedded LearnHigher activities at Brunel. An increasingly useful feature of the (developing) question database is that a large number of the topic areas occur repeatedly in quantitative method (quants), maths or core skills modules so that the (decontextualised) questions serve many modules across the university. However, it is worth remarking that engaging some of the above departments was much more difficult than expected.

Described in more detail in the above references, several features of Mathletics are worth emphasising:

1 Question Mark Perception allows authors 'authoring access' to some underlying code. This means that question authors can go beyond the standard question templates, writing their own Javascript to allow different question functionality.
2 Each question is actually a short Javascript program that incorporates random parameters, so that each question style produces many thousands, or even millions of question realisations, allowing the student to attempt apparently new questions each time, but testing the same underlying skill(s). The random parameters carry through from the question stem to all aspects of the question (key, distracters, feedback and answer file data).
3 When students get mathematics wrong, they often do so for a specific reason; such incorrect reasons are known as mal-rules and can be

algebraically encoded. This means that we can infer from a student's response the nature of their incorrect thinking and offer tailored feedback. Students typically spend the majority of their time studying this feedback (Gill and Greenhow, 2007). Moreover, students often guess or knowingly put in a wrong answer simply to read the feedback – they are, in fact, using the assessment as a learning resource.

Our experience with Mathletics is that it is generally robust, but not completely foolproof. Discussion of issues and some of the educational spin-offs can be found in Greenhow (2008).

To demonstrate the efficacy of using CAA, we can look at the largest cohort – some 300 first year economics students. A 'before/after CAA' comparison of **examination** marks showed that the mean increased from 48% (count=243, stdev=22%) to 53% (count=286, stdev=25%). With the CAA component included, the mean mark moved to an even more respectable 56% (count=304, stdev=24%).

That this increase might reasonably be attributed to the introduction of CAA is supported by examination of the circa 15,000 answer files this cohort produced during the academic year. This wealth of data gives some fascinating statistics on which questions/topics pose the greatest difficulty, which questions discriminate best, and how the question type affects these measures. Detailed analysis is beyond the scope of this chapter, but we should note that the sequence of marks obtained at each attempt shows that most students seriously engaged with the tests and especially the feedback, using it to improve their subsequent performances. Although more analysis is needed using data from future academic years, the CAA prepared students well for their exam by building confidence and engagement with mathematics, especially in the first semester. How students improved their performance is probably discernible from their own perceptions of the CAA, of which the following are typical:

> You can practise and learn at the same time. It helps students gain more confidence as most of the students struggle with maths.

> No stress. You can do them whenever you like. Helped me understand certain concepts better and in depth. Interesting, challenging questions.

> Gives a range of questions. Answers are easy to follow. It has increased my confidence in my mathematical ability and increased my curiosity of maths in general. It is a safe way of studying without being hit by the teacher.

Figures 10.3 to 10.5 demonstrate the opportunities for feedback and the types of problems which are used.

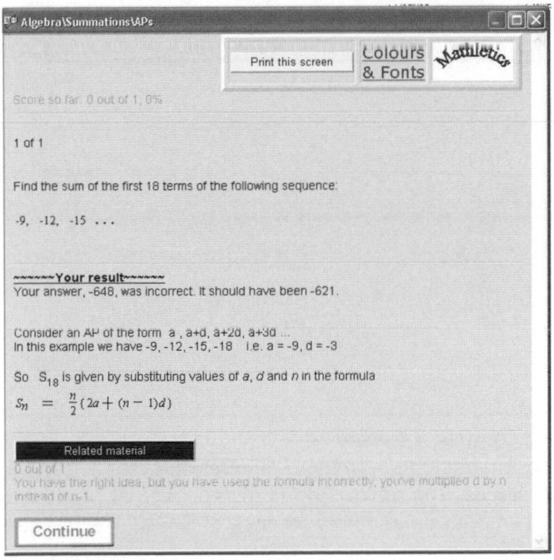

Figure 10.3 The feedback screen
The feedback screen from a simple responsive numerical input question with random parameters a, d and n, comprising general feedback and responsive feedback specifically triggered by the students' input and based on a known mal-rule. The 'Related material' button automatically links to a variety of web resources (pdf files, web pages, videos) on this topic.

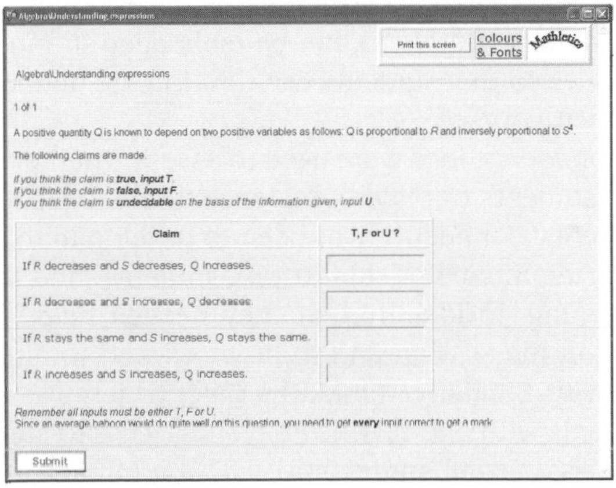

Figure 10.4 Algebraic question
A true/false subject/property question. Here the student is first required to formulate the relationship between Q and R and S mathematically (making this question harder than its clone, where the relationship is displayed) and then to interpret the meaning of this relationship. Each claim splits into two parts; a randomly chosen subject, and a randomly chosen property. (In the first claim, the subject is 'If R decreases and S decreases' and the property is 'Q increases'.) Although students are not required to do any mathematical manipulations, the answer files show that these types of questions are demanding for all students (and hence do not provide a high level of discrimination). A student needs to get all entries correct (i.e. input U, T, F, U) to get the mark.

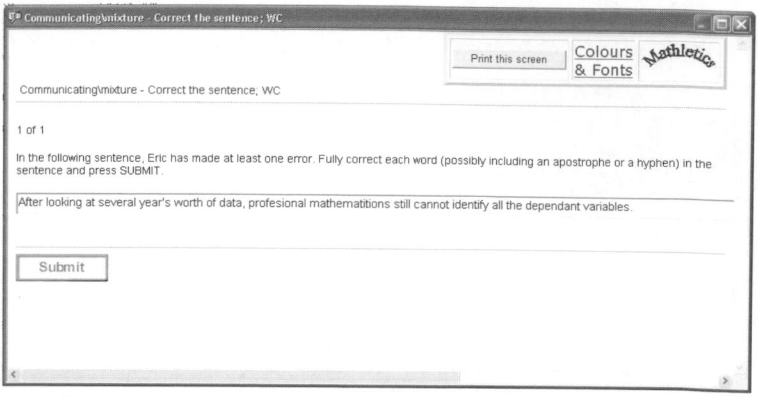

Figure 10.5 A word correction question
A randomly chosen sentence has a random number of errors in certain positions: here errors occur in four places. The name 'Eric' is also chosen at random from a list of names that reflect the gender and ethnic balance of British 16–25-year-olds.

▶ Conclusion

The need to develop resources to aid students in building confidence and bridging knowledge gaps in mathematics in higher education is no longer as pertinent as it once was. What is necessary is to understand how widely available resources can be embedded in modules/courses across disciplines so that students can develop the mathematical skills required for their course.

At Brunel, confidence logs were used to assess whether weekly workshops helped students to build confidence in the skills being covered. Although students' confidence was seen to develop in this small group environment it required students to take initiative and take charge of their own learning, to identify that they needed help with the skills being covered in the session and to be motivated to attend this extra curricular activity. Similarly, the Maths Café, which was a project that provided students with one-to-one help and access to paper-based and online resources, needed students to take the initiative to attend and engage with the activity. Although both of these projects were aimed and focused at the target group (non-mathematicians) and were successful in helping those students that attended to bridge knowledge gaps and build confidence with mathematics, not all students who needed the extra help accessed this additional support.

More successful at identifying 'at risk' students were the Computer-Aided Assessments (CAA), which have been used across disciplines and levels for diagnostic, formative and summative purposes at Brunel University. The introduction of CAA into a large, Level 1, quantitative methods module has increased overall module marks by giving students the opportunity to interact and engage with a resource which provides them with ample feedback and gives them the opportunity to repeat the testing of a skill without them seeing exactly the same question again.

▶ References

Biggs, J. (2003) *Teaching for Quality Learning at University* (Buckingham: Society for Research in Higher Education and the Open University Press).

Brown, G., Bull, J. and Pendlebury, M. (1997) *Assessing Student Learning in Higher Education* (London: Routledge).

Bull, J. and Mckenna, C. (2004) *Blueprint for Computer-Assisted Assessment* (London: RoutledgeFalmer).

CALM (2001) *Computer Aided Learning in Mathematics*, Department of Mathematics, Heriot-Watt University. Available at: www.calm.hw.ac.uk (last accessed 29/3/10).

Cannon, R. and Newble, D. (2000) *A Handbook for Teachers in Universities and Colleges*, 4th edition (London: Kogan Page).

Coventry University (2009) Faculty of Engineering and Computing, Mathematics Support Centre. Available at: http://cuportal.coventry.ac.uk/C13/MSC/default.aspx (last accessed 29/3/10).

Gill, M. (2007) *Issues with Teaching Mathematics to Non-mathematician Undergraduates*, LearnHigher CETL. Available at: www.learnhigher.ac.uk/learningareas/numeracymathsstatistics/home.htm (last accessed 29/3/10).

Gill, M. and Greenhow, M. (2007) 'Learning and teaching via online maths tests: update and extensions', *Proceedings of the Science Learning and Teaching Conference 2007* (Keele: Keele University Press).

Gill, M. and Greenhow, M. (2008) 'Maths Café – an initiative to help non-mathematicians', *CETL–MSOR Conference Proceedings* (Higher Education Academy, Maths, Stats and OR Network).

Greenhow, M. (2008) 'Mathletics – a suite of computer-assisted assessments', *MSOR Connections* 8 (3), 7–10.

Greenhow, M. (2009) 'Mathletics – downloads for private study'. Available at: http://people.brunel.ac.uk/~mastmmg/./Downloads/entry.htm (last accessed 29/3/10).

Griffiths, S. (2003) 'Teaching and learning in small groups', in H. Fry, S. Ketteridge and S. Marshall (eds) *The Effective Academic: A Handbook for Enhanced Academic Purpose* (London: Kogan Page).

Hawkes, T. and Savage, M. D. (eds) (2000) *Measuring the Mathematics Problem* (London: Engineering Council).

HELM (2009) 'Helping Engineers Learn Mathematics'. Available at: http://helm.lboro.ac.uk (last accessed 29/3/10).

LearnHigher (2009) 'Learnhigher – Centre for Excellence in Teaching and Learning'. Available at: www.learnhigher.ac.uk/ (last accessed 29/3/10).

mathcentre (2009) Website: www.mathcentre.ac.uk (last accessed 29/3/10).

Mathematics Learning Support Centre (2009) 'Mathematics Learning Support Centre – a centre for excellence, Loughborough University'. Available at: http://mlsc.lboro.ac.uk (last accessed 29/3/10).

McDonald, G. (2009) 'Mathematics Hyper-Tutorials, University of Salford'. Available at: www.cse.salford.ac.uk/profiles/gsmcdonald/PPLATO.php (last accessed 29/3/10).

Metal (2009) 'Mathematics for Economics: enhancing Teaching and Learning'. Available at: www.metalproject.co.uk (last accessed 29/3/10).

Moxley, D., Najor-Durack, A. and Dunbridge, C. (2001) *Keeping Students in Higher Education* (London: Kogan Page).

Pell, G. and Croft, T. (2008) 'Mathematics support – support for all?' *Teaching Mathematics and its Applications* 24 (4), 167–73.

QuestionMark (2009) *Questionmark Computing Limited.* Available at: www.questionmark.com/ uk/perception/index.aspx (last accessed 29/3/10).

Sangwin, C. and Grove, M. (2006) 'STACK: addressing the needs of the "neglected learners"'. *First WebALT Conference and Exhibition, January 5–6, Technical University of Eindhoven, Netherlands* (Helsinki: Oy WebALT Inc., University of Helsinki) pp. 81–95.

Sim, G., Holifield, P. and Brown, M. (2004) 'Implementation of computer assisted assessment: lessons from the literature', *ALT-J, Research in Learning Technology* 12 (3), 215–29.

Smith, A. (2004) *Making Mathematics Count: The Report of Professor Adrian Smith's Inquiry into Post-14 Mathematics Education* (London: The Stationery Office).

11 Negotiating and Nurturing: Challenging Staff and Student Perspectives of Academic Writing

Rebecca Bell

▶ Summary

This chapter summarises major current issues concerning student academic writing, reviews the three major approaches that have been proposed to solve them, and then evaluates the approach adopted by one UK university to address these problems in a way which effectively complements established methods. Using a communities of practice approach, learning developers have been able to forge new and more productive relationships with academic teaching staff. The teaching staff have developed new insights and the confidence to change their approaches and practices.

▶ Introduction

Although often seen as dusty, dry and problematic by both students and staff, academic writing is an important aspect of the university experience. Effective communication is often cited as a primary graduate attribute (QAA, 2009). However, the poor levels of student literacy identified in many undergraduate essays does not support such alleged development (*TES*, 2007; *Independent*, 2006). The use of academic writing as the primary tool for assessment also ensures that this issue cannot be easily ignored by those in the sector.

Confusion over who 'owns' the problem of academic writing, and therefore who should address it, is just one of the many issues up for debate. This confusion leaves students and staff feeling frustrated and powerless, unaware of the ways in which writing can be developed and the additional support available. As such, any sense of development is often neglected in favour of a 'quick fix' approach.

Working closely with academics, support staff and students, learning developers are privy to most sides of the learning process. Being in a unique position; they are often able to see the whole picture, mediating between the often competing perspectives of students and staff. As a learning developer based centrally within the Centre for Academic Standards and Quality (CASQ) at Nottingham Trent University (NTU), I have established a number of initiatives with colleagues to help them engage and support their students' writing development. This chapter explores two of them: the Academic Writing Readers' Group (AWRG) is a reading group for academics, examining the current theory and debates surrounding student academic writing; whilst the Writing Across the Curriculum (WAC) project has a more practical approach. These projects provide colleagues with the time and space to discuss discipline-specific curriculum-based practical writing activities. Both groups provide a forum for discussion between learning developers and academic staff, whilst feedback from students also influences the discussions. These projects offer a valuable insight into student academic writing within contemporary higher education, allowing student writing to be viewed as an opportunity and not a problem.

This chapter has been written to encourage interaction with the reader. Please consider the questions at the beginning of each section in response to your own situation, as it was answering similar questions that allowed for a greater understanding of academic writing at our own institution.

▶ Why is academic writing important?

What's important to you about academic writing and why do you care?

Academic writing is important as the lynchpin holding together much of the university experience. It allows students to summarise and develop their knowledge, express themselves and ultimately receive a degree classification based on how they master these processes. It is also important as an area where students often struggle and where they are not necessarily well prepared via their previous educational experiences. The writing process that students experience at university is often very different from that experienced in post-16 education (Foster, Bell and Salzano, 2008). The transition between the two sectors in many instances is poorly managed, leaving students inadequately equipped to cope with the heightened expectations (Cook and Leckey, 1999).

▶ What is the problem? Twenty-first-century issues with academic writing

What do you perceive as being the main problem with academic writing in your situation?
My conversations with staff and students uncovered primary concerns that fuelled the establishment of the two projects. One concern raised by colleagues is the lack of student knowledge about what is required of their writing at a higher education (HE) level. Academic staff were also concerned about whether academic writing fell under their remit, with some stating that their expertise lay in their subject area as opposed to teaching academic writing. The majority of staff are therefore often unaware of their students' writing ability until the marking of the assessment. Consequently, students may be referred for writing support at quite a late stage, overriding any sense of development with one of crisis management. This approach also ensures that the problem is perceived as a remedial one – students have to make a mistake before they can begin to develop their writing.

Students leaving post-16 education may be asked to do very little writing in HE until their first assessment – only then perhaps realising that they are struggling to cope. Colleagues report that some student work is laden with errors, and this may be because they are given very few chances to practise and develop outside the pressure of assessment. Another primary concern is that once students receive a pass grade they do not consult the assignment feedback again (Burke, 2009). The module tutor, who may never see the student again, marks the paper, advises on certain areas, and also moves on. The tutor does not know if feedback has been digested and addressed, and the student may not see its relevance to future modules. Consequently the process becomes disjointed and development of writing rarely takes place.

The issues highlighted above are wide ranging and cover everything from preparation to long-term development, assessment and feedback. Students are often caught in a relentless cycle of assessment with little awareness of how to develop their writing and little motivation to do so beyond their next assignment. But by providing students with few opportunities or incentives to practise the craft of academic writing, staff leave themselves open to masses of poorly written manuscripts. For writing development to take place, there are two major issues that need addressing: staff need to provide opportunities for students to write more frequently; whilst students need to value and engage with those opportunities to enhance their writing beyond assessment.

▶ How, as a sector, are we currently addressing the issue of student academic writing in higher education?

How are you currently addressing the issue you highlighted earlier? Is it working?

There are three main approaches to academic writing in higher educa- tion: the skills model, the socialisation model and the academic litera- cies approach. These three approaches form the bedrock of writing support in many institutions.

The skills model

Often referred to as the deficit model (Lea and Street, 1998), this perceives writing as a skill to be learnt. It involves the teaching of vari- ous study skills (including writing) through individual one-to-one support sessions or group workshops. Such classes are usually based in the student support centre and often conducted by non-academic staff. Sessions focus on generic-based support outside of the subject discipline and tend to focus on individual projects or assignments where students may be struggling. Historically, academic writing has been identified as a student-centred problem (Lea and Street, 1998), with the deficit model suggesting that failings are caused by students' lack of education or motivation.

Consequently, the skills model offers practical solutions. Although imperfect, this model does have an important role to play and is main- tained by most institutions as a vital area of support. It provides staff with a place to refer students, thus removing the pressure of additional writing tutoring in an already crowded curriculum, and provides moti- vated students with an opportunity to develop their writing.

Socialisation

The socialisation model (also known as the institutional default model) suggests that students acquire academic writing skills through 'implicit induction' (Ganobcsik-Williams, 2006, p. 32). As such, the socialisation model is more concerned with issues of context and culture than the skills model, and challenges the presumption that academic writing is solely an individual issue. This approach assumes students will develop knowledge and skills in their chosen subject simply through being immersed in the culture of higher education.

The socialisation model has its roots in constructivist education methods. By identifying that 'Learning is a social activity' (Hein, 1991, p. 2), socialisation into the higher education culture is given an important role in student development. However, analysis from linguistics (Spack and Zamel, 1998) suggests that, given the complexities of language, we cannot assume that students will simply soak up the language of a complex discourse that may have taken their lecturers many years to understand.

Academic literacies

Limitations of the above models led to the development of the academic literacies approach to student academic writing. This approach highlights the institutional culture and context in which writing takes place and the ways this may encourage or hinder writing development, examining the ways in which current models and practices may need to be adapted in order to accommodate the changing culture of higher education. By building on and developing both the skills and socialisation models, academic literacies has begun to question the very nature of academic writing and consequently the very nature of higher education itself. Research has also examined issues of identity and writing with regard to class, race (Lillis, 1999, p. 24) and gender (Francis, 2005), highlighting the effects of increasing diversity within the field of higher education.

Students may feel isolated and disengaged from their writing and need to find their own identity and voice within their discipline. Lillis (1999) found that some students were actually fully aware of the correct styles and technicalities of writing academically. Despite this, they felt that writing in such a manner did not reflect their personal voice. These findings challenge both skills and socialisation approaches, instead providing sound evidence for a more holistic model, which examines the wider context in which writing takes place.

Resolving the differences?

None of these methods alone is sufficient to tackle the issues identified earlier and institutions need to be aware that the models, 'are not mutually exclusive and do not follow a simple linear pattern' (Ganobscik-Williams, 2004, p. 36). The three models interlink and each plays an important role in the various facets of academic writing. Despite their differences, the approaches confirm that writing needs to be made a clear part of the learning process, not simply something that can be soaked up, or 'solved' at a one-off support session. This requires a holistic approach that engages both staff and students in developing and valuing student writing. In an already crowded curriculum, this is clearly a difficult thing to achieve.

▶ How are we addressing the issues at Nottingham Trent?

How could you address the issue at your institution? Is there anything here that you could use or that you hadn't considered before?

Two new approaches to academic writing have been adopted at Nottingham Trent University: the Academic Writing Readers' Group and the Writing Across the Curriculum project. Both are targeted at staff and have been developed to run alongside traditional models of support. This section will look at the ways in which these groups have been established to help engage with and develop students' academic writing.

The Academic Writing Readers' Group

The Academic Writing Readers' Group was initially set up in 2007 as a forum for academics to discuss student academic writing issues. However, it soon developed into a social network in which staff discuss, explore and highlight current practice in this area. The sessions are promoted via the university's intranet and last approximately 1–2 hours once a term. Each session attracts approximately 15 attendees from a variety of disciplines and departments.

The sessions are based around a relevant paper, which staff are required to read prior to attending. Over the last 12 months, the papers have covered academic literacies, writing across the curriculum, plagiarism and a number of other topics, reflecting current research and theoretical debate in the field. For example, one session examined a chapter from a popular writing development book (Bean, 2001) that suggested a number of short in-lecture writing activities may help students to develop their writing. Subsequently, many attendees trialled the resources and provided useful feedback on their practical applicability. Such comments are invaluable to learning developers as they assist with resource development. Discussion topics can fire colleagues' imagination, with some even drafting their own response to the paper, thereby adding a new perspective to consider.

Evaluation of the project indicates that colleagues find the group an environment in which they can develop their understanding and teaching of academic writing. The group also links staff with the central funding and development opportunities available to enhance writing development. The link to the LearnHigher CETL also provided colleagues with a sense of autonomy from the university whilst directing them towards another valuable resource bank.

I was drawn to the Academic Writing Readers' Group project to discover what kinds of problems other professionals were encountering with their students. It has been very interesting to see the range of problems reported by academics, from students writing incoherent sentences because of poor grammar, punctuation and expression to higher level problems with formulating a logical argument or being sufficiently critical. This diversity of problems has led to some lively discussions when some participants have felt that correct grammar and spelling are decidedly less important than the higher skills of logical and persuasive writing, while others have experienced that students' expression is so poor that no sense can be discerned. This can make the meetings frustrating as it seems that participants are starting from such very different standpoints that they can have no real grasp of the problems each is encountering. A valuable aspect of the meetings is sharing expertise and practice with other professionals and also just conversing with others with similar roles as my role can be quite isolating.

(Sian Trafford – Learner Support Coordinator, School of Social Sciences)

As you can see from the above vignette, the project is not without its problems but it does seem to achieve its overall goal, which is essentially to get colleagues talking and sharing perspectives about what good academic writing is, and also how to achieve it. It helps staff to reflect on their own practice and reassess what constitutes 'good' academic writing whilst breaking down the isolation felt by many colleagues.

The Academic Writing Readers' Group acts as a stepping stone to introduce academic staff to alternative ways of teaching and thinking about academic writing. The group helps to identify academic writing as something that can be developed in a variety of ways, dismissing the notion of there being a single right way and thus lessening the pressure on staff. This allows colleagues to feel at greater ease when trialling academic writing activities and helps to build confidence in those who may feel they have little knowledge in this area. One of the approaches discussed in the group was that of Writing Across the Curriculum, and this provoked such interest that it fuelled the second project.

The Writing Across the Curriculum (WAC) project

The WAC project is an action research project that utilises the WAC philosophy (The WAC Clearinghouse, 2009). This approach is very popular in the USA and uses writing as a tool to develop learning. Whilst most courses in the UK already include writing for assessment, WAC uses writing-based activities not only to help students learn, but also to help students learn to write in their discipline. The approach consists of two strands: Writing to Learn, and Writing in the Disciplines.

- Writing to Learn uses informal, generic, short writing tasks, to help students structure their thoughts and ideas. These activities tend to be short and impromptu and are often undertaken in the early part of a course, enabling students to identify key theories and grasp difficult concepts.
- Writing in the Disciplines (WiD) uses writing activities to teach students the discipline specifics of writing in their field. Discipline-focused activities develop students' writing so that they are able to communicate as scholars in their field. These tend to be undertaken in the second or third year of a programme.

WAC adopts an academic literacies approach in that writing is not just a skill to be learnt or socialised into but a tool for learning and communicating ideas.

The WAC project at NTU provides a UK version of the approach, offering academics resources and support to enable them to develop academic writing in their sessions. Staff are encouraged to engage as little or as much as they like. Those interested in the project currently meet once a term to discuss, trial and develop writing activities. The group is supported by a learning developer who facilitates the meetings and offers resources, ideas and support. In many instances, staff may not be aware of ways to enhance and develop their students' writing – this project provides them with a range of information and ideas. Colleagues can work together on developing generic resources, tailor them to their own disciplines and even trial them in their sessions all as part of a supportive professional network. The group can also help in encouraging each other to 'stick with it', and share ideas about what has worked in other contexts and disciplines.

The project in particular helps to address issues raised previously regarding staff and student expectations of writing both in and outside of assessment. By prioritising writing, the approach provides space for staff to discuss academic writing with students; particularly what is expected from them in higher education. The consistent use of writing also allows students to practise using it as a learning tool and to begin to grasp the disciplinary specifics of writing in their field. This use of writing also allows staff and students to address concerns early on in the module, allowing any additional support to become part of a developmental process as opposed to a last-minute solution.

My interest in Writing Across the Curriculum came about as I realised that as a module leader, I focused on delivering and assessing subject-based outcomes, but as a Programme Leader, I needed also to be addressing transferable skills; most notably effective written and oral communication. Our campus receives no direct writing support, so it falls on the programme team to address issues of writing style. I felt several students were struggling to move from writing for clarification to writing for communication, in addition to having little awareness of the need to improve their writing style. WAC and WiD are useful for developing writing skills in a subject-specific context, enabling students to develop their scientific writing by focusing on the subject, not the written communication. I have used WAC at all three levels of the BSc and I have received positive feedback from all cohorts.

(Dr Sarah Broadberry – Programme Leader, School of Animal, Rural and Environmental Sciences)

▶ How have these projects created change and what lies in the future?

What challenges might you face in implementing your project, and how can you meet them? Who might be able to support you in your project?

Both groups display numerous characteristics associated with communities of practice (Wenger, 1998). Participants have a *shared repertoire* in that they use similar language and have stories and events that bond them. They also share a *joint enterprise* and mutual engagement – they connect to each other in a range of ways and ultimately share the responsibility of maintaining the group. They bring to the group a *range of identities* that includes not only their participation in the project but also their role as lecturer or learning developer and this diversity enriches the group.

Participants report raised awareness of academic writing issues: they feel confident to look more closely at how academic writing is taught in their field and to question and develop the way that this is done. They have helped to build a community of practitioners where more confident staff members can advise and mentor those who may be new to the field.

These new communities have provided learning developers with a pool of staff to trial new approaches and activities. By bringing together colleagues from a range of fields, we are also developing staff knowledge of the issues encountered by international students or those struggling with dyslexia or mental health issues. Students have benefited through the opportunities created for them to encounter a range of writing techniques and methods, something that many students have responded very positively to. This combination of staff and student feedback enables resources to be tailor-made for specific contexts. Consequently a collaborative working relationship has developed between students, staff and learning developers. This has helped to foster a more holistic approach to student writing support and has placed the responsibility for its development evenly between all the involved parties.

▶ Conclusions

The groups that have been established are in themselves an act of linking writing and the thinking process. Encouraging colleagues to question the point and use of academic writing, to examine what we truly use it for and how it could be developed, has made it possible for writing to be reconstructed in the eyes of all participants.

These projects also demonstrate new ways in which learning developers can help support colleagues. Learning developers have a very important central role to play not only in the creation and support of teaching resources, but also in challenging teaching and learning methods and perspectives. They can bring new concepts and approaches to the attention of time-poor colleagues and help them discover new ways to develop and enhance their teaching. For learning developers who may have little understanding of a particular discipline themselves, simply bringing colleagues together in an open discussion can discover and promote ideas and approaches that others may be involved in. There are many important aspects which need to be discussed and better understood in order for us to develop and enhance the way that academic writing is taught and supported in higher education. Questions such as how and why students learn to write academically, what difficulties they encounter, what kinds of support students access and why they access this kind of support all require answers in order for us to move forward. It is also imperative that the role of teaching staff is not overlooked; how academics respond to student writing issues and how they can assist in the development of academic writing are key factors. Only when these issues are discussed between academic colleagues, learning development staff and ultimately students, can we start to truly understand the nature of academic writing.

▶ References

Bean, J. (2001) *Engaging Ideas: The Professors' Guide to Integrating Writing, Critical Thinking and Active Learning in the Classroom* (San Francisco, CA: Jossey Bass)

Burke, D. (2009) 'Strategies for using feedback students bring to higher education', *Assessment and Evaluation in Higher Education* 34 (1), 41–50.

Cook, A. and Leckey, J. (1999) 'Do expectations meet reality? A survey of changes in first year student opinion', *Journal of Further and Higher Education* 23, 157–71.

Francis, B. (2005) *University Lecturers' Constructions of Undergraduate Writing: A Gender Analysis*. ESRC report. Available at: www.esrcsocietytoday.ac.uk/ESRCInfoCentre/index_academic.aspx (last accessed 29/3/10).

Foster, E., Bell, R. and Salzano, S. (2008) '"What's a Journal?" – Research into the Prior Learning Experiences of Students Entering Higher Education'. *European First Year Experience Conference, 7–9 May 2008*, University of Wolverhampton.

Ganobscik-Williams, L. (ed.) (2006) *Teaching Academic Writing in UK Higher Education* (Basingstoke: Palgrave Macmillan).

Ganobscik-Williams, L. (2004) 'A Report on the Teaching of Academic Writing in UK Higher Education'. Unpublished research project, University of Warwick.

Hein, G.E. (1991) Constructivist Learning Theory. Available at: www.exploratorium.edu/ifi/resources/constructivistlearning.html (last accessed 29/3/10).

Independent (2006) 'University students: they can't write, spell or present an argument'. Available at: www.independent.co.uk/news/education/higher/univesity-students-they-cant-write-spell-or-present-an-argument-479536.html (last accessed 29/3/10).

Lea, M. R. and Stierer, B. (eds) (2000) *Student Writing in Higher Education: New Contexts* (Buckingham: Open University Press).

Lea, M. R. and Street, B. V. (1998) 'Student writing in higher education: an academic literacies approach', *Studies in Higher Education* 23 (2), 157–71.

Lillis, T. (1999) 'Re-defining the problem of student writing', in M. Graal and R. Clark (eds) *Partnerships Across the Curriculum*. Proceedings of the 6th Annual Writing Development in Higher Education conference, University of Leicester Teaching and Learning Unit, pp. 15–32.

Orr, S. and Blythman, M. (1999) 'Have you got ten minutes? Can you just sort my dissertation out?' in M. Graal and R. Clark (eds) *Partnerships Across the Curriculum*. Proceedings of the 6th Annual Writing Development in Higher Education conference, University of Leicester Teaching and Learning Unit.

QAA (Quality Assurance Agency for Higher Education) (2009) 'Understanding qualifications – The frameworks for higher education qualifications'. Available at: www.qaa.ac.uk/students/guides/UnderstandQuals.asp (last accessed 29/3/10).

Spack, R. and Zamel, V. (eds) (1998) *Negotiating Academic Literacies: Teaching and Learning Across Languages and Cultures* (Mahwah, NJ: Lawrence Erlbaum Associates).

TES (Times Higher Educational Supplement) (2007) '"Appalling" writing skills drive tutors to seek help'. Available at: www.timeshighereducation.co.uk/story.asp?sectioncode=26&storycode=208242 (last accessed 29/3/10).

The WAC Clearinghouse (2009) *An Introduction to Writing Across the Curriculum*. Available at: http://wac.colostate.edu/intro (last accessed 29/3/10).

Vogt, E. E., Brown, J. and Isaacs, D. (2003) *The Art of Powerful Questions: Catalysing Insight, Innovation and Action*, California: Whole Systems Associates. Available at: www.theworldcafe.com/involved.htm (last accessed 29/3/10).

Wenger, E. (1998) *Communities of Practice: Learning, Meaning and Identity* (Cambridge: Cambridge University Press).

12 Learning Resources that Students will Use: Producing a Web-based Multi-media Resource to Improve Group and Teamwork Skills

Carol Elston, Peter Hartley and Julia Braham

▶ Summary

This chapter analyses and evaluates the production and outcomes of 'Making Groupwork Work', the LearnHigher web-based multimedia learning resource designed to help students understand and reflect upon their group dynamics and development.

We describe the design process and explain the rationale for its structure, demonstrating how it enables flexible use by students and staff and facilitates the future expansion of supporting materials. Our evaluation is based on the feedback which has been provided by the growing number of universities who are using the resource in different ways.

Given the increasing use of open educational resources in HE, this chapter suggests useful pointers to help learning developers and academics who wish to develop flexible learning resources within limited budgets.

▶ Introduction

The increase in collaborative learning opportunities has created greater expectations of students to be able to perform effectively in groups, yet students continue to report problems associated with group dynamics and a general negativity when approaching group-work (Lerner, 1995). Studies show that, by understanding group dynamics and the process by which a group develops, students know what to expect and are better prepared for the challenges they are likely to face (McGraw and Tidwell, 2001). However, the means of developing this understanding differ (Douglas, 2000). Some advocate 'throwing them in at the deep end', suggesting that the group project provides the necessary 'on the job' development opportunities in a safe environment. Others challenge the assumption that students will develop skills simply by completing group projects and suggest that students need some 'up front' development before embarking on a group project (Ettington and Camp, 2002). Our experience favours this second view and this is supported by evidence from team development in other contexts, such as management or business. Unless team members have the resources and support to develop ideas and reflections on which they can improve their performance then they are likely to repeat the same, or similar, mistakes.

The LearnHigher CETL supported the collaborative project between three universities to produce a web-based multimedia learning resource to help students understand their group dynamics and development. Particular design features were considered vital: the resource should be suitable for 'up-front' development and as a point of reference during a project; the design should allow further development of the supporting materials; and the resource should offer scope for inter-activity and encourage active reflection.

The sections of this chapter follow our journey through the key stages of planning, production and evaluation and, through example, review the issues and concerns that web-based resource developers need to consider before embarking on such an ambitious project.

As with any project, resource development must have an underlying purpose, and this purpose must be based on research and evidence rather than intuition. The first section of this chapter identifies the questions we were keen to ask and considers the impact the answers to these questions had on the resource's rationale and design specification.

The second section advocates a project-planning approach to the development and production processes that is suitable and feasible within the imposed constraints. In its early stage, this needs to estab lish clear boundaries associated with budgets, resources and timescales, before continuing to consider the roles and responsibilities of the key players involved. We do not advocate a formal approach (such as the Prince 2 Methodology which many universities have used recently) as this can be inflexible and may introduce unnecessary levels of bureaucracy. One key lesson we have learned is the need to be flex-ible at all stages.

The third section highlights issues relating to the production process; we allocated roles and responsibilities to a media services department for filming and editing and to an educational technologist for produc-ing the episode template. We had to resolve issues of planning (e.g. the use of scripts versus free speech, and whether to use actors or enthu-siastic students!), scheduling and coordination (e.g. harmonising the demands of video production and web streaming). Underpinning these are issues of finance and budgets – we had to decide what was possi-ble within very limited constraints of both time and money.

Arguably the most important phase of resource development is eval-uation. This feeds back into the development phase, providing a cycli-cal process for improving and enhancing the resource. The final section of this chapter explains how evaluation was built in to all the stages of the project and how our responses to this feedback have improved the resource.

▶ Determining our purpose

The key question for any resource is whether it is truly needed – will it be used by the intended audience, and in what circumstances? Members of the development team had previously identified the main issues confronted by student groups and the need for good resources to help students and tutors manage the challenges associated with group projects (Hartley, 1997 and 1999; Hartley and Thorpe, 2001). Groupwork plays an integral part in many undergraduate programmes of study, fuelled by the pressures to develop 'key skills' and employa-bility. However, this increase in the use of group projects is often coupled with decreasing staff support. Studies indicate that in many cases educators are choosing not to include groupwork development sessions either prior to or during practical groupwork tasks; this defi-ciency in developing skills is frequently attributed to lack of time

(Chapman and Van Auken, 2001). Where tutors are able to point students to supporting resources, they often direct students to texts which may not offer alternative models for interaction or relate to current evidence on student behaviour. For example, the common 'recipe' for group development in many texts is the 'forming/storming/norming/performing' set of stages which dates back to summaries of group studies which were typically not comprised of students (Tuckman, 1965). Alternative models may be ignored (Hartley et al., 2005), and recent studies of student groups can give a much more complex picture (Lindsey and Hartley, 2006).

This lack of pre-project preparation by students, alongside some frustration with current sources and the growing evidence that many students harbour a negative attitude to groupwork, prompted the conception of the 'Making Groupwork Work' resource. An earlier survey by Hartley and Thorpe (2001) identified eleven key issues facing students. The issues range from group dynamics and control, to equity of assessment and allocation of marks:

I didn't like it last year when the tutor put us with people we didn't know, this time we could work with friends, I didn't like that either!

It is hard getting all the group members together, hard to contact and unreliable.

I wasn't really impressed because Jo didn't show the same commitment to the project as the others and she got the same mark.

The eleven identified issues, ranked in order of importance, were classified as follows. This ranking was not the same as in some previous studies.

1 Membership of the group itself.
2 Social aspects.
3 Issues of control and influence.
4 Equity of the allocation of marks.
5 Maintaining momentum.
6 Time management.
7 Product versus process.
8 Equity of the assessment method.
9 Public nature of the work.
10 Reciprocal nature of groupwork.
11 What happens in meetings.

The content of the resource was driven by this data, supplemented by the practical experiences of the other members of the team and a quick survey of other LearnHigher partners to make sure that we had not neglected a critical issue.

The decision to develop a web-based resource was driven by a number of factors.

- The subject lends itself to the online environment from a pedagogical viewpoint, allowing a mix of video playback, supporting resources and interactive elements.
- Web access means that the resource can be used world-wide, offering 'any place any time' learning to a mass audience; a growing requirement for students who expect flexible learning.

Another important consideration was cost; by uploading the resource to a website there are no reproduction and distribution costs, allowing the resource to be free of charge.

From a development viewpoint, the web-based interface also allows the resource to evolve with time; the aim: to develop an initial resource that can be enhanced by additional resources designed to reinforce learning outcomes relating to the areas of groupwork, listening and interpersonal skills, and oral presentations.

Everything seemed to be in favour of using the web as a means of delivery, but we were aware that, however good the resource, it would have little impact unless it was embraced by educators. In the wake of pressures to re-evaluate learning routes and adopt cost-effective technology, the majority of universities are now actively integrating, or considering the integration of, web-based learning within educational practice (Salmon and Jones, 2004). This trend has been reinforced recently by the call for more use of 'open educational resources' (as witnessed by the range of submissions to the OER 2010 conference, including one based on this resource – Hartley, 2010). As a result, we were confident that the audience was ready and our challenge was to publicise the resource and ensure that the content was educationally robust as well as stimulating and fun to use.

Having established a need, outlined the subject content and decided on a delivery medium, the next stage was to ensure that the resource met its purpose, the engagement of students; our audience. Our rationale for using video clips was based on the ease with which the progress of a group of students could be followed though viewing snippets of their meetings. This method of communication enabled the introduction of many of the issues and challenges faced by students. It also provided a focus for follow-up face-to-face discussion and collaborative learning. From the outset, the intention was for the resource to be used as part of a blended learning programme rather than purely as an online experience.

The use of video also provides settings where users can learn in authentic contexts with supporting tools and scaffolding (Kong and So, 2008). With groupwork, either students need to learn by trial and error or they can prepare for the experience through other static learning media such as books and handouts. Although no substitute for learning through experience, quality video can provide the next best thing. If the video clips were sufficiently authentic so that students could relate to them, we knew that we could engage the student and would have a valuable learning tool.

▶ Planning the resource

Do as I say and not as I do! Our project team, initially six, was a geographically disparate group with masses of enthusiasm and little time; our issues and challenges were just the same as those of our audience. Obviously we scoured the literature for the latest advice on effective teamwork, contextualised this for our purposes, and implemented a reflective and adaptive group process, before submitting a thorough and detailed application for funding. Such were our dreams! Unfortunately, we only had one initial meeting, where the original suggestion for paper-based resources turned into the ambition to produce a flexible online resource, and the funding bid was due in the following week! So our group process was rather more spontaneous and emergent. Fortunately, we didn't face any conflict, but time management and maintaining momentum were definite challenges. Our group dynamics and development were probably unconventional and not what we would advocate to others, but they worked for us. And we do have some explanations for our effectiveness, which we will return to later. With just a handful of face-to-face meetings during the project, the majority of our communication was via email; a successful medium for focused exchanges yet a poor vehicle for dynamic discussion.

The face-to-face meetings we did have were driven and exceptionally productive; the key to success was a focused agenda with clearly defined required outcomes. It was during these meetings that the resource evolved; decisions were made, tasks allocated, and budgets agreed. As with any group, the members brought with them particular strengths and experiences, from research experience to knowledge of e-learning development. They also brought varying levels of time and commitment; for one of us, the project was a major part of their role (although only working part-time); for others, the project played a small part in a varied and pressured working schedule. We didn't look for an equal allocation of tasks; it would not have been practical and neither would we have met our deadlines. The project team also experienced long-term sick leave and two members leaving their respective universities, and the project, in pursuit of new challenges. Thankfully the latter was in the later stages of the project, and the impact minimal. As with all projects, the journey was seldom smooth. However, we did exhibit, throughout, several characteristics of effective teams as highlighted in the literature: a high level of commitment to the overall goals; a range of expertise; flexible problem-solving and decision-making; and mutual respect (West, 2003). This also influenced our approach to the resource itself – we did not want to suggest 'one best way' of effective teamwork – more important is the ability of members to reflect on what is (or is not) working and adapt accordingly.

Our project plan was effectively one document, starting with a timeline of 'typical issues' in a sequence that many staff and students recognised, we produced a document that outlined the episodes and their associated learning outcomes. This became our point of reference and it took on several reincarnations as the project evolved. This episode planner was interspersed with milestones such as three filming dates (March, June and September 2007). The other key aspect of the project plan was to turn this 'story' into a resource with a clear structure and underpinning educational rationale.

Working as a group involves students engaging in a series of choices, including how to form, engage and then maintain the group (Lizzio and Wilson, 2006). This resource needed to firstly address these choices and then move on to help the students explore their options and ultimately find a way to connect and progress. To do this we needed to inter-relate the developed learning objects within a learning design or pedagogical strategy (Nicol, 2003). This required a logic that we could use to aggregate learning objects to support the episodes. One of the most difficult parts of the project was achieving the agreement on the structure and the main focus of the resource which is now represented in Figure 12.1.

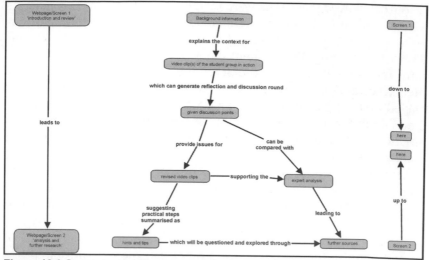

Figure 12.1 Concept map of the resource structure

This approach meant that we visualised the resource in terms of two main web pages or 'screens'. The idea of the two screens came from the pedagogic distinction between 'reviewing' and 'analysing' each episode. We wanted students to review each episode – appreciate the context, watch the video and discuss their initial reactions – and this is the format of Screen 1. For Screen 2, we wanted students to explore the situation in more depth, comparing their reactions with other 'expert' analysis and looking for further sources and materials to develop a more informed view of the episode and the group dynamics involved. The two screens in the final web resource went through several redesigns within this broad framework and a typical example of each is given in Figures 12.2 and 12.3 below.

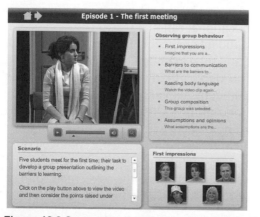

Figure 12.2 Screenshot showing Screen 1 of Episode 1

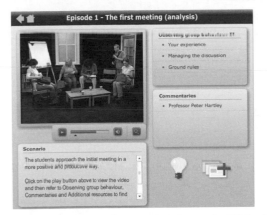

Figure 12.3 Screenshot showing Screen 2 of Episode 1

The other advantage of this design is that the two web pages allowed us to bring together materials from different sources, as discussed in the following section.

▶ Producing the materials

Having defined the structure of the resource and the learning outcomes for each episode, the next stage was to develop video clips, the main feature of each episode, designed to fit along a timeline. The aim of the clips was to develop the characters of the students and hopefully draw in the audience in much the same way as a TV soap opera. To film the clips we needed content and this involved preparing scripts. This stage of the development was a steep learning curve for all involved. In many ways we were now practising what we preached; we were learning to work as a group, maximising on strengths and delegating tasks to match availability and skills.

Keeping an eye on the bottom line, we decided to use 'real' students rather than actors. We did have some doubts about this, and so decided to advertise for performing arts students or at least students with an interest in acting; however, the results were far from ideal. After some disastrous auditions we decided to employ 'real' actors, probably the best decision we made. We also decided to produce a pilot episode, another sensible decision when 'learning on the job'.

The script for the pilot episode was very 'loose' and did not include specific dialogue. On the filming day, the actors managed extremely well but we found that we were adapting their assumed dialogue to cover the desired learning points. This was both time-consuming and frustrating for all involved, causing particular difficulty for the filming crew. Without a tight script they were having to try to 'capture everything' and could not guarantee the smooth transitions and well-framed shots, which was their natural inclination. We learnt a valuable lesson from this and the next nine episodes where tightly scripted.

Another issue for this production stage was the level of 'realism' or 'authenticity' in the video clips. Shooting the clips in a real classroom or library study room might have added to the feeling of authenticity but would have created technical challenges and added to production costs. Shooting in the studio guaranteed technical quality but the set is obviously stylised and artificial. Our choice of this studio location has been vindicated by reactions to the clips. Users have focused on the characters, and the setting has been suitably anonymous.

Alongside the video production was the web design and we needed to ensure very clear lines of communication between video producer and web designer to ensure that the clips were produced in the appropriate format.

The other main feature of the web design was the linking between the main resource and the web pages of additional materials which were located on the web servers of the different partners. Although the video element of the resource is unlikely to be developed further, the episodes are regularly enhanced through additional resources that reinforce the highlighted learning points. The videos include the majority of the generic challenges identified by research; however, there are some more discipline-specific or student-specific challenges that can also be identified through the development of additional resources.

▶ Evaluation: What do users do with the resource and what do they think about it?

Evaluation was seen as fundamental to this project from day one and each stage of the project has been subjected to different levels of external scrutiny:

- The original timeline was discussed with LearnHigher partners.
- The interface design was piloted with different groups and presented at several events to gain feedback.

- A pilot episode was produced and tested with different groups at several universities.

The feedback was constructive and resulted in positive changes to the structure and navigation of the resource. The evaluation phase also provided an insight into the different ways in which the resource is used by tutors (Elston, 2009):

1   Students are provided with the web address of the resource either directly or through a virtual learning environment (VLE). They are expected to refer to the resource independently if and when needed.
2   Students are referred to the resource and directed to watch one or more of the episodes before a face-to-face or online discussion session.
3   Students are referred to the resource on a needs basis; if they identify a problem, they are signposted to the relevant episode.

We have since become aware of further variations in tutors' practices and will be investigating these as part of our plans for further development.

Observing different ways in which students are introduced to the resource led us to questions regarding student engagement and the effectiveness of the content. Student evaluation began early in the project; as a result of demonstrating the resource at a number of conferences and LearnHigher evaluation sessions, several colleagues volunteered to trial the resource during the first semester of the 2007/8 academic year. At this stage, only the video clips were available but nevertheless a total of seven institutions were keen to include the clips within learning programmes. The majority of the feedback was brief and anecdotal but overwhelmingly positive.

One institution, the University of Manchester, found an innovative way to encourage student feedback; students were required to take part in a discussion forum (blog) as part of their coursework. The students were instructed to watch the video clips for all ten episodes before contributing to an online discussion forum. In total, 67 students took part in the forum; the transcript data from the blog were analysed using a combination of inductive and deductive approaches to establish whether the students picked up on the main learning points and whether they showed any intention of using this knowledge in the future to change their practice (Volet and Mansfield, 2006).

The findings show that a majority of students felt able to relate to the scenarios portrayed by the clips and were also able to relate to the characters and identify with their patterns of behaviour. This was reinforced by their ability to identify individual and group strengths and weaknesses and provide opinions about the development of the group process.

All the students gave a positive response to the resource, with the majority indicating that it had increased their understanding of group process or had provided a reminder of the issues involved. Although only 13.5% categorically stated that it would result in a positive change in practice, it can be inferred from the data that the resource informed or reminded many more students of scenarios and behaviours to be avoided.

▶ Conclusions: lessons learned

Perhaps the most important lesson we have learned is that a committed team can produce a quality multimedia learning resource at relatively modest costs of technical production (assuming that staff with the appropriate pedagogic skills are prepared to give sufficient time to the enterprise).

However, to ensure a quality resource we quickly learned the importance of a clear specification for the technical production which emphasised usability and accessibility from the user's perspective.

Our assertion that this is a 'quality' resource is supported by the feedback we have received from staff and students. Making Group-work Work is an award-winning resource, recognised by e-practitioners as being an innovative example of using video in an educational context. Having been shortlisted for the Learning on Screen Awards in 2008, we achieved a 'double first' in 2009, winning both the Jorum Learning and Teaching Competition and the ALT/Epigeum Award for the most effective use of video in an educational or training context.

This success has reinforced our view that a good resource must satisfy certain criteria that we embodied in the group-work resource: interactivity; flexibility; potential for expansion; and that no resource will survive unless it satisfies a genuine need from its student audience. As with any technology-based resource it is important to keep in tune with user trends. One next step is to investigate the challenges of adapting the resource for mobile technologies.

▶ Further sources and suggestions

The Making Group-work Work resource can be accessed from:
www.learnhigher.ac.uk/students/group-work

LearnHigher listening and interpersonal skills pages are at:
www.learnhigher.ac.uk/students/listening-and-interpersonal-skills

▶ References

Chapman, K. and Van Auken, S. (2001) 'Creating positive group project experiences: an examination of the role of the instructor on students' perceptions of group projects', *Journal of Marketing Education* 23 (2), 117–27.

Douglas, D. (2000) *Basic Groupwork* (London: Routledge).

Elston, C. (2009) 'Making Group-work Work – an overview', *Journal of Learning Development in Higher Education* 1.

Ettington, D. R. and Camp, R. R. (2002) 'Facilitating transfer of skills between group projects and work teams', *Journal of Management Education* 26, 356–79.

Hartley, P. (1997) *Group Communication* (London: Routledge).

Hartley, P. (1999) *Interpersonal Communication*, 2nd edn (London: Routledge).

Hartley, P. (2010) *Supporting Student Groupwork through Multimedia and Web Software*. Paper presented to first national conference, OER 2010. Slides available at: www.ucel.ac.uk/oer10/index.html (last accessed 29/3/10)

Hartley, P. and Thorpe, L. (2001) *'Groupwork!' groaned the students. 'As if we haven't enough to do.' An Examination of the Key Issues Surrounding Assessed Groupwork from the Student Perspective*. Paper presented to ILT Annual Conference, University of York.

Hartley, P., Woods, A. and Pill, M. (2005) *Enhancing Teaching in Higher Education* (London: RoutledgeFalmer).

Kong, S. C. and So, W. M. W. (2008) 'A study of building a resource-based learning environment with inquiry learning approach: knowledge of family trees', *Computers and Education* 50 (1), 37–60.

Lerner, L. D. (1995) 'Making student groups work', *Journal of Management Education* 19 (1),123–25.

Lindsey, N. and Hartley, P. (2006) *Development of Student Groups*. Paper presented to HEA Annual Conference, Nottingham University.

Lizzio, A. and Wilson, K. (2006) 'Enhancing the effectiveness of self-managed learning groups: understanding students' choices and concerns', *Studies in Higher Education* 31 (6), 689–703.

McGraw, P. and Tidwell, A. (2001) 'Teaching group process skills to MBA students: a short workshop', *Education and Training* 43 (3), 162–71.

Nicol, D. (2003) 'Conceptions of learning objects: social and educational issues'. Commentary on Charles Duncan, 'Granularisation', chapter 2 of A. Littlejohn (ed.) *Reusing Online Resources: A Sustainable Approach to eLearning*. Special issue of the *Journal of Interactive Media in Education*. Available at: www-jime.open.ac.uk/2003/1/ (last accessed 29/3/10).

Salmon, D. and Jones, M. (2004) 'Higher education staff experiences of using web-based learning technologies', *Educational Technology and Society* 7 (10), 1007–114.

Tuckman, B. (1965). 'Developmental sequences in small groups', *Psychological Bulletin*, 384–99.

Volet, S. and Mansfield, C. (2006) 'Group-work at university: significance of personal goals in the regulation strategies of students with positive and negative appraisals', *Higher Education Research and Development* 25 (4), 341–56.

West, M. A. (2003) *Effective Teamwork: Practical Lessons from Organizational Research*, 2nd edn (London: Wiley-Blackwell).

13 The Student as Producer: Learning by Doing Research

Andy Hagyard and Sue Watling

▶ Summary

The idea of encouraging students to engage in research activity, becoming 'knowledge producers' rather than consumers of an educational 'product', is central to a number of recent initiatives aimed at tackling the historic dichotomy between research and teaching in higher education.

This chapter examines the development of research-based learning in higher education and analyses the experience of one university which has introduced a research bursary scheme for undergraduate students. This case study is used to identify the implications of research-based learning for the practice of learning development.

This chapter also identifies the key issues students doing research will need to become familiar with, including methods of collecting and analysing data, and an understanding of the nature of research within the context of their discipline.

▶ Introduction

Research is at the heart of academic life. Universities have traditionally existed as organisations concerned with the creation of knowledge, where students learn not only about their discipline but also to think critically and to conduct their own investigations and inquiries. Yet in a rapidly changing higher education environment, research and teaching came to be seen as competing priorities, with no clear evidence of any mutually beneficial relationship between them (Hattie and Marsh,

1996). The UK Government even came close to formalising the divide between teaching and research, with its White Paper on 'The Future of Higher Education' (HMSO, 2003) suggesting that certain institutions should be designated as 'teaching only' universities. Ultimately, opposition from the sector led to the abandonment of this idea.

Recent initiatives have attempted to tackle the historic dichotomy between teaching and research, emphasising instead the complementary nature of these two facets of university life and exploring various ways of creating linkages between them. Central to many of these initiatives is the idea of encouraging students to engage in research activity, becoming 'producers' of knowledge (Neary and Winn, 2009) rather than consumers of an educational 'product'.

This chapter explores the development of research-based learning and consider its implications for learning development. It will describe recent trends in the USA and the UK (Boyer Commission, 1998; Jenkins et al., 2007), and focus on the experience of one university in introducing a research bursary scheme for undergraduate students. The scheme was successful but relied on external funding support. The more recent challenges have been to develop a sustainable strategy so that the benefits extend into mainstream delivery, and to develop further ways of integrating research-type activity into the curriculum.

The chapter also considers the impact of this 'reinvention' of the curriculum on the learning development needs of students. As the teaching paradigm shifts to a research-based learning approach, students need support to understand the nature of research and the range of methods required to engage fully in research within their discipline. Learning development must also adapt to support these demands.

▶ The development of research-based learning

In 1998, the Boyer Commission in the USA published a seminal report in this area. It acknowledged serious failings in research universities, with thousands of students graduating:

> without ever seeing world-famous professors or tasting genuine research [...] and still lacking a coherent body of knowledge and any inkling as to how one piece of information might relate to others. (Boyer Commission, 1998, p. 6)

It recommended that every university should provide 'opportunities to learn through inquiry rather than simple transmission of knowledge', that research-based learning should become the standard, and that every degree should culminate in a major project to bring together all the research and communications skills that students had developed.

Echoing the Boyer recommendations, the Higher Education Funding Council for England (HEFCE) published its strategic priorities for learning and teaching (HEFCE, 2006). These included the aim of 'ensuring that teaching is informed and enriched by research', with one of the areas where institutions should seek to invest funds being 'students experiencing research, and developing research skills' (p. 5). As significant ring-fenced funding was attached to these aims, institutions across the country began exploring a range of strategies to link research and teaching, summarised in the report commissioned by the Higher Education Academy (HEA) (Jenkins and Healey, 2005).

At the same time, a number of Centres for Excellence in Teaching and Learning (CETLs) were set up to promote inquiry-based learning and the development of undergraduate research skills. These included the Reinvention Centre based at the universities of Warwick and Oxford Brookes, the Applied Undergraduate Research Skills CETL at Reading, the Centre for Inquiry-Based Learning in Arts and Social Sciences in Sheffield and the Centre for Excellence in Enquiry-Based Learning in Manchester. The LearnHigher CETL also identified 'doing research' as one of the learning areas within its definition of learning development.

Healey (2005) neatly demonstrates the various ways in which research and teaching can be linked in the curriculum. The model contains four quadrants with two axes. These are defined by the emphasis on the content or processes of research, and students as participants or as the audience.

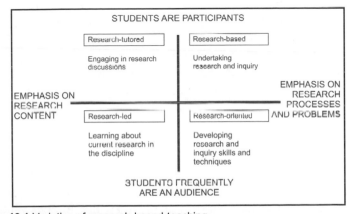

Figure 13.1 Varieties of research-based teaching
Source: M. Healey and A. Jenkins, *Developing Undergraduate Research and Inquiry* (York: Higher Education Academy, 2009). Reproduced with kind permission.

After three years of ring-fenced funding from HEFCE, there was clear evidence of a growing preference for what we define as research-based learning (Healey and Jenkins, 2009). This places the emphasis on students as active participants, with a focus on research processes rather than content.

The concept of the 'student as producer' (Neary and Winn, 2009) not only encapsulates the sense of students being actively engaged in knowledge production, it also comes as a welcome antidote to the growing tendency to portray students as consumers of some sort of higher education product.

With dedicated funding allocated to strengthening the links between research and teaching, the University of Lincoln, a post-1992 higher education institution, developed a learning and teaching strategy for 2007–9 which included a research bursary project for students; the Undergraduate Research Opportunities Scheme (UROS). Analysis of this scheme highlights both the benefits and challenges for institutional adoption of research-based learning.

▶ UROS at Lincoln

UROS is underpinned by Boyer's proposal that every university should provide 'opportunities to learn through inquiry rather than simple transmission of knowledge' (Boyer Commission, 1998). It is also aligned with HEFCE's strategic priorities for ensuring that teaching is informed and enriched by research (HEFCE, 2006). UROS epitomises the cultural shift from the student as the recipient of knowledge to the student as researcher and producer of knowledge. Other higher education institutions that run similar undergraduate research schemes include Warwick, Reading and Imperial College, London. Faculty-based bursary schemes can be identified at a number of other institutions, but Lincoln was one of the first of the new universities in the UK to implement the scheme across all faculties and departments. The UROS pilot ran in 2007 with five students, one per faculty, being awarded a bursary of £1500 each for their participation in the research work of the university. Further details of these projects are on the UROS website (www.lincoln.ac.uk/cerd/UROS/Uros2007.htm).

The pilot was judged successful on all the key criteria: student engagement; quality of the project outputs; and staff involvement. As a result, UROS 2008 provided opportunities for a wider number of undergraduate students to engage in a real research project. Staff were asked to identify existing research projects and invite student applications for placement. Where students had ideas of their own for research projects they were invited to contact an appropriate member of staff for further discussion. A key feature of UROS was to ensure students were fully supported throughout their research. All projects had an academic member of staff in a supervisory role; helping students to enhance not only their own understanding of the research process but their knowledge of their own discipline as well.

Publicised through posters, leaflets and the university radio station (Siren FM Radio), the launch event was open to staff and students across the university and included presentations from students and their supervisors from the pilot scheme. A feature of UROS was that it replicated a genuine research experience as far as possible starting with the invitation for interested students to fill in a bursary application form. This went before a UROS panel, which included the Dean of Teaching and Learning and the Dean of Research, who awarded individual bursaries of £1500 to a total of 30 projects. Some projects involved a single student; some consisted of groups of students who shared the bursary between them. A UROS website was set up (at www.lincoln.ac.uk/cerd/UROS.htm) and each project was provided with an online blog for reporting and reflection (at http://earninglab.lincoln.ac.uk/blogs/uros2008/).

A networking event was held to maintain cohesion and provide an opportunity for sharing experience. The event included short presentations on creating a research poster and setting up a blog. For example, a group from the Lincoln School of Performing Arts had used their UROS bursary to research into Victorian Melodrama, following the discovery of a rare version of the drama *Sweeney Todd*. This had been produced by the Lincoln Performing Arts Centre, and the group, the first of the UROS projects to complete that year, gave a presentation on their research experience.

A dissemination event was held at the end of the year. Over 100 people from across the university met with the students and viewed their research posters before attending a series of student-led presentations. The aim was to provide the students with a replica conference environment where they could gain the experience of participating in a poster display and giving a presentation in a friendly, supportive atmosphere; 28 out of the 30 funded projects had completed; 25 posters were displayed and 16 presentations took place. During the event, UROS students were invited to consider their research findings for submission in *Neo*, the university's new online, refereed journal, aimed at promoting and celebrating student work, and giving an opportunity for UROS research outputs to be recognised as professional academic work (http://neo.lincoln.ac.uk).

Evaluation and impact

This enhancement of links between teaching and research in the undergraduate curriculum creates a win–win situation. By becoming involved in the research work of the university, students not only enhance their research skills and experience, they also gain insights into the processes and practices of research, the experience of working effectively with colleagues and staff, and the opportunity to improve their employability.

The following quotations from our evaluations illustrate the impact and effectiveness of UROS.

> Research seems like a much more do-able thing now whereas before I wouldn't have thought I could do my own research project.

> It further backed up my opinions that research is stressful, frustrating yet incredibly interesting and important.

> I have learned a lot about topics related to my degree subject by doing research and not simply being told about it.

Students were also successful with external dissemination of their research findings. A UROS student and supervisor presented their research findings at the International Conference on Software Maintenance (ICSM) in Beijing, China (Capiluppi and Knowles, 2008). Collaboration between two UROS groups took place on a research paper for the International Conference of Open Source Systems (OSS) in Sweden (Boldyreff et al., 2009). Internally a number of UROS students presented their work to research seminars and events within their own departments.

Staff involved as supervisors on UROS projects have gained the opportunity to work with a keen undergraduate on a research project. They also report a range of positive outcomes and advantages, including a recommended way of undertaking small pieces of research and writing articles that might not otherwise get completed.

> A breath of fresh air to share research interest and expertise with a different category of student and a real pleasure to see them working so productively ... helped me to help students develop – which after all is my job.

Despite the undeniable success of the UROS scheme and the obvious benefits for staff and student participants, it is clearly impossible to give every student a genuine research experience through this scheme alone. Consequently a range of other strategies need to be considered, and a number of these are documented in various sources (Jenkins et al., 2007; Healey and Jenkins, 2009).

▶ Other ways of integrating research

Cornell University includes all first year biology students in a small-scale research investigation by allocating them in small groups to researchers. Students then play an active role in the 'exploration', giving them insight into typical research problems in biological sciences. In this way, up to 900 students each year benefit from active participation in genuine research (http://BioG-101-104.bio.cornell.edu).

An increasingly popular way of promoting student research is through journals of student work. One of the first and best-known is the *Origins* journal at the University of Chester, but similar projects have emerged, such as the *Reinvention* journal from the CETL of the same name. The great attraction of a journal is that it demonstrates to students that research can have a purpose and an audience. In contrast, the traditional final-year dissertation can be a lonely and isolating experience, with the end product never being read other than for assessment purposes.

Another innovative project at the University of Lincoln was the development of an online conference as part of the assessment in a final-year Tourism module. Students have to submit a paper to a website (www.cometravel.lincoln.ac.uk) and then review the work of their fellow students by posting online comments. Not only has this proved extremely popular with students, it also demonstrates once again the public aspect of research publication and the role of peer review in the research process.

▶ The present and future for UROS

The importance of integrating research into the mainstream undergraduate curriculum is underlined by the resource-constrained climate that higher education is entering. With the end of HEFCE's Teaching Quality Enhancement Fund (TQEF) and CETL funding, there are now financial as well as pedagogical motivations for finding alternative ways for undergraduate students to experience research. The experience of UROS has contributed at the University of Lincoln to an initiative termed 'research-engaged teaching and learning': an institution-wide strategy aimed at making research-based learning the dominant paradigm for all aspects of curriculum design and delivery. While UROS-type activities will continue, they are more likely to be embedded into the curriculum and contribute to credit-bearing modules than to exist as separately funded projects.

Lincoln is not alone in pursuing the mainstreaming of undergraduate research. Healey and Jenkins (2009), in their latest report commissioned by the HEA, argue that 'all undergraduate students in all higher education institutions should experience learning through, and about, research and inquiry', and refer to numerous examples from institutions across the country.

▶ Implications for learning development

The growing interest in research-based learning has serious implications for learning development. 'Study skills' resources have generally been organised around traditional learning areas such as note-taking, academic writing, referencing, etc. While these undoubtedly remain important, a new paradigm of research-based or inquiry-based learning introduces a whole new set of issues. From the beginning of their undergraduate studies, students will need to become familiar with research processes and skills.

In many areas, this represents a significant shift in thinking. Many undergraduates' only experience of independent research currently comes by means of a final-level dissertation, and even then it can be argued that these are rarely based on any 'real' research effort. It is not uncommon to hear staff express the view that students are only capable of genuine research at postgraduate level. An investigation of current practice (Hagyard, 2010) in preparing students for dissertations revealed significant variability, with much 'research skills' training being concerned largely with information retrieval and writing skills. But if subject areas embrace research-based learning as defined in schemes such as UROS, students from the start of their studies may be learning through a process of inquiry and will need a certain understanding of both methodology and methods of collecting and analysing data. Perhaps most importantly, they will need to appreciate the nature of the research within the context of their discipline.

The UROS scheme described above provided us with a valuable opportunity to investigate the experience of students engaging in research projects and to assess its impact both on students' knowledge of their discipline and also on their understanding of research processes.

Our survey of UROS students asked them about the research skills they had developed, as well as those where they would like further support (see Fig. 13.2).

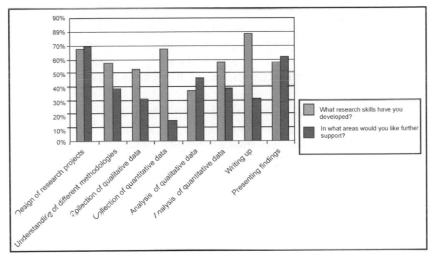

Figure 13.2 Skills developed by UROS

The results suggest that students develop a wide range of skills through engagement in research projects. The students involved felt generally more comfortable with methods of data collection and analysis but wanted more help with designing research projects, and also with presenting findings. This suggests that new resources need to focus on promoting understanding of research approaches and concepts more than on specific methods. It was interesting to note the high levels of anxiety amongst some students when faced with the prospect of presenting their work. While the traditional dissertation is typically an isolating experience shared only between the student and the supervisor, research-based learning allows students to experience the full research process, culminating in publication and presentation of findings. Despite the associated anxiety, it was also clear how much the students appreciated this opportunity, and there was an almost tangible 'buzz' of excitement at the UROS dissemination event.

Disciplinary differences

Evidence from further interviews with students also confirms the extent to which notions of research are interpreted differently within different disciplines. In the sciences, research is typically concerned with experimental design and statistical analysis, whereas interpretations will be very different in subjects such as drama, journalism, law or social work. This is epitomised by the reaction of a psychology student, who felt that research-based learning could be very appropriate in her subject, but 'couldn't imagine how it would work in a subject like history'. This echoes the 'academic literacies' approach in writing (Lea and Street, 1998), where development work is considered to be done best within the context of the discipline. Nonetheless, increased awareness of research processes should ideally encompass an understanding of different research traditions and research methodologies.

Supporting research practice through learning development

From the early days of the LearnHigher CETL, 'doing research' was included as one of the learning areas. The initial challenge was to define the area. While 'Research Methods' can represent up to one year of postgraduate study, it was clearly unrealistic to produce resources to cover the full breadth and depth of the topic. Instead the learning area was conceived as supporting the strategic development of research-based learning in the undergraduate curriculum.

If students are to learn through a process of inquiry, then there is a clear pre-requisite to develop a general awareness of research. They need to understand research processes and be aware of alternative approaches and research paradigms. They need to be able to critically evaluate research and apply research findings to practice. Collectively, this can be termed 'research-mindedness', a concept first developed in social work (www.resmind.swap.ac.uk) but which is equally relevant to other disciplines.

The most effective way to introduce students to researching and developing research-mindedness is to focus on real and topical examples of research which have an impact on everyday lives. Research is all around us: searching for the phrase 'according to research' on any news website will reveal a range of stories of immediate interest and/or relevance to students. Whether it is a report on the health effects of mobile phone usage, analysis of binge-drinking among young women or research into the relative happiness of different nationalities, students can appreciate the real-life relevance of research. Critical analysis can then be developed by asking students to consider a series of questions around the methods used and the conclusions drawn:

- What is the research question?
- How was the data collected?
- Was the sample representative?
- Could the question have been investigated in a different way?
- Do you agree with the findings?

Examples of bad research are a good way of introducing students to the need for rigour, and developing understanding of basic concepts such as validity and reliability.

Barriers and challenges

The critical first step is to break down barriers to students' understanding of research and challenge their perceptions that research is something beyond their capability. A key part of this 'demystification' process involves helping students to make sense of the language of research, which can often present a seemingly impenetrable barrier. The actual language required will vary according to the research traditions of the discipline, and at times the preferences of the lecturer. While it is unusual to explicitly introduce undergraduates to terms such as 'ontology' and 'epistemology', much of the research methods literature to which they are directed will be couched in those terms, and also refer to phenomenology, interpretivist and positivist approaches, and many more.

From a learning development perspective, we need a scaffolded approach to the acquisition of research language, and this was one of the key objectives of the LearnHigher area. At an initial level, almost all students will need to distinguish between essentially qualitative and quantitative approaches, as well as key concepts such as 'validity' and 'reliability'. Where a largely scientific approach dominates, concepts of sampling, significance, probability and other statistical terms need to be grasped. In disciplines which adopt a more philosophical approach, students may be asked to consider the very nature of truth, reality and knowledge, and therefore grapple with the complex vocabulary used to describe alternative research paradigms. As before, it is essential for these complex notions to be supported by real examples in order for students to make sense of them.

LearnHigher resources developed for the learning area of 'doing research' have been designed to take into account these considerations and build on the lessons learnt from UROS. The 'understanding research' workshop, in particular, attempts to present basic concepts and language of research through the use of real-life examples, but also needs the flexibility to incorporate discipline-specific examples. Similarly, the 'analyse this' and 'collect this' resources introduce students to basic concepts and methods of data collection and analysis, using practical examples and activities to reinforce understanding.

▶ Conclusions

Momentum is gathering in the UK for the development of research-based learning as a principle of curriculum design from the beginning of undergraduate studies. This is a model which engages students as active participants in their learning, bringing with it the pedagogic advantages associated with all forms of active learning. The experience of students in undergraduate research schemes demonstrates the potential of such schemes to significantly enhance students' development of subject knowledge and research skills. Even more significantly, engagement with research can transform students' conception of their educational experience, the relationship between students and staff, and ultimately their view of themselves as members of an academic community.

As research-based learning becomes more commonplace, there are clear learning development implications. Research methods which may previously have been introduced only for final-level dissertations, or even neglected until postgraduate study, will need to be introduced from the beginning of undergraduate study.

Yet, like academic writing, doing research is a learning area that is best learned within the context and academic traditions of each discipline. The challenge for the learning development community is to produce support materials and learning resources which support the development of 'research-mindedness' through understanding general concepts, methods and critical thinking, while allowing these resources to be adapted for use in a range of disciplinary contexts.

▶ Further sources and suggestions

For details of all LearnHigher resources in this area, see: www.learnhigher.ac.uk/ students/doing-research

SWAP (Social Work and Social Policy) subject centre, research-mindedness website: www.resmind.swap.ac.uk/

Centres for Excellence in Teaching and Learning (CETLs) promoting research-based learning:

* The Reinvention Centre for Undergraduate Research
  www2.warwick.ac.uk/fac/soc/sociology/rsw/undergrad/cetl
* Centre for Excellence in Applied Undergraduate Research Skills
  www.reading.ac.uk/cetl-aurs/
* Centre for Inquiry-based Learning in the Arts and Social Sciences
  www.shef.ac.uk/cilass/
* Centre for Excellence in Enquiry-Based Learning
  http://www.campus.manchester.ac.uk/ceebl/

Other UK Undergraduate Research Schemes:
www2.warwick.ac.uk/fac/soc/sociology/rsw/undergrad/cetl/resources

All the above URLs were last accessed on 29/3/10.

▶ References

Boldyreff, C., Capiluppi, A., Knowles, T. and Munro, J. (2009) 'Undergraduate Research Opportunities in OSS', in C. Boldyreff, K. Crowston, B. Lundell and A. Wasserman (eds) *Open Source Ecosystems: Diverse Communities Interacting*, 340–50.

Boyer Commission (1998) *Reinventing Undergraduate Education: A Blueprint for America's Research Universities* (Stony Brook, NY: Carnegie Foundation for the Advancement of Teaching).

Capiluppi, A. and Knowles T. (2008) *Maintenance and Evolution of Free/Libre/Open Source Software*, presentation to ICSM 2009, Beijing. Available at: www.icsm2008.org/ (last accessed 29/3/10).

Hagyard, A. (2010) 'Doing Research: literature review'. Available at: www.learnhigher. ac.uk/staff/doing-research (last accessed 29/3/10).

Hattie, J. and Marsh, H. (1996) 'The relationship between research and teaching: a meta-analysis', *Review of Educational Research* 66, 4.

Healey, M. (2005) 'Linking research and teaching: exploring disciplinary spaces and the role of inquiry-based learning', in R. Barnett (ed.) *Reshaping the University: New Relationships between Research, Scholarship and Teaching* (Maidenhead: SRHE).

Healey, M. and Jenkins, A. (2009) *Developing Undergraduate Research and Inquiry* (York: Higher Education Academy).

HEFCE (Higher Education Funding Council for England) (2006) *Teaching Quality*. Available at: www.hefce.ac.uk/pubs/hefce/2006/06_11/ (last accessed 6/7/10).

HMSO (2003) *The Future of Higher Education*, Government White Paper, January 2003 (London: The Stationery Office).

Jenkins, A. and Healey, M. (2005) *Institutional Strategies to Link Teaching and Research* (York: Higher Education Academy).

Jenkins, A., Healey, M. and Zetter, R. (2007) *Linking Teaching and Research in Departments and Disciplines* (York: Higher Education Academy).

Lea, M. R. and Street, B. V. (1998) 'Student writing in higher education: an academic literacies approach', *Studies in Higher Education* 23 (2), 157–72.

Neary, M. and Winn, J. (2009) 'Student as Producer', in L. Bell, H. Stevenson and M. Neary (eds) *The Future of Higher Education – Policy, Pedagogy and the Student Experience* (London and New York: Continuum).

14 Visualising Learning

Pauline Ridley

▶ **Summary**

This chapter argues that visual knowledge and skills are an essential element of all subject disciplines in higher education. It describes the approach adopted by LearnHigher, working with subject staff to raise awareness of the visual dimension of their subjects, and to explore how these skills can be taught and assessed. Curriculum innovation through funded projects and initiatives, involving still and moving images and student drawing, has demonstrated significant impact in a range of disciplines. Examples of project outcomes are summarised to demonstrate the benefits for both staff and students.

▶ **Introduction: defining the territory**

When the idea of LearnHigher was first proposed, the suggested learning areas included most of the elements a student might expect to find in a general study guide. However, there was no 'visual' learning area. I was invited to join the group after suggesting that this was a serious omission; visual competence is not a marginal concern, nor is it confined to students of art and design.

As an art historian, I had spent most of my teaching career developing students' abilities to look carefully at different kinds of images and artefacts, to draw inferences from what they see, and to use this visual evidence rigorously in developing their ideas and arguments. Similarly, scientists, geographers, and health professionals need to learn to observe and interpret visual evidence, as do historians, anthropologists and researchers in many other disciplines.

Visual knowledge and skills can sometimes be taken for granted in practice-based courses; but equally they may be ignored or undervalued in other disciplines. Both positions, by failing to make these elements explicit, lead to missed opportunities for student learning. First, we needed a name to denote this learning area.

'Visual literacy' is an established term, particularly in the US, where its wider currency has generated a variety of useful resources available through the International Visual Literacy Association (www.ivla.org/). Thibault and Walbert (2003) define it as:

> the ability to see, to understand, and ultimately to think, create, and communicate graphically ... while accurate observation is important, understanding what we see and comprehending visual relationships are at least as important. These higher-level visual literacy skills require critical thinking, and they are essential to a student's success in any content area in which information is conveyed through visual formats such as charts and maps.

'Reading' images is a learned and culturally mediated activity, but the analogy with spoken or written language can also mislead, by blurring the very real structural and neurological differences between visual and verbal modes of communication. More importantly, the concept is too narrowly focused on the ability to decode human-made images or artefacts. The spectrum of visual knowledge and skills relevant to higher education also includes observation of human subjects or natural phenomena (in clinical settings, laboratories or in the field) and the ability to use visual evidence to develop new ideas and understanding. A well-known example is the part played by Darwin's close attention to natural phenomena in the development of his theory of evolution.

We also needed to encompass the complex processes involved in learning, mastering and demonstrating all kinds of practical and technical procedures (Sennett, 2008). Eventually we decided on 'Visual Practices' to embody the full range of meanings.

▶ Engaging with subject needs

Subject-specific skills and knowledge, as articulated in a representative sample of the 57 Subject Benchmark statements for

UK higher education (QAA, 2002 onwards, see www.qaa.ac.uk/
academicInfrastructure/benchmark.asp [last accessed 26/7/10]), helped
us to map the territories outlined above. I also surveyed academic
colleagues on the visual skills they required of their students and how
they developed and assessed these. Initially this seemed irrelevant to
some subjects but consideration of the challenges faced by blind or
partially-sighted students could open up new insights. For instance,
the importance of diagrammatic visualisation for computer
programming design is highlighted by the need for tactile alternatives
for visually impaired students.

It is clear that visual/tactile knowledge and skills of some kind play a
part in most disciplines, so it may seem surprising that they are not
taught more directly and explicitly. There are complex historical
reasons for this undervaluing of sensory knowledge. Often linked to
the rise of academies in the eighteenth century, it may be traced further
back in Western thought:

> The nature of experiential knowledge is shrouded in a cultural fog
> stemming from our continuing ... admiration for the ancient
> Greeks [whose] philosophy valued the life of the mind over the life
> of the body. [Since then], experiences have been marginalised and
> thought to be imperfect or second rate in comparison with intel-
> lectual pursuits. We see it in Cartesian dualism [and] Locke's
> notion of primary innate ideas. (Biggs, 2004)

However, there are more practical reasons for the regular omission of
visual skills from generic study guides. Where these are taught explicitly, it is usually done 'live', through demonstration, discussion and
example. Written advice alone is much less useful than for other study
practices, and the development of effective multimedia resources
requires a longer lead time and careful planning.

At the same time, most resources in this area, where they exist at all,
tend to be subject-specific, closely linked to particular curriculum
activities and not immediately transferable to other contexts. One of
the major challenges for this area has been to decide on the appropriate balance between specific and generic resources. Too specific and
they have limited relevance for students on a different course in the
same subject, let alone another discipline; too generic and they may be
of no use at all.

The LearnHigher strategy here, therefore, differed from other learning areas whose focus was the creation and testing of resources for

students. Instead, we worked with subject staff to raise awareness of the visual dimension of their subjects, and to explore how these might best be taught and assessed. The purchase of specialist equipment such as cameras and visualisers to support teaching in particular subjects also helped to raise awareness, with early projects generating such interest that most subsequent funding was used to support additional fellowships.

▶ Themes arising from the projects

Information about all the projects can be found through the Visual Practices website created to house resources and case studies (details at the end of the chapter); the examples outlined here illustrate some key themes.

Creativity, criticality and identity

One clear lesson has been the interdependence of technical, creative and critical learning, and the contribution these make, not just to students' subject knowledge, but to their own sense of self.

For instance, students from a variety of Information Studies courses were offered a digital photography option. Outlining her aims, the tutor described their core curriculum as 'theory-heavy and essay/exam based [with] few outlets ... to explore their own creativity' so, as well as developing their technical skills, she wanted students to understand:

- that real seeing is actually an acquired skill, rather than a given fact ... to learn to carefully observe their surroundings ... to imagine, and then to express their ideas visually.
- that the image making process is complex; that images are made, rather than taken ... to gain the necessary skills to analyse images and read them as texts. To ask the 'why' questions: who, what, why etc.
- that having a creative mind can be useful in many parts of their lives as well as other areas of study. (Winckler, 2007)

Interspersed with seminars on relevant contemporary and historic photographers, students undertook individual and small group tasks around an underlying theme of portraiture and identity, deliberately chosen to support their transition into higher education and develop their self-awareness. Student workbooks (which housed their ideas and storyboards, technical notes, drawings and ideas maps) provided a space to organise their material and critically reflect on their work, but also helped them:

> to develop their creativity, learn to make sketches and explore ways of visualizing and recording the world around them. (Winckler, 2007)

Learning to Look

Photography's potential for developing visual awareness and observational skills and enabling explorations of professional and personal identity has proved even more valuable for medical students. Learn-Higher, in conjunction with Inqbate (the CETL in Creativity) and Brighton Photography Biennial, helped Brighton and Sussex Medical School (BSMS) to develop a photography course, 'Learning to Look', which is now an approved option for third year medical students.

Weekly seminars encourage students to analyse the relationship between medicine and photography, with a focus on perception and observation in art and science, and particularly the contribution these make to diagnosis. Students are expected to discuss critically the work of relevant photographers and relate this to their own experiences, while acquiring practical skills through learning to take, upload, edit and print digital colour photographs. Crucially, they also take and develop black and white photographs in darkroom sessions; student feedback has demonstrated the value of this experience in sensitising them to subtle tonal variations, thereby improving their ability to interpret x-rays and other medical imagery.

Medical students are unaccustomed to open-ended assessments with no right or wrong answers, so some were initially uncertain about submitting a logbook of images and reflections. However, discussions about subjectivity and objectivity in photography, medicine and science have helped their understanding of the ways in which perceptions of patients may be distorted by their own assumptions, and equally that patients' own subjectivity affects the histories they give to doctors:

> Observations are a key element when examining a patient; taking a history is like taking a snapshot. It is a small part of their lives captured. A history also involves bias depending on the patient's mind state or if someone else is giving the history, their perspec-

tive. Their history is subjective to a point of view as is a photo-graph.

I believe [that] standing back from scientific theory and developing the creative side of my mind has aided my perception.

I have learned more about the kind of person that I am with the images I shoot. In my opinion it will help in being a better doctor. (Student comments, in Jones, 2007)

The ambition of 'Learning to Look' is indeed to make better doctors, and the project has sparked wider debates about the role of visual arts practice within clinical education. To accompany an exhibition of work from the project, LearnHigher sponsored a national conference for arts practitioners and medical educators to explore the evidence for this approach. Cardiac surgeon Francis Wells, whose own pioneering prac-tice has been influenced by the anatomical drawings of Leonardo da Vinci, spoke eloquently about how new medical students need to process their experiences in creative as well as academic ways:

[Medicine] is an emotionally exhausting subject so this business of looking and really seeing is potentially dangerous as well as extremely exciting ... because you're asking people who have been trained to be objective to suddenly open their hearts to what's around them. ... I was inspired by [a student comment that] '[Learning to Look] has made me look, listen and think' ... That's it – you've done your job! ... when you take the lid off people's minds at that age, you can never put it back on again – they will never see life in the same way again. I think that's a massive achievement.

Visual assessment

Many other projects demonstrated the transformative potential of creative visual practice, but this was not their main focus of attention. Instead, practical assignments were often designed to develop specific critical skills and understanding, with photographic or video projects supported by LearnHigher proving an effective way to bring visual analysis and theory to life.

For instance, 'See What I'm Saying' (co-funded with the CETL in Design) brought together students from three-dimensional design practice with others studying the history of design and visual culture. They worked in pairs to produce short films exploring the process of creation and placing of objects in museum collections. These interdisciplinary collaborations helped both groups to develop fresh ways of examining and articulating their response to objects. The course tutors reported:

a noticeable development in the use of critical language to express ideas in conjunction with visual media, which was evidenced in the questionnaires, evaluative form returns and especially in the 200 word moving image analysis reports. The content and visual quality of the films also developed in sophistication as the project progressed. (Letschka and Seddon, 2006)

Tourism students also need to develop a critical view of the way that artefacts and images create and communicate meaning in the tourism industry, but it is often hard to persuade vocationally-oriented students to engage with challenging and often dry texts on semiotics. To help make these ideas more tangible, tutors devised a fieldwork task using still images or video to construct a visual 'essay' about Eastbourne, the students' home campus, as a seaside town and holiday destination. Introducing practical tasks as alternatives to writing poses unfamiliar challenges for staff and students, so we helped the course team to draw up the brief and devise clear, but not over-prescriptive, assessment criteria. As one student commented afterwards,

once the assignment was explained to the group my first feelings were those of excitement because we were trying something new and we were left to use our imagination to construct a visual essay. Although I was excited I was also unsure about the initial idea and was a bit wary of what the lecturers wanted.

These initial misgivings were overcome through reassurance and feedback on work in progress, and the final levels of achievement and enthusiasm have been so high that the tutors are continuing to develop this approach (Burns and Lester, 2007).

Not all assessment projects involved digital technology. One study explored the use of handmade posters as an alternative to Power-Point® for student seminar presentations (Cattaneo, 2008). Students were asked to compare their experience of the two formats at each stage of preparing, delivering and listening to seminar presentations in a Cultural Studies module.

Just over half the students found that preparing a poster to accompany their seminar presentation helped them to organise their ideas, particularly those who identified themselves as dyslexic or visual thinkers, though some preferred the linearity of PowerPoint: *'my brain is chaotic and PowerPoint organises it'*. When it came to delivering their presentation, three-quarters preferred using posters as a visual aid, typically reporting that they *'felt more focused and in control'* and *'It was good to have all the information on view at the same time.'*

The most compelling results related to the value of posters for the audience and the quality of discussion generated. Almost all the audience members found the posters a more interesting and engaging visual accompaniment to the talks, perhaps because of the greater confidence felt by the speakers. Significantly, 100% of presenters said they had found the poster discussions useful, compared with just 25% after delivering with Powerpoint:

'There was discussion, rather than just questions & answers'; *'people seemed to be more involved'*, *'discussions were of a more dynamic nature'*. Students on this course are now offered experience of both formats and then choose their own presentation mode – two-thirds of them opt for posters.

Drawing: making learning visible

The poster study highlighted a number of interesting questions about the value for students of being able to see information all at once rather than sequentially, which are also reflected in our recent work on the role of drawing in higher education.

The cognitive value of drawing is recognised at primary school, where children are encouraged to draw from life and to copy and colour maps and diagrams across all subjects. Despite this, most students have long since abandoned drawing by the time they come to university – either because they have come to believe they are 'no good' at it or because they think it is irrelevant to learning at this level.

Digital technology has accelerated this process. One lecturer in biomolecular science deplored the fact that so many of her students arrive with no experience of drawing what they see while looking down a microscope, having been accustomed to using digital microscopes at secondary school. Yet drawing is an essential tool for sharpening observation skills:

In my experience, the only way to be sure I'm looking carefully enough at something – particularly something with lots of detail – is to draw it. The vital importance of this is that there may be something new and unexpected there; unless I draw I won't look carefully enough to see the unexpected. (Genetic scientist, quoted in Phipps, 2006)

Drawing is also a vital part of the thinking process for many scientists. Previous studies (Tasker and Dalton, 2006) have shown that chemistry students often fail to grasp the complex relationship between symbolic representations of molecular structures and the phenomena described. Devising their own versions helps build more sophisticated understanding, as demonstrated in another initiative at Brighton where pharmacy students create short animations to explain chemical processes (Elsom, 2009). Similarly, in Harvard University's 'Picturing to Learn' project, part of their Envisioning Science Program, science majors create freehand drawings to represent a given topic (such as the quantum behaviour of particles). These are rigorously assessed on the extent to which they demonstrate and clarify key scientific concepts.

Tho Big Draw

To help raise awareness of drawing as a tool for learning and research, we organised a month-long series of activities in 2007, linked to the National Campaign for Drawing's annual Big Draw event. 'Big Draw @ Brighton' was designed to encourage people to rediscover the pleasures of drawing and explore the role it could play in their own subject – not only to improve observation skills, but also to generate and communicate ideas and offer new perspectives on experience.

Confidence-building was important, so we included games and online resources as well as explaining the rationale for drawing as a legitimate university activity. Hundreds of students received specially designed folding sketchbooks, and visiting artists led subject-based workshops. In one session, engineering students experimented with different ways to move between two- and three-dimensional representations in order to improve their ability to visualise structures. Midwifery students produced some stunning drawings based on visualisations of the pregnant body and the child in the womb, while a workshop for physiotherapists and other health professionals explored experiences of illness, injury and recovery. One participant wrote later:

it showed [us] that drawing depicts concepts in a very emotionally raw way, and that people are accessing their thoughts and feelings via quite a different route than when verbalizing ... iterative drawing exercises allowed us to push through one-dimensional stereotypes of particular illnesses or conditions into a more multi-faceted understanding of the relationship between illness, internal and external perceptions of illness, treatment, aftercare and identity ... a lot more we could explore ...

Feedback for all these events was excellent, but it is worth remembering that not all students will find expressive, arts-based approaches equally helpful. We offered an artist-led workshop on mark-making for geology students, in preparation for a field trip where they would be drawing rock exposures and landscape features. Though they enjoyed the session, most students found the demonstrations by their tutors more relevant. These used a LearnHigher visualiser to project geologists' field sketchbooks and drawings of mineral samples as they were being made.

The University received the national Drawing Inspiration Award for the Big Draw @ Brighton. Our subsequent work in this area has reinforced the value of drawing in higher education, not just to improve observation skills, but also to generate and communicate ideas.

Conceptual drawing

During the Big Draw, new students on a sociology module were invited to make drawings and diagrams to represent 'society', which they revisited later to see how their ideas had changed. Getting students to visualise abstract concepts is an invaluable way to help them recognise tacit assumptions and theories, enabling them to see and explore areas of disagreement and debate.

This approach is equally productive with staff. At recent workshops, academics from different subject areas have been asked to brainstorm words associated with higher education and then draw these. The activity vividly exposes the range of tacit and conflicting meanings they themselves attach to terms such as 'critical' or 'argument', and shows them how difficult it can be for their students to understand these.

Concept mapping software can offer similar benefits (Novak, 2009), but our experiences indicate that the immediacy of handmade drawings and maps carries some important additional advantages for learning. Just as copying and colouring in primary school help reinforce memory, so the physicality of drawing and other forms of image making such as collage can assist more complex learning and reflection, and help to tease out emergent insights. For instance, recent workshops for research students have exploited the possibilities of collage:

> This collage process breaks away from the linearity of written thoughts by working first from feelings about something to the ideas they evoke, instead of the reverse. The resulting visual juxtapositions frequently reveal new connections and understandings that have previously remained tacit. (Butler-Kisber and Poldma, 2009)

Physical image making can also help to engage students in personal and professional development. One successful induction activity for courses with a strong vocational element starts by asking students to draw round each other on large sheets of paper. They then use a variety of materials to represent, on and around these life-size outlines, the attributes of the 'ideal' professional in their field – an effective way to prompt discussion of their expectations and whether these are realistic. This can be followed by a collective mapping of their imagined journey towards that goal. As the health professionals discovered through the Big Draw, such 'embodied' reflection often elicits insights that may be unavailable through other means.

► Conclusions

LearnHigher projects have demonstrated the potential scope of work in Visual Practices and this learning area continues to expand rapidly. Working closely with subject staff has enabled us to highlight the importance and relevance of visual practices in different disciplines and to develop case studies and other resources. The agenda for the next few years is to develop more sophisticated and flexible versions of student-facing resources and to evaluate their long-term impact on student learning.

Though we began by considering different types of visual knowledge and skills in relative isolation from each other, our experience has increased our understanding of the interlocking relationship between creative and academic practice and their role in students' conceptual, critical and emotional development.

It has also reinforced the importance of thorough preparation when introducing any new form of assessment. Visual assessment formats such as posters, websites, presentations, film and photographic assignments are on the increase in many subjects. Whether (as in some of the examples here) they are designed to develop and assess analytic or generic skills, or recommended as 'reasonable alternatives' to written essays for students with disabilities, their potential value may be lost unless lecturers are equipped to set appropriate tasks and mark them fairly and rigorously. Staff and students have equal need of specialist assistance to build confidence until they are more experienced.

Through work around visual knowledge mapping, whether in the more intimate form of small scale drawings described here, or the giant 'info-murals' used to support collective analysis and understanding of complex global problems (Horn and Weber, 2007), it is also becoming clear that the ability to make ideas visible and concrete is a powerful route to new knowledge. As such, it is an essential element of learning development.

▶ References

Biggs, M. (2004) 'Learning from experience: approaches to the experiential component of practice-based research', in H. Karlsson (ed.) *Forskning-Reflektion-Utveckling* (Stockholm: Swedish Research Council).

Burns, P. and Lester, J. (2007) 'Living in a material world: visualising tourism', in J. Barlow (ed.) *Making Teaching More Effective* (Brighton: University of Brighton Press).

Butler-Kisber, L. and Poldma, T. (2009) 'The power of visual approaches in qualitative inquiry: collage making and concept mapping in experiential research', *Design Research Society Experiential Knowledge Conference 2009*.

Cattaneo, J. (2008) *Assessment through Posters*. Available at: http://staffcentral. brighton.ac.uk/learnhigher/LHVPCattaneo.html (last accessed 29/3/10).

Elkins, J. et al. (2007) *Visual Practices Across the University* (Munich: Wilhelm Fink Verlag).

Elsom, J. (2009) 'A creative assessment strategy to improve student motivation and engagement in biochemistry', in J. Barlow, G. Louw and M. Price (eds) *Social Purpose and Creativity: Integrating Learning in the Real World* (Brighton: University of Brighton Press).

Harvard University (n.d.) 'Envisioning Science Program: Picturing to Learn'. Available at: www.picturingtolearn.org/ (last accessed 29/3/10).

Horn, R. and Weber, R. (2007) 'New Tools for Resolving Wicked Problems'. Available at: www.odnetwork.org/events/conferences/conf2008/pdf/artclHORN-WEBER-NewToolsWickedProblems.pdf (last accessed 29/3/10).

Jones, P. (2007) 'Learning to Look: Interim evaluation report. Brighton Photography Biennial' (unpublished).

Letschka, P. and Seddon, J. (2006) 'See what I'm saying'. Available at: http://cetld.brighton.ac.uk/projects/completed-projects/see-what-i-m-saying/results (last accessed 26/7/10).

Novak, J. D. (2009) *Learning, Creating and Using Knowledge: Concept Maps as Facilitative Tools in Schools and Corporations*, 2nd edn (London: Routledge).

Novak, J. D. and Cañas, A. J. (2008) 'The Theory Underlying Concept Maps and How to Construct Them', Florida Institute for Human and Machine Cognition. Available at: http://cmap.ihmc.us/Publications/ResearchPapers/TheoryUnderlyingConceptMaps.pdf (last accessed 29/3/10).

Phipps, B. (2006) *Lines of Enquiry: Thinking through Drawing* (Cambridge: Kettle's Yard).

Sennett, R. (2008) *The Craftsman* (London: Allen Lane).

Tasker, R. and Dalton, R. (2006) 'Research into practice: visualisation of the molecular world using animations', *Chemistry Education Research and Practice* 7 (2), 141–59.

Thibault, M. and Walbert, D. (2003) *Reading Images: An Introduction to Visual Literacy*. University of North Carolina. Available at: www.learnnc.org/lp/pages/675 (last accessed 29/3/10).

Winckler, J. (2007) *Developing Critical and Visual Literacy Skills*. Available at: http://staffcentral.brighton.ac.uk/lcarnhigher/LHVPWinckler.html (last accessed 29/3/10).

Section D

Students and Technology

15 When Worlds Collide: the Paradox of Learning Development, E-Learning and the 21st-Century University

Debbie Holley, Tom Burns, Sandra Sinfield and Bob Glass

▶ Summary

This chapter reviews the socio-political context for e-learning and argues that the temptation to approach new technology from economic or managerialist perspectives must be resisted. Rather, e-learning must be seen as an important aspect of a new and emergent pedagogy.

Paradoxically, whilst the student has the illusion of 24/7 access to 'the mind of the tutor' via hyperspace, the reality of higher education (HE) is a world of diminishing resources, larger classrooms and increasing central control.

However, pockets of good practice persist. To demonstrate what we regard as good practice in the use of e-learning, we review specific examples of resources. These were mostly created within a community of practice that firmly places students at the centre of developments, and engages them with a series of practices that will enable them to gain access to 'the academy'.

▶ Introduction

Government policy and resulting strategy documents (e.g., Dept for Education and Skills – DfES, 2005; HEFCE with JISC and the Higher Education Academy – HEA, 2005), coupled with recent funding initiatives (e.g. the HEA Benchmarking and Pathfinder initiatives and recent funding calls from JISC), are encouraging more universities to develop far-reaching e-learning strategies within, or alongside, their traditional institutional learning and teaching strategies. See, for instance, the recommendations of the JISC-funded Bradwell Report (Bradwell, 2009). Whilst ICT and e-learning may offer wide-ranging and exciting educational possibilities, the resulting demands that this makes on students, staff and resources need to be carefully considered; as do the challenges it poses for learning development and learning development practitioners.

This chapter will examine the implications of enhanced dependence on information and communications technology (ICT) for staff and students, with a special focus on e-resources and e-resource development. The first part discusses the theoretical assumptions underpinning ICT policy agendas and the dissonance this generates. In the latter part of the chapter, we review several resources that we have been involved in, revealing our rationale and underpinning methodology and philosophy.

Whilst the opening of the chapter highlights the negative aspects of this changing landscape, we conclude with an emphasis on good practice and collegiality that is designed to inspire and engender hope.

▶ The socio-political context

Government policies are a key driver for e-learning. This is demonstrated in the 2005 (revised 2008) DfES report, *Harnessing Technology*: a document disturbing for its lack of educational vision and its contrary emphasis on the ICT skills required for business (Sinfield, Holley and Burns, 2009). Whilst the form and content of any organisation, and educational ones in particular, should arguably be shaped by all its stakeholders (Crowther and Mraović, 2005), *Harnessing Technology* gives voice only to business (via government policy) and to senior management in universities; staff and students are rendered voiceless and powerless in the process. Pedagogy, once purely the concern of the academics directly involved in course delivery, has now become an issue for government policy – implemented by senior management via university strategy (Sinfield, Burns and Holley, 2004, p. 3).

The right to manage
Newman and Clarke (1994) suggest that this new managerialism within

the public sector stresses the 'right to manage' and reflects other changes therein initiated by centre right governments. concern about the economic costs of the state sector and the power of bureaucrats and professionals. The rise of new managerialism coincides with the move to a mass HE system and the arrival of the 'widening participation' student from working-class and other 'non-traditional' backgrounds, 'consistently ... classified as dangerous, polluting, threatening, revolutionary, pathological and without respect' (Skeggs, 1997, p. 1). The more cynical amongst us would argue that disregard for these students ushers in the new, digital university where the non-traditional student can access *only* virtual learning environments (VLEs), a scenario anticipated by the work of Noble (2002) on the commercialisation of education.

21st-century university blues

Thus the new university is to be opened up through e- and distance learning packages allowing students to choose *how* and *where* to learn, and even *when* to learn: but nowhere is there to be a choice or discussion about *what* and *why* students learn (Sinfield, Holley and Burns, 2009). In this vision of ICT, training and skills replace Anthony Giddens' (1996) reflexive agent and reduce the 'learner' (student) to automaton (Noble, 2002). To compound this reductionist view of the learner (as needy, deficit and atomised; classless; dislocated and dismembered), *Harnessing Technology* also embodies a reductionist view of education *per se* which accords with Noble's (2002) assertion that e-learning is inextricably bound up with the denaturing and de-professionalising of higher education itself. Indeed, the push for e-learning typically coincides with an emphasis on cost cutting, staff reduction, increased class sizes and so forth (Bennett, 2002).

When the issue of cost is raised in relation to online learning, many people in HE focus on the question: Does online learning cost more or less than traditional instruction? The predominant belief is that it costs significantly more – and without resources of time and creativity, institutional pushes for e-learning silence, disassemble and de-skill both the academic professional and the student (Sinfield, Holley and Burns, 2009).

The tensions of pedagogic practice

Despite a rapidly emerging body of literature about the benefits of e-learning and blended learning, what evidence is there that a blended-learning approach makes a difference to the student experience? Are tutors convinced by the government rhetoric of e-learning being 'as good as' traditional education (that is, a classroom-based experience), as has been argued by some authors? For instance, in *The No Signifi-cant Difference Phenomenon* (1999), Russell surveyed 355 research reports, summaries and papers from 1928 onwards, reviewing the impact of different methods of delivery (with a focus on technology) on the learning process of distance learners. Student learning outcomes, grades, interactions and frequency of interaction between students and staff, as well as other measures, were all reviewed and the conclusion was that there was no significant difference in outcome from different modes of delivery. This work focused on distance learners rather than using the blended approach that is the focus of this chapter; however, there is applicability to students in other spaces and places. Moreover, given the additional resources that have to be directed to producing high quality e-learning materials, this is a cause of concern in a higher education environment under threat of spending cuts.

Russell's work has been criticised by other researchers. Phipps and Merisotis (1999) pointed out a number of shortcomings, namely lack of control over extraneous variables; lack of randomness in the selection of subjects; validity of instruments; and the under-weighting of the importance of staff and student perceptions. They called for further research exploring differences within groups of online learners (see Chapter 16 of this book), and considering why drop-out rates are significantly higher in distance education programmes. In turn, Brown and Wack (2005) critique the Phipps and Merisotis paper, commenting that it is very difficult for any research outcome to predict the experi-ences of an individual learner if all learners learn differently. They conclude it is not 'the pitting of face-to-face conventional instruction against technology-enhanced and distance strategies' that is the issue, but that the 'educational researcher's most pressing and persistent challenge is ... not that we don't have the insight into ways to assess and enhance the art of teaching, but that educational research has for all but a few failed to inform teaching practice' (Brown and Wack, 2005, p. 6).

Resistance is useless

The move from educational settings where staff are at the centre of models of teaching and learning can cause anxiety for staff and students: a factor that can come as a surprise to early enthusiasts implementing technological innovations (Akerlind and Trevitt, 1999). The apprehension of faculty who anticipate losing status and power is a key theme of Talbot's work (2007) and Twigg (2001, p. 2) comments, 'Leaders of the old paradigm community have a tremendous amount of time and energy invested in using the old rules. Consequently, they are often resistant to change ... '. There is also well-documented evidence about the role of tutors changing with the introduction of web-based technology, especially within the context of sharing course access and design (Allison, McKechan, Ruddle and Michaelson, 2001).

Smith and Oliver's 2002 survey of staff attitudes to technology set a critical context to the debate about the use of ICT. Tentative findings indicated that staff respondents were broadly in favour of using technology in the context of their subject teaching; however, these were staff who saw themselves as 'above average' in using ICT. Other academic colleagues were viewed by enthusiasts as hostile or unwilling to use learning technologies, not as colleagues who have a different set of equally valid priorities. An alternative explanation may be that those that traditionally hold power are reluctant to share it, and thus the new technologies and their enthusiasts are viewed as a threat to the *status quo*.

Or is it?

We have argued that there is a deficit model emerging amongst influential decision makers, with e-learning as a 'quick fix' for the financial woes of the academy (Sinfield, Holley and Burns, 2006) where students are the absent, or least valued, stakeholder. However, as Beetham and Sharpe (2007, p. 6) comment, there *is* a need to rethink pedagogy for a digital age, and they posit the idea of digital design as a means of reclaiming the scholarship of teaching. And whilst there might be a tension around the drivers of e-learning, it can also involve a creative and responsive approach to meeting the aspirations of both students and academic staff (Beetham and Sharpe, 2007, p. 8).

Using an emergent design framework, and working within a community of practice (Wenger 1999), the initiatives we discuss below were designed with the intent to embody and enact the best practices of learning development's work with students and other stakeholders. We hope that the strength of our approach is our emphasis on working with the wider stakeholder body: students, discipline- and learning-development academics and learning technologists. This enables teams to come together and work in a creative and non-competitive environment. It offers a contrast to the binary opposition model set up and encouraged within current UK higher education policy and does not load all the ideological apparatus against the student.

▶ Web-based delivery of learner development information and learning materials

Learning Development Units have been providing web-based materials since the early 1990s. These originally comprised static information pages, downloadable documents, links to other internal and external resources and so on. More recently, Web 2.0 technologies have seen the addition of interactivity and enhanced engagement possibilities. Blogs (e.g., Blogger, Wordpress), social networking sites (e.g., Facebook, MySpace and Bebo) and wikis (e.g., PBwiki, Wetpaint) have all been utilised as methods of information delivery and to encourage interactivity between students, discipline- and learning-development academics. Second Life sites have been developed by a number of universities (including London Metropolitan University and Manchester Metropolitan University) to address some key student issues. These include getting access to learning resources and information literacy when students are already 'juggling' complex lives, with commitments that may include work, study and family (Holley and Oliver, 2010). There are some really interesting and exciting web developments taking place at present, and with the advent of Web 3.0 promising open access to a wide range of document formats and 3D spaces, the possibilities seem almost endless. However, there is a worrying trend in which some universities are choosing to put less on their websites (open access) and more inside their password protected VLEs. This may protect intellectual property, but means that opportunities for cooperation and sharing good practice are diminished.

Open access sites that provide some really useful links to web-based learning development resources and also provide examples of good practice for practitioners include LearnHigher (www.learnhigher.ac.uk), Intute (www.intute.ac.uk), the Joint Information Systems Committee (JISC) (www.jisc.ac.uk), the Higher Education Academy (www.heacademy.ac.uk) and the Re-usable Learning Objects (RLO)-CETL (www.rlo-cetl.ac.uk). The remainder of this chapter will focus on four interesting examples of relatively recent open access resources, and an example of how a resource can be used, and extensively adapted for use by a myriad users.

Example 1: *The Internet Detective*
Available from www.vts.intute.ac.uk/detective/

> Students are increasingly turning to the Internet to find information for their coursework or assignments, but they can be naïve in the sources they choose. There is concern among lecturers and

librarians that students often degrade their work by referencing inappropriate information sources and by failing to use the key scholarly materials that they should be using. (Place, 2006)

Now in its second edition, *The Internet Detective* is a free online tutorial, designed by Emma Place and Margaret Kendall for Intute, to help students develop the critical thinking required for their internet research. The tutorial offers practical advice on evaluating the quality of websites and highlights the need for care when selecting online information sources to inform university or college work (Place, 2006).

The Internet Detective embodies the metaphor of research as informed detection by taking the literary genre of Philip Marlowe's detective fiction and applying this very effectively to each of the sections on the website. The style is eye-catching, the sections easy to use, and there is a degree of interactivity provided via sectional quizzes. The content is also available on CD for download and use within VLEs and other electronic environments. This has been a very successful resource and is used in many UK and non-UK universities. The next stage with this resource is to create an m-learning version for users to access the site via mobile phones and personal digital assistants (PDAs).

Example 2: The Book and the NoteMaker
Available from www.learnhigher.ac.uk (see Fig. 15.1)

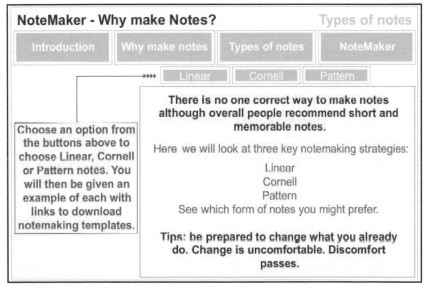

Figure 15.1 The *NoteMaker* resource

Both developed at London Metropolitan University, the 'speaking' *Desk* and interactive *NoteMaker* give very quick, user-friendly and non-patronising introductions to key study practices. The *Desk* proves revelatory when used with students in sessions on organisation and time management for study. The simple design and easy-to-see 'tips' can be returned to by students as and when they need them. Similarly the *NoteMaker* is designed as a revision and extension aid to taught sessions covering note-making as learning. This resource covers the why, what and how of note-making; with links to additional web materials including Tony Buzan's Mindmap lectures and open source mindmapping resources. Feedback collected from learning development staff through the Learning Development in Higher Education Network (LDHEN) mailing list (www.jiscmail.ac.uk/ldhen) indicates that this can facilitate experimentation and inquiry about the note-making process.

Example 3: Preventing Plagiarism
Available from www.learnhigher.ac.uk

With the expansion of higher education, concern about plagiarism and the lack of literacies found among 'new' students has reached hysterical proportions (see the first section in this book). This pathologises our students as deficient – even criminal. Developed at London Metropolitan University, this resource sets out, not to further demonise students, but to link anti-plagiarism practice to the development of student agency through successful study practices. Rather than duplicate effort extant in the wider community, newly-developed materials were married with existing good resources from the RLO-CETL, exit tests developed by Colin Neville (University of Bradford) and the University of Leicester's *Don't Cheat Yourself* tutorial.

Example 4: *Quickstart*
Available from http://learning.londonmet.ac.uk/LMBS/quickstart

The *Quickstart* project was an early attempt to provide students with an integrated learning environment where lectures, seminars and online activities were all designed to complement each other and offer students the ability to start on their academic studies from the first day they arrived in class. It is based on a visit to the

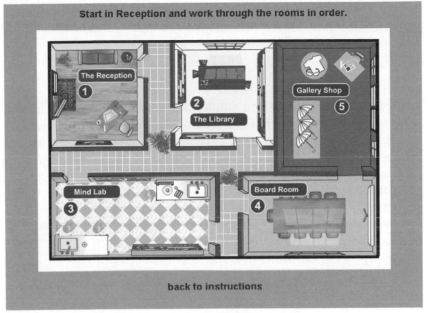

Start in Reception and work through the rooms in order.

The Reception
1

2
The Library

Gallery Shop
5

Mind Lab
3

Board Room
4

back to instructions

Figure 15.2 Snapshot of the entry to the *Quickstart* materials

Tate Modern art gallery, where students select an inspirational piece of art work and present to their peers their ideas of how the artefact could be adapted as a 'real' item for sale in the art gallery shop. This resource has been extensively evaluated with three cohorts of students, and the technology shared with other universities (Holley and Dobson, 2008; Cavanagh, Dobson and Holley, 2007; Holley, Dobson and Yau, 2005).

The institutional drivers for the project were influenced by the positioning of a post-1992 university within a competitive league table, hence recruiting many of its students from 'clearing' (a process in the UK where students who have not been offered a place at their first choice university are centrally processed to 'match' places at other institutions). The course team teaching the first semester 'Higher Education Orientation' module therefore had students attending class for the first time up to teaching week six. Offering students the *Quickstart* resources gave individuals the opportunity to feel part of the academic community straight away, as they could work through the interactive online materials.

► The defining characteristics of 'good' resources

These four examples all illustrate the characteristics we associate with good e-resources:

- Use technologies to be subversive: let them work *for* you.
- Create and work with a community of practice: technologies enable us to do this even when we are not in the same physical space.
- Engage students within that community – find creative ways to involve them.
- Develop enabling tools that encourage inquiry.
- Share the tools.
- Challenge assumptions about what we can do, how we 'should' do things and, most of all, assumptions about our students made by policy advisers.
- Enjoy playing, experimenting, developing and sharing.
- Reuse and recycle.

► Conclusions

Political issues and the subsequent commercialisation of education have led to many 'new managerialism' policy practices being introduced to the public sector arena. For universities, the consequences are obvious: silencing staff and students, de-professionalising staff, and the marketisation and commodification of HE itself. In terms of our students, instead of universities being there for education, they are there for the 'UK plc' skills agenda, set out by David Blunkett:

> The powerhouses of the new global economy are innovation and ideas, skills and knowledge. These are now the tools for success and prosperity as much as natural resources and physical labour power were in the past century. Higher education is at the centre of these developments ... It is therefore at the heart of the productive capacity of the new economy and the prosperity of our democracy.   (David Blunkett, Secretary of State for Education, Speech at the University of Greenwich, 15 February 2000. Available at http://cms1.gre.ac.uk/dfee#speech [last accessed 29/3/10])

Those lacking in the 'skills' of business are labelled as deficient, and handed over to agencies for treatment: hence the paradox of learning development (typically a place where any student could go for assistance) being asked to 'fix' low-achieving students. The wonders of Web 2.0 technologies are often barred from universities by firewalls, and the 'quick fix' for the student is the locally controlled Virtual Learning Environment, where academics are exhorted to deposit their 'knowledge' in a format the student can 'collect' later – thus offering the 24/7 illusion. The VLE monitors and controls – the academics can watch and monitor the students, the managers can watch and monitor the academics, the funding council can garner statistics to 'prove' learning is now taking place ...

We have suggested that a more optimistic vision is possible, one where collegiate teams can come together to reinvigorate their own practice and develop useful resources for themselves and their students.

▶ References

Akerlind, G. S. and Trevitt, C. (1999) 'Enhancing self-directed learning through educational technology: when students resist the change', *Innovations in Education and Teaching International* 36 (2), 96 106.

Allison, C., McKechan, D., Ruddle, A. and Michaelson, R. (2001) 'A group based system for group based learning', in P. Dillenbourg, A. Eurelings and K. Hakkarainen (eds) *European Perspectives on Computer-supported Collaborative Learning: Proceedings of Euro CSCL 2001* (Maastricht: Maastricht McLuhan Institute).

Atkinson, D. (2006) 'School art education: mourning the past and opening a future', *International Journal of Art and Design Education* 25 (1), 16–27.

Beck, U., Giddens, A. and Lash, S. (1996) *Reflexive Modernisation: Politics, Tradition and Aesthetics in the Modern Social Order* (Cambridge: Polity Press).

Beetham, H. and Sharpe, R. (2007) *Rethinking Pedagogy for a Digital Age: Designing and Delivering E-Learning* (London: Routledge).

Bennett, R. (2002) 'Lecturers' attitudes to new teaching methods', *International Journal of Management Education* 2 (1), 42–58.

Bradwell, P. (2009) *The Edgeless University: Why Higher Education Must Embrace Technology* (London: Demos). Available at: www.jisc.ac.uk/media/documents/publications/edgelessuniversity.pdf (last accessed 18/12/09).

Brown, G. and Wack, M. (2005) 'The difference frenzy and matching buckshot with buckshot', *The Technology Source*, May/June 1999, University of North Carolina.

Cavanagh, G., Dobson, C. and Holley, D. (2007) '"A little less conversation, a little more action please." Using multimedia to engage the first year student during Induction and post induction: lessons learning from a twin institution collaboration', *The First Year Experience in Continuing Education: Conference Proceedings* (Bristol: HEA Subject Centre for Education).

Crowther, D. and Mraović, B. (2005) 'Network semiology: a vehicle to explore organizational culture', in D. Crowther and R. Jatana (eds) (2005) *International Dimensions of Corporate Social Responsibility*, Vol. 2 (Hyderabad: ICFAI University Press).

Department for Education and Skills (2005) *Harnessing Technology: Transforming Learning and Children's Services* (Nottingham: DfES Publications, DFES-1296-2005).

Giddens, A. (1996) *In Defence of Sociology* (Cambridge: Polity).

HEFCE with JISC and the Higher Education Academy (2005) *HEFCE Strategy for e-Learning*. Available at www.hefce.ac.uk/pubs/hefce/2005/05_12/ (last accessed 29/3/10).

Holley, D. and Dobson, C. (2008) 'Encouraging student engagement in a blended learning environment: the use of contemporary learning spaces', *Learning, Media and Technology* 33 (2), 139–50.

Holley, D., Dobson, C. and Yau, H. (2005) 'Using multimedia to engage marketing students: a case study of collaboration with industry', in S. Greenland and N. Caldwell (eds) *Contemporary Issues in Marketing* (London: London Metropolitan University).

Holley, D. and Oliver, M. (2010) 'Student engagement and blended learning: portraits of risk'. To be published in *Computers in Education* (Amsterdam: Elsevier Publishing).

Laurillard, D. (2002) *Rethinking University Teaching: A Conversational Framework for the Effective Use of Learning Technologies*, 2nd edn (London: RoutledgeFalmer).

Leathwood, C. and O'Connell, P. (2003) '"It's a struggle": the construction of the "new student" in Higher Education', *Journal for Education Policy* 18 (6), 597–615.

Lillis, T. (2003) 'Student writing as "academic literacies": drawing on Bakhtin to move from critique to design', *Language and Education* 17 (3), 192–207.

Mitchell, S. (2003) *Developing the Potential of Student Writing for Learning in the University*. Presented to Student Learning Network, Queen Mary University of London, 2003.

Newman, J. and Clarke, J. (1994) 'Going about our business? The managerialisation of public services', in C. Clarke, A. Cochrane and E. McLaughlin (eds) *Managing Social Policy* (London: Sage).

Noble, D. (2002) *Digital Diploma Mills: The Automation of Higher Education* (New York, NY: Monthly Review Press).

Phipps, R. and Merisotis, J. (1999) *What's the Difference? A Review of Contemporary Research on the Effectiveness of Distance Learning in Higher Education* (Washington, DC: Institute for Higher Education Policy).

Place, E. (2006) *The Internet Detective: Back on the Case*. Press release dated 13 June 2006. Available at: www.vts.intute.ac.uk/detective/downloads/press_release_Internet_Detective_June_2006.doc (last accessed 29/3/10).

Rogers, C. (1994) *Freedom to Learn*, 3rd rev edn. (Upper Saddle River, NJ: Merrill).

Russell, T. (1999) *The No Significant Difference Phenomenon: A Comparative Research Annotated Bibliography on Technology for Distance Education* (Raleigh, NC: North Carolina State University).

Sinfield, S., Burns, T. and Holley, D. (2004) 'Outsiders looking in or insiders looking out? Widening participation in a post-1992 university', in J. Satterthwaite, E. Atkinson and W. Martin (eds) *The Disciplining of Education: New Languages of Power and Resistance* (Stoke-on-Trent: Trentham Books).

Sinfield, S., Burns, T., Hoskins, K., Holley, D. and Smith, C. (2008) *The contested terrain of notemaking: the development of a web and mobile based tool enabling students to gain their own voice through recontextualising their own notes and ideas*. Paper presented at Discourse, Power and Resistance Conference, Manchester Metropolitan University

Sinfield, S., Holley, D. and Burns, T. (2006) *The Silent Stakeholder: An Exploration of the Student as Stakeholder in the UK Government E-learning Strategy 2005*. Paper presented at the 4th International Corporate Social Responsibility Conference, Idrine, Turkey.

Sinfield, S., Holley, D. and Burns, T. (2009) 'A journey into silence: students, stakeholders and the impact of a strategic governmental policy document in the UK', *Social Responsibility Journal* 5 (4), 566–74.

Skeggs, B. (1997) *Formations of Class and Gender* (London: Sage).

Smith, H. and Oliver, M. (2002) 'University teachers' attitudes to the impact of innovations in ICT on their practice', in C. Rust (ed.) *Proceedings of the 9th International Improving Student Learning Symposium* (Oxford: Oxford Centre for Staff and Learning Development).

Talbot, C. (2007) 'State Building'. Available at: www.nottingham.ac.uk/npc/publicpolicy/content/point_of_view.pdf (last accessed 22/08/07).

Twigg, C. A. (2001) *Innovations in Online Learning: Moving Beyond No Significant Difference* (New York, NY: National Center for Academic Transformation (NCAT), Rensselaer Polytechnic Institute).

Wenger, E. (1999) *Communities of Practice: Learning, Meaning and Identity* (Cambridge: Cambridge University Press).

16 Defining and Supporting the New Digital Students

Neill Currant, Becka Currant and Peter Hartley

▶ Summary

Like many areas of learning development, the use of learning technologies impacts on a range of academic and support services: individual lecturers, learning technologists, IT services and so on. It is important that the 'learning development community' is aware of how these technologies affect student learning as we may find ourselves supporting learners who are struggling with the demands placed on them from the academic use of such technologies. This chapter suggests that students are not one homogeneous group of 'tech-savvy' learners. It proposes a simple typology to help us understand the different needs of students with regards to learning technologies and suggests ways to support these diverse students.

▶ Introduction

It seems inevitable that ICT and learning technology will be an increasing aspect of the higher education learning experience. Therefore, it seems only a small jump to assume that it will become an increasing part of the work of learning development and learning development practitioners. Not only does it provide challenges for resources but the rhetoric of the so-called 'digital native' or 'Google Generation' could lead us into making assumptions about the best way to support learners' use of learning technology that may be a waste of time or even detrimental to their learning.

Exploring the 'Google Generation' rhetoric

Prensky coined the phrase 'digital native' in 2001. He posited the notion that these natives were different in how they learned because of technology. Whilst it was an interesting idea, it was not founded on any hard evidence and has been widely discussed and criticised (e.g. Siemans, 2007). However, the catchy moniker seems to have passed out of the realms of the educational technology world into popular consciousness. It has been joined by a band of such catchy titles: Google Generation, Millennials, Generation Next, Generation Y and so on. The ideas bring with them an assumption of what young people and students today are like and how they might learn. One of those assumptions can be summarised as: 'Students today are technology savvy and therefore they can arrive at university and easily transfer their technology know-how to using technology in the formal learning environment.' However, whilst we know that technology has become an integral part of their everyday experiences to the extent that they do not see it as technology (Oblinger and Oblinger, 2005), it is by no means certain that the social and personal use of technology equates to effective use of technology for learning. We must remember and plan for the fact that: 'data suggests that they [adolescents] are both comfortable with new technologies, and yet not always as technically savvy as we collectively believe them to be' (Pew Research Center, 2008). This is also mirrored by Lei (2009, p. 87) who found that trainee teachers, who had grown up with technology, were savvy at using communication technologies, but: 'their technology proficiency is limited by both the narrow scope and the lack of depth of their technology activities'.

As well as our own assumptions, students may have assumptions about the technology used in higher education and their own competence with technology: 'students view their computer competence differently depending on whether they are using the technology for personal or course-related tasks' (Messineo and DeOllos, 2005, p. 50). This can be partly explained because the technology tools used in the formal setting of university are often different from those being used in the everyday world of the student (Ipsos Mori, 2008). The Ipsos Mori report highlighted the fact that technologies that might be used for learning, such as wikis, podcasts and online assignment submissions, were unfamiliar to students and they were uncomfortable in using them. Additionally, using their own social networks for formal learning was not something that they were comfortable doing either.

Of course, it is not just the 'Google Generation' that are students in our universities. In an era of widening participation in higher education we have a diverse range of learners including mature learners and those from less advantaged socio-economic backgrounds. In the general population, 'age has a dramatic impact on digital choices' (Dutton, Helsper and Gerber, 2009, p. 4) although it appears this effect is less dramatic for university students (White, 2007). However, it may still be the case that older learners have less experience of, or less confidence in, the use of technology. Background can also play a part: Facer and Furlong (2001) raise the issue of social inequality as a force that may affect confidence and competence in using technology, with children who had limited access to computers and who saw little relevance of computers to their daily lives. Today, addressing the digital divide is still a policy driver for the UK Government, 'we are clear that the digital divide has not been entirely overcome and persists in several dimensions: in access to technology and also in operational capability' (CLEX, 2009, p. 3).

Learner preferences and styles will also influence how well technology is used for learning. Heaton-Shrestha et al. (2007) found that the use of a virtual learning environment (VLE) did not influence the approach to learning; but the approach to learning, i.e. whether deep or strategic (Entwistle, Tait and McCune, 2000), influenced the use of the technology. Chen and Macredie (2002) suggest that different styles require different approaches to educational technology. For example, more dependent learners may require a very structured approach to online learning with guidance from either the tutor or the system. It is not just learning styles or technical ability that can have an effect on the use of technology. We are increasingly finding that the 'skills' which underpin the effective use of technology are lacking, for example, information literacy (Brabazon, 2007) and group-work (Alexander, 2001; Currant and Whitfield, 2007; Hammond, 2005).

In summary, students, just as they may be unfamiliar with studying and learning in the higher education environment, may not be comfortable using some learning technologies and, possibly more importantly, they may lack the underpinning skills to work and participate effectively in collaborative online environments. Further, as indicated above, student diversity is also a factor we need to bear in mind: different learners will have different preferences for how they use learning technology and will have different levels of experience and confidence with such technology. In this chapter we explore how we can understand this diverse mix and how to plan to support learners and learning.

▶ Towards a new typology of digital learners

From our experiences as part of the JISC Enhancing Learner Progression 2 (ELP2) project, LearnHigher, and other work looking at the use of Web 2.0 technologies with students, we found that, despite the expectation that young people were digitally adept, some learners struggled with using tools such as wikis and blogs and using social networking on formal courses, particularly in group-work. In order to understand what was happening, we developed a typology that reflected the differences we could see between students.

The most obvious differences were in experience, confidence and competence in using technology. As already noted, some learners will be less confident ICT users and some will be unfamiliar with certain tools that are used in an educational setting (Ipsos Mori, 2008). This forms one dimension of the typology: 'experience of technology'. This dimension is about whether the technology itself presents barriers to learning for some learners.

The second dimension is labelled 'degree of educational contribution' to reflect the degree to which students are able to contribute to their formal learning using technology. This refers to how the technology is used in the formal educational setting and whether students have the skills needed to use the technology effectively for learning. It also considers the underpinning skills, such as interpersonal and group-working skills, that are implicit in collaborative web-based technologies, and raises questions: How do those underpinning skills impact on the learner's effective use of technology? Are they likely to engage with technology and see the benefits of its use in their educational experience? This is captured in the idea that students need 'self-efficacy as learners and technology users' (JISC, 2009, p. 1).

There is a link between this dimension and what are referred to as field-dependent and field-independent learners (Witkin et al., 1977) in the sense that the 'field' in this case is the context of use for the technology. So a field-dependent learner familiar with the social use of technology may struggle with the educational use of the same technology because of the different context.

There may be a link between this second dimension and educational experience per se; however, other factors such as learning styles may also play a part. For example, an active learner may contribute more than a reflective learner, regardless of previous educational experience. An older student, with less formal educational experience, may contribute more because they have the necessary 'life skills' to

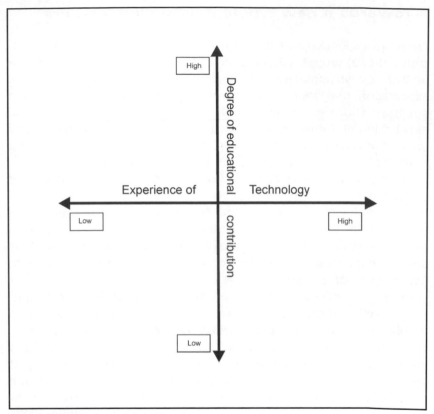

Figure 16. 1 Typology of digital learners

contribute. Thus education experience may be one factor among many that influence 'educational contribution' using learning technology. 'Educational contribution' simplifies the model and is easier to observe than trying to factor in the complicated interrelated factors which may influence this dimension. Putting these two dimensions together you can create four quadrants (Currant et al., 2008) to provide a simple model of four different types of learners, each of which requires a different approach to learning technology (see Fig. 16.1). We outline that approach below, drawing on student voices from our 'Develop Me' and JISC Enhancing Learner Progression projects to underline our arguments.

▶ 'Digitally Reluctant'

These learners fall into the lower end of both continua – they are not confident or experienced technologically and can find the idea of technology frightening and off-putting. They cannot see the potential educational benefits. They are unlikely to use technology within an educational context as they lack the confidence to be able to engage effectively.

> [I thought] you don't know how to do it [use the online learning environment], just switch it off, get out of here. (Lynne)

Lynne is a mature student. She has used computers in employment but uses them in very specific ways. Lynne finds using new web-based tools a big challenge and has limited knowledge of using technology for her own learning. She struggles to see how technology can help other than in ways similar to how she has used technology before, such as word processing, or the web as a source of basic information.

'Digitally Inexperienced'

These are students who have lower levels of experience of technology but score higher on the degree of educational contribution. The 'digitally inexperienced' are willing to try using technology within an educational setting but lack the experience to do so. They may be very enthusiastic about their learning and keen to engage with different approaches, but their lack of technological expertise is a barrier to their engagement.

> I was really keen to do it [a wiki] but I don't think I really understood what would be involved in it and how to use it properly'. (Liz)

John, a postgraduate student, is another example of this type. John can see how collaborative technologies can be used but is very reluctant to engage because of his limited experience in online interactions. John is uncomfortable in an online social environment and with giving his opinions in this way:

> if I felt confident enough about what I was blogging [but] I don't think I'm ready for it at the moment.

'Digital Socialites'

In our experience, 'socialites' are drawn from the so-called 'Google Generation'; high on the experience of technology but low on the educational contribution. They have grown up with technology but tend to use it for social and entertainment reasons. They prefer face-to-face educational settings over e-learning (Oblinger and Oblinger, 2005; Ipsos Mori, 2008): 'Imagining technology used for social purposes in a study context presents conceptual difficulties to learners' (CLEX, 2009, p. 6). They are likely to be as described by Ipsos Mori thus (2007, p. 5):

> young people automatically think of ICT improving their learning through giving them more access to data and research resources, rather than imagining totally new methods of teaching, learning, or interacting with peers and lecturers.

They may use technology to support aspects of learning but do not automatically take full advantage of the opportunities afforded by the technology. An example is Usman, a first year undergraduate student. Usman downloads music to his mobile phone and watches YouTube videos. He makes prolific use of synchronous chat tools and his mobile for chatting/texting his friends. He is happy to exchange thoughts with them about his latest music acquisition. He is not afraid of technology; however, when asked in an educational setting to view an online video and then discuss its contents in an online discussion group he finds it difficult to know what to post. He is inclined to ask the tutor what he needs to write. He might post a short sentence with fairly general thoughts, and make no response to other posts, or he waits until others have contributed and then replies with a short statement along the lines of 'I agree'. He struggles to apply his day-to-day electronic communication skills within an educational context.

'Digitally Experienced'

For this group, technology is a major part of everyday life and they are comfortable with using different applications simultaneously and collaboratively. With a high score on both dimensions, these students are well equipped for making effective use of learning technology but there is a risk of them being disaffected by poor use of technology at university. Tony is comfortable with technology and is a self-directed autonomous learner. He can see the benefits of collaboration online and gets frustrated when his peers are reluctant to engage with him.

I'm concerned, however, while some of us are having regular exchanges of views, other colleagues are keeping low profiles ... such a small number of us are contributing [online] that I wonder what the point is sometimes.

Implications for learning

The digitally inexperienced and reluctant need to become familiar with the learning technology. Lack of confidence can be a significant barrier to their learning because they are worrying about what to do with the technology rather than concentrating on how to use it to support their learning. A patient, supportive approach is needed which may include taking them through which buttons to click, reassuring them that their work is safe and that they are not going to 'break anything'. There is a sense of palpable relief from students who are struggling with technology once you take them through how to use the technology for the purpose that they need to use it for. We need to remember that working on high-stakes assessment or tasks using technology can be a cause of stress for students (Lawless and Allan, 2004).

Both the digitally reluctant and digital socialites need to understand the purpose of using the technology. The context for use is very important. Why are they being asked to use the technology? How does it relate to their course? They will also benefit from development to increase their learning autonomy, such as the use of e-portfolios to support informal learning, and learning across the curriculum rather than the modular focus which partitions so much of the learning. The socialites may not see that using technology is a problem but can end up using it for surface learning only (Currant and Whitfield, 2007). Helping them develop a deeper understanding of processes such as personal development planning can help them gain a broader perspective of how the technology can help their learning.

▶ Good practice in learning support

Having identified the types of learners on the basis of how they use learning technology, we need to ask whose job it is to support them in their academic use of technology. Is it the individual academics? Is it ICT services? Is it learning development? Is it the students themselves? In reality, it is all of the above and more. The following examples are drawn from a range of different approaches, many of which are not within the traditional domain of learning development services; this only serves to highlight the overlapping domains of learning development with other services and provision. We have identified a number of benefits that come from such inter-agency working. These include ensuring different staff are aware of the types of support available from complementary services; 'joined up' thinking in supporting students, which helps students to develop trust and confidence about the types of support they are receiving; reducing the number of inappropriate referrals/duplicate referrals between services; highlighting additional support and help which is available.

Madden (2009) suggests four ways to engage learners in education using new media:

- encourage creativity;
- encourage conversations;
- augment offline relationships online;
- use semi-public online spaces.

It is the latter three that the Develop Me social network at the University of Bradford hopes to engage. The site is an 'official' but informal (Hartley, 2007; Hartley and Currant, 2008) university social network originally created to ease the transition of new students into higher education by providing a space where they can build relationships with fellow students prior to arrival on campus. It has been particularly popular with international students and has been effective in engaging staff and students alike. The site is not just the preserve of the younger tech-savvy students, who are more used to Facebook and similar sites. One of the most active student-led groups is for mature students.

Bridging the social and the academic

The Develop Me social network site acts as a bridge between the social use of technology and the academic use. Staff can communicate with students and vice versa. Course-specific information is available to students prior to their arrival and some departments have used it for pre-induction activities.

Students helping students

CLEX (2009, p. 28) recommends that 'students' practical skills with ICT can be harnessed by staff to good effect in both domains – operation and effective use'. Those students who are the digitally experienced understand both the technology and the reasons for its academic use and can therefore support other students in getting to grips with the tools and help explain the purpose of tools in the academic context. For example, the University of Wolverhampton employ Blended Learning Technical Support delivered by students experienced in using the university's learning technology systems. These students proactively support others (staff as well as students) to use the e-portfolio and VLE with the help of staff in the Blended Learning Unit. It is effective because these students have successfully used the technology for their own academic study and understand both the technical and the academic issues that may arise.

Embedding peer support

Peer support can be embedded within a course as well as being part of a central service, as above. The University of Bradford's BSc Midwifery Studies course has second year students supporting first year students in their use of learning technology. For the digitally inexperienced and reluctant, the peer support gives them the confidence to use the technology. In many cases the students giving the support were themselves uncomfortable using the technology at the start of the course. For the digital socialites, the support can help explain the purpose of using the technology so that the students can see the end point of the processes; the answer to 'why am I using this technology?'

The Midwifery course uses an e-portfolio for development and collaboration in a lifelong learning module which is embedded into each year of the course. This embedded nature of the technology in the course allows students to learn effectively. There is a clear reason for using the e-portfolio. The use of technology is congruent with the learning outcomes and staff are confident enough in using the technology to be able to support students, or know where to get help quickly by working with central support services.

Embedding ICT literacies

The 'Communicating in an Information Age' module at Bradford University couples learning about modern communication tools with learning about group-work and communication skills. This first year module gives students the chance to explore the similarities and differences in working collaboratively online and face to face. It uses a range of features such as wikis, blogs and e-portfolios to help them learn about the technologies and how they can be used. The module makes extensive use of online resources to support both the learning aims. On this module the skills of using technology are embedded as part of the content of the curriculum.

There are many approaches to supporting the effective use of learning technology; we are sure you have your own examples, but context is very important for some students and for others it is confidence and comfort that matter. As with all other areas of education, it is in combining good pedagogy, high-quality resources and the expertise of staff and students where success is to be found.

▶ Conclusion

Hopefully, this chapter has shown that our universities have a diverse range of learners when it comes to using technology and that a one-size-fits-all approach is not likely to work. JISC (2009) recommend integrating the digital into existing skills support, using e-portfolios for development, and building online communities for study support, amongst many other suggestions for supporting digital literacies. Moreover, if handled well, the introduction of blended learning can allow:

> The renegotiation of the relationship between tutor and student ... a relationship in which each recognises and values the other's expertise and capability and works together to capitalise on it. (CLEX, 2009, p. 38)

In fact, it should extend beyond this relationship. It is through working in partnership with academic staff, learning development, educational development, ICT services and students that effective use of technology takes place in the academic realm; 'work towards an integrated strategy across departments and services' (JISC, 2009, p. 3). Who better to foster those partnerships than learning developers?

▶ Further sources

Typology stories can be found at:

www.elp.ac.uk/stories

The Develop Me social network is an open network for all staff and students at the University of Bradford, and can be found at:

http://developme.ning.com/

Online resources used from Develop Me can be found at:

www.bradford.ac.uk/developme/

and the LearnHigher website:
www.learnhigher.ac.uk/
All URLs last accessed on 29/3/10.

▶ References

Alexander, S. (2001) 'E-learning development and experiences', *Education and Training* 43 (4/5), 240–8.

Brabazon, T. (2007) *The University of Google: Education in a (Post) Information Age* (Aldershot: Ashgate).

Chen, S. Y. and Macredie, R. (2002) 'Cognitive styles and hypermedia navigation: development of a learning model', *Journal of the American Society for Information Science and Technology* 53 (1), 3–15.

CLEX – The Committee of Inquiry into the Changing Learner Experience (2009) *Higher Education in a Web 2.0 World*, final report (Bristol: Department for Employment and Learning).

Currant, N. and Whitfield, R. (2007) 'Students aren't prepared for Web 2.0 learning, are they?' Presentation to Association for Learning Technology Annual Conference, at University of Nottingham. Details available at: www.alt.ac.uk/altc2007. Presentation available at: www.slideshare.net/ncurrant/altc-2007-presentation-neil-currant (last accessed 26/7/10).

Currant, N., Currant, R., Whitfield, R. and Hartley, P. (2008) 'Defining Generation Y: towards a new typology of digital learners', in J. Pieterick, R. Ralph and M. Lawton (eds) *EFYE Conference Proceedings 2008*.

Dutton, W. Helsper, E. and Gerber, M. (2009) *The Internet in Britain 2009: Oxford Internet Survey* (Oxford: Oxford University Press).

Entwistle, N., Tait, H. and McCune, V. (2000) 'Patterns of response to an approaches to studying inventory across contrasting groups and contexts', *European Journal of the Psychology of Education* XV (1), 38.

Facer, K. and Furlong, R. (2001) 'Beyond the myth of the "Cyberkid": young people at the margins of the Information Revolution', *Journal of Youth Studies* 4 (4), 451–69.

Hammond, M. (2005) 'A review of recent papers on Online Discussion in Teaching and Learning in Higher Education', *Journal of Asynchronous Networks* 9 (3), 9–23.

Hartley, P. (2007) 'Keynote presentation'. Presentation at JISC 'Next Generations' conference. Availalable at: www.jisc.ac.uk/news/stories/2007/04/news_nextgen.aspx (last accessed 29/3/10).

Hartley, P. and Currant, N. (2008) 'How many virtual learning spaces do students need?' Presentation at SOLSTICE Conference, Edge Hill University. Available at: www.edgehill.ac.uk/solstice/conference2008/documents/session14ProfessorPeterHartley_NeilCurrant.pdf (last accessed 26/7/10).

Heaton-Shrestha, C. et al. (2007) 'Learning and e-learning in HE: the relationship between student learning style and VLE use', *Research Papers in Education* 22 (4), 443–64.

Ipsos Mori (2007) *Student Expectations Study,* JISC. Available at: www.jisc.ac.uk/media/ documents/publications/studentexpectations.pdf (last accessed 29/3/10).

Ipsos Mori (2008) *Great Expectations of ICT,* research study report (Bristol: JISC).

JISC (2009) *Responding to Learners Guide 4: A Guide for Learning Developers and Learning Support Staff* (Bristol: JISC).

Lawless, N.and Allan, J. (2004) 'Understanding and reducing stress in collaborative e-learning', *Electronic Journal on e-Learning* 2 (1), 21–128.

Lei, J. (2009) 'Digital Natives as Pre-service Teachers', *Journal of Computing in Teacher Education* 25 (3), 87–97.

Madden, M. (2009) 'Eating, Thinking and Staying Active in New Media'. Presentation, 2/6/09, at NICHD Media-Smart Youth Meeting.

Messineo, M. and DeOllos, I. (2005) 'Are we assuming too much? Exploring students' perceptions of their computer', *College Teaching* 53 (2), 50.

Oblinger, D. and Oblinger, J. (2005) 'Is It Age or IT: first steps toward understanding the Net Generation', in D. Oblinger and J. Oblinger (eds) *Educating the Net Generation* (Washington, DC: Educause).

Pew Research Center (2008) *Pew Internet and American Life Project.* Available at: www.pewinternet.org/topics/Teens.aspx (last accessed 28/8/09).

Prensky, M. (2001) 'Digital natives, digital immigrants', *On the Horizon* 9 (5), 1–6.

Siemans, G. (2007) *Digital Natives and Immigrants: A Concept Beyond its Best Before Date.* Available from: http://connectivism.ca/blog/2007/10/digital_natives_and_ immigrants.html (last accessed 14/3/2008).

White, D. (2007) 'Results and analysis of the Web 2.0 services survey undertaken by the SPIRE project', project report. Available from: www.jisc.ac.uk/media/documents/ programmes/digitalrepositories/spiresurvey.pdf (last accessed 29/3/10).

Witken, H., Moore, C., Goodenough, D. and Cox, P. (1977) 'Field-dependent and field-independent cognitive styles and their educational implications', *Review of Educational Research* 47 (1), 1–64.

17 Friend or Foe? The Impact of New Technologies on Student Time Management at University

Kim Shahabudin

▶ Summary

This chapter discusses difficulties faced by students in managing their time at university, and considers the role of 'new' technologies including Web 2.0 tools, mobile phones, laptops and Personal Response Systems (PRS), in both creating and solving these difficulties.

The widespread use of these technologies for study and leisure will be considered in the context of typical learning cultures for recent 18–21 student cohorts, as well as traditional academic practices and expectations. A range of case studies are discussed, in order to explain and share interventions that have been effective in helping students to develop better time management strategies.

▶ Introduction

> *Time management is the skill which above all others can make the difference between graduating and drop out.* (Pickford and Brown, 2006, p. 4)

Good time management is crucial for independent learning, and independent learning is an increasingly significant element of university life. In a Higher Education community which is more than ever focused on both student retention and student success, this is a concern not just for individual students, but also for their tutors, and for learning developers working with both students and tutors to maximise study success. An inability to manage study time can lead to under-achievement and late or non-submission of assignments, and causes considerable stress. Early guidance towards independent study as part of university induction can be invaluable. However, as students progress through their degree courses, new challenges can sabotage even the most carefully organised study schedule (JISC, 2007, p. 9) – and the encroachment of the digital in both social and educational spheres can pose some of the most beguiling challenges of all.

Despite widespread acknowledgement of its importance to student success and retention, effective time management is rarely taught within subject disciplines. However, learning developers are uniquely placed to advise students on this topic, as time management strategies can be shown to relate to the whole range of practices essential for study: from focused active reading and effective note-making through to good practice in exam preparation and academic writing. Developing effective interventions for problems prompted by new technologies may become increasingly important as budgets are squeezed, and there is more reliance on virtual delivery methods for teaching and resourcing courses.

This chapter will describe strategies to support student time management, developed through practice-led research for LearnHigher, illustrating them with anonymised case studies based on professional experience working with students as a learning development adviser. These will be set in the context of the widespread use of new technologies, new student learning cultures and the conflicts these can provoke with traditional academic expectations.

► Digitally challenged

New technologies offer particular challenges to student time management. On the one hand, they are increasingly used in universities as effective communication and teaching tools: for instance, communicating administrative information via email or text, or providing virtual tutorial support through podcasts, interactive web pages and online forums. Blogs and wikis are used for group-work, and social bookmarking to update reading lists. Students are themselves organising online study groups to share ideas and resources (Ipsos MORI/JISC,

2008, p. 7). However, the devices through which these virtual learning arenas are entered are tools for leisure as well as study. This blurring of boundaries can provoke difficulties.

For recent 18–21 cohorts in higher education, devices like laptops, mobile phones, Personal Digital Assistants (PDAs) and iPods are not 'new' technologies: they are the necessary tools of everyday life (JISC, 2007, p. 4). The 'digital native' tag applied to these students (Prensky, 2001) is now widely recognised as over-simplistic (see, for instance, Currant et al. in Chapter 16 of this volume). However, the impact of technologies on learning cultures is undeniable. The easy accessibility, interactivity and high level of customisation offered, especially by Web 2.0, have prompted consumer expectations of variety, stimulation and flexibility in all areas, including universities. These can conflict with academia's more hierarchical structures (CLEX, 2009, pp. 39–40), and with traditional ideas about effective learning, which demand periods of focused attention in order to research, process and communicate complex ideas.

Throughout our research for LearnHigher, teaching staff from both learning development and subject disciplines have reported an increasing need for advice for students on managing time more effectively, in order to meet deadlines and achieve academic success. What kind of strategies and interventions can we offer in this increasingly digital age to enable students to negotiate boundaries between study and leisure, exploit and allow their new expertises, and encourage them to achieve their academic potential?

▶ Focusing on study

I think there might be something wrong with me – I get to the end of a page and I can't remember a word I've just read. (2nd year Geography student)

Traditional academic notions of focused periods of study to develop deep understanding are in sharp contrast to prevalent habits of consumption of contemporary popular culture (both on and offline), which offers hyper-stimulation and instant gratification through short bursts of content. Students in the current 18–21 cohort have been negatively labelled 'the MTV generation' for their short attention spans and constant need for novelty. They have grown up finding immediate answers to any question, from the internet; maintaining constant inter-personal contacts through mobile phone texts and instant messaging; and personalising entertainment choices through the use of iPods, multi-channel and on-demand television. Even their food is fast, with microwave meals, online supermarket shopping and a choice of takeaways from every corner of the globe.

There can be great advantages to this new culture in terms of creativity, cultural knowledge, aspiration and the ability to multi-task. A report on 18–34-year-olds gives the example of a moderator who, 45 minutes into an online discussion on technology at university, asked student participants how many other windows they currently had open on their computers: answers ranged from 4 to 9 (Castell et al., 2008, p. 16). This activity is also multi-modal, with one survey noting that a third of students surveyed:

> regularly access the internet during lectures or seminars – for general use as well as specifically for university work. (Ipsos MORI/JISC, 2008, p. 15)

However, some find that this has an impact on their ability to give undivided attention to study. Students report difficulties in maintaining concentration, both in relatively passive study situations (e.g. taught lectures) and in more active ones (e.g. researching, reading and writing assignments, preparation for exams). This can cause problems with managing studies even if there is good time planning, with tasks taking much longer than expected because of the constant need to repeat and refocus. The consequence can be late submission or non-submission of assessed work, and under-achievement.

Active learning has long been known to promote better engagement with study, encourage focus and increase retention of new knowledge; new technologies can be used in teaching to make learning more active. For instance, Personal Response Systems (PRS) can be utilised to get students interacting with lecture topics by asking them to express their opinions through 'voting'; this enacts, in learning, the culture of consumer choice that they experience in other spheres. A brief case study from the University of Reading on the use of PRS with Chemistry students to encourage active learning reported advantages including instant feedback, and anonymity of response (Page, n.d.). Some students use Twitter (Ramsden, 2009) and Google Docs (Ipsos MORI/JISC, 2008, p. 40) to create notes on lectures that can be shared and compared with those of other students at the same lecture, giving them a multi-perspective overview (see Moon, 2004).

This kind of initiative tends to be driven by individual enthusiasts (students and staff); when new technologies and e pedagogy are imposed without adequate training, resources or contextualisation, they can have a negative effect on engagement. (See Chapter 15 for more discussion and suggestions to combat this.) Students tend to disengage if they feel staff are not competent with technologies (Castell et al., 2008, p. 30). In addition, some students, especially those from non-traditional backgrounds, can have their already fragile academic confidence further dented if asked to use technologies that are unfamiliar to them.

Dissertations, research projects and revision schedules are especially challenging if students cannot plan and pace work over time. Providing electronic interactive framework plans that students can use to structure their work schedule can be a way of mediating planning while encouraging the move towards more independent working. Such plans are likely to be more successful if they have an element of flexibility built in, and show students how to break down larger pieces of work into their individual tasks, enabling them to establish a series of short-term targets to retain focus (see, for instance, www.learnhigher.ac.uk/ask).

Case study. Anil   focusing on revision

Anil was a final-year student having difficulty concentrating on revision. Although he felt that he was working all the time he was not getting anything accomplished. His usual plan was to get up early and set himself up in the library for the day, using his laptop to access lecture notes and online articles: but his attention often wandered. This was made worse by constant text alerts on his mobile phone from friends who were also revising, checking on progress. Switching his phone off made him worry that he might miss something important. Even after he returned home, he felt that he ought to carry on studying to make up for his earlier lapses. He had made a revision plan, but was already well behind on what he had hoped to achieve. The consequent anxiety and general tiredness from late-night studying were making his concentration worse.

We suggested a more active revision strategy: working out first what he already knew about each topic, looking for information to fill any gaps, then using what he had learned, to answer a practice exam question. Each task was allocated a bounded amount of time to create a series of achievable short-term targets. Anil identified his best time for concentration as being first thing in the morning, while his worst time was after lunch. We suggested that he printed off any texts he needed to read in the afternoon, rather than trying to read onscreen. This change of reading mode offered variety as well as a rest for tired eyes. A study timetable for each day was devised including some designated time off. In addition to avoiding the '24/7 study trap', we explained that this break would help him to process the information he had read.

His mobile phone was enlisted as a tool to help him control his time, rather than something which was contributing to him losing control. The organiser function was a convenient and portable way to keep a list of targets for each day's revision; an alarm was set to remind him to take his daily 'time out' period. During this time, he used the voice recorder to record any brief reflections and thoughts he had about his revision. By being shown how his phone could be a tool which aided rather than sabotaged learning, Anil was better able to return his focus to study after his friends texted, instead of surrendering to a more social mode of thinking.

Encouraging students to make more use of personal technological devices might feel counter-intuitive in terms of focusing on study. However, these are potential learning tools which students already own and are familiar with using – and that they are highly unlikely to relinquish, however distracting. Recruiting them to the cause of study can offer new possibilities for creative solutions to support time management.

▶ Learning to be selective

> *The books are never in the library, so I usually research online. I get thousands of hits, so I just pick the first five.* (1st year Politics student)

With student numbers increasing, the lament of the late-submitting student has often been, 'I couldn't get hold of the texts on the reading list!' This no longer holds water; e-journals and the internet mean today's students can access information for academic research more simply, quickly, and in greater quantity, than any previous generation of learners. Quantity does not equal quality, and concerns in this area have focused on students' uncritical acceptance of online information and lack of academic rigour when selecting 'evidence' to support written discussions (CLEX, 2009, pp. 22–3). However, there are also implications for student time management in the sheer volume of sources and the concomitant need to practise selectivity.

Of all the new technologies available to support learning, internet searching is the most widely used. The Great Expectations survey observes that:

> Students tend to head to the internet as a first port of call for academic research, and predominantly use generic search engines such as Google, but are then likely to check the information they find against other sources such as the library. (Ipsos MORI/JISC 2008, p. 34)

Finding and accessing information online is more easily achieved than traditional searching and sourcing of library resources. The large quantities of information produced then need sifting and evaluating. However, students who are conscientious, or lack confidence in their ability to select, can find themselves overwhelmed by the quantity of information. They can become paralysed into inaction, or feel unable to start writing until they have read 'one more source'. The well-known problem of the perfectionist student, who feels compelled to read every text on the reading list in case they miss something important, is massively compounded when a Google search can instantly produce thousands of pages on any topic.

Tutors may intervene by directing students to authoritative online resources such as peer-reviewed e-journals, conference proceedings or government reports. Better still, students may be offered training to develop more effective search strategies by limiting the sites they search and using academic search engines and databases. However, once texts have been sourced, they must be read and processed. Again, problems can arise for students who are more familiar with using online information in non-academic contexts: made visually appealing, written in accessible language, and organised in small digestible chunks. Ease of access does not necessarily equate to 'accessibility' in writing style or content. Students confronted with online academic texts may be as overwhelmed by expectations of content as by quantity; this can have a substantial impact on time management.

Case study: Belinda – reading too widely?

Belinda was a second year undergraduate student who wanted advice on speed-reading, to help her complete the reading for her seminars in a particular module. The time she spent reading for these weekly meetings was so extensive that she was getting behind with her coursework assignments. Belinda's reading list for each week comprised a dozen (and sometimes more) articles from academic journals, all available electronically. Although her tutor's (implicit) expectation was that students would read selectively, Belinda's usual practice was to download all the articles, then read through each in detail, making copious notes. To save money on printing, she was reading on-screen. When she came for advice, Belinda was exhausted and demoralised by her inability to keep up with what she believed to be normal academic demands.

We began by explaining to Belinda that the purpose of reading for seminars was to prepare her for discussion rather than testing. This boosted her academic confidence generally, and dispelled the idea that she might be underprepared if she did not read everything. We also explained that the purpose of university study is rarely to find a single right answer: increasing the number of texts read will not make this more likely. Belinda was shown how to read more actively, considering the purpose of each seminar and how her reading might link with that purpose. Using online resources for reading was modelled against study for other modules where resources were mostly paper-based; in these, she was used to reading a few accessible sources. We suggested Belinda practise more selective reading: focusing on reading and understanding more discursive sections (e.g. introductions and discussion sections) when preparing for seminars, and drilling down to the detail (e.g. methods and data sections) only when conducting more in-depth research.

Finally we suggested that Belinda select three articles to read, and then assess what she had learnt and whether she needed to read more to feel prepared for the seminar. This developed her ability to select suitable materials. Limiting reading also meant that she could afford to print and read the articles in a paper format, which she found aided her reading speed and comprehension and helped her to think of reading e-resources as an equivalent to reading paper-based resources. Belinda reported feeling more in control of her reading, and was able to reduce the time she spent on it to a manageable level.

As more resources become digitised (and as digitised resources become more widely recommended because of cost considerations), the ability to select will become increasingly important, if our students are not to become overwhelmed. However, being able to select is inevitably bound up with academic confidence. Clearly communicating our expectations to students will be essential in achieving this. The traditional exhortation to 'read widely' may need to be more carefully framed in the future.

▶ Defining boundaries

Giving Students Facebook Chat is Like Giving a Hyperactive Child Crack. (Title of Facebook Group with 1,938 members in August 2009)

Much use of social and educational technologies takes place in a single shared online space: the personal computer or laptop. This can prompt issues about setting boundaries to balance the use of time for study and for leisure and to avoid distraction (JISC, 2007, p. 19). While mobile phones and iPods are primarily seen as personal communication and entertainment devices, personal computers (PCs) were from early days associated equally with work and leisure. Early use of PCs as gaming and word processing machines has been extended to include the capacity to create a range of digital products (including PowerPoint® slides, websites, videos and music), and the interactive technologies of Web 2.0 used for leisure as well as study (interactive online gaming, social networking and instant messaging, blogs, wikis and social book-marking). Though some students can develop good multi-tasking skills, such distractions are irresistible for all students at some time; for some they become overwhelming. For these students, strategies for establishing boundaries are crucial to academic success.

Setting boundaries is essential for effective independent study. However, this is the generation whose schooling has been dominated by league tables and tests: as a consequence, the current 18–21 cohort are used to having time scheduled for them by schoolteachers and parents. Boundary-setting has become more significant because of the continuing trend in universities towards more on-screen communications and resources. Students receive administrative information via email, find course resources on Virtual Learning Environments, and submit assignments online. With study tasks conducted using the same technology as social and leisure practices, running programs for both simultaneously is usual. Coupled with poor concentration, the temptation to abandon complex study tasks in favour of checking Facebook or dropping in on an ongoing role-playing game is almost irresistible. There is an apparent gender division here, with female students more likely to spend time on social networking sites and male students more likely to spend time gaming (CLEX, 2009, p. 22). This temptation to distraction is cited as one reason students are wary of social networking groups for study, with one student worrying that she'd 'probably get distracted by other stuff on Facebook and not end up doing anything' (Ipsos MORI/JISC, 2008, p. 37).

Case study: Calvin – overcoming game addiction

Calvin was a first year student who had suspended his studies after becoming obsessed with online gaming. His re-entry was conditional on him seeking support to overcome this, and to establish good time management practices. It emerged that Calvin had had difficulty making friends when he started at university. Consequently, he had spent increasingly long periods in his room in Hall, where the combination of free internet access and his own laptop (bought by his parents to help him with his course) had resulted in his immersion in a Massively Multi-player Online Game (MMOG). These games take place in real time, with new participants constantly joining and leaving. As a result, there is no natural 'finish' to the game: like an alternate reality, the game simply continues in the background with the player giving it more or less attention. Calvin was away from the structuring framework of home and school for the first time and had not yet had the opportunity to develop his self-management skills. Without the incentive of an exciting new social life (experienced by most of his peers), he had no reason to leave the game. He stopped attending lectures and lab sessions, and even skipped meals and sleep to continue playing.

In Calvin's case, things had clearly gone beyond being just a learning development issue. Our intervention was just one part of a coordinated support programme which included counselling, peer supporters, his personal tutor, the department's administrative team and Hall wardens. This integrated approach tackled both Calvin's obsessive behaviour and the difficulties in socialising that had prompted it originally. Working with Calvin to empower him by letting him develop his own solutions (rather than imposing rules) was key in reinstating habits of independent study, as his inability to stop playing the game had prompted feelings of power-lessness and lack of control. He felt that he would be less likely to lapse if he was in a very public place, so a temporary desk was found in his department (out of sight of other students, but in sight of office staff). Calvin tried using software that blocked certain websites, but reported that he felt again as if he lacked power to determine his own actions, in this case because the software program was telling him what he could and couldn't do. However, with the support of all parts of the integrated support team, he made progress. Once Calvin felt ready to work more independently, he was helped to devise a study timetable which included time for independent study but also ring-fenced time when he would not study, for socialising, sports and relaxing generally. Even so, Calvin felt that multi-tasking in several windows made distraction too tempting for him, and preferred to work on one task at a time.

Although such extreme cases are rare, the strategies that work for students in these situations can help us understand the needs of all students. Importantly though, if we want students to become inde-pendent learners, we must enable them to develop their own solu-tions, and not simply impose rules on them, however welcome a fixed framework might seem to be.

▶ Conclusions

Studies of recent student cohorts and new technology have tended to focus either on the problems new learning cultures present for tutors, or on e-pedagogy. The persistent notion of 'digital natives' has encour-aged assumptions that current students will naturally be able to use, manage and innovate in their handling of technology. However, although the 18–21 cohort has grown up with technologies, it is more as consumers than as creators. Inequalities of both access and compe-tence remain (CLEX, 2009, pp. 20–1), and these can be magnified in less mainstream groups, like mature and international students. More recent studies have noted the need to guide students to expand their recognition of the potential of new technologies for learning, and to develop 'new conventions from learning using digital media' (Ipsos MORI/JISC, 2008, p. 13).

The spaces where new technology, current students and the demands of academic study seem to mesh most productively are those created by the students themselves and are seldom recognised by their users as explicit learning tools: for instance, discussions using instant messaging, or the numerous and often temporally brief study groups and message threads set up on social networking sites like Facebook. These practices have been described as an 'underworld of communication' about learning (JISC, 2007, p. 21). In one study, three-quarters of students surveyed were using social networking sites to discuss coursework, but did not perceive this as learning (Ipsos MORI/JISC, 2008, p. 7). Students felt uncomfortable with the lack of hierarchy if tutors interacted with them through Facebook: for new undergraduates especially, learning is still seen as a process in which teachers impart knowledge rather than one of joint knowledge creation (Ipsos MORI/JISC, 2008, pp. 10, 32).

The interactions we have had as learning development advisers with students learning to manage their time suggest that many of them do recognise the possible difficulties posed by new technologies, and are looking for guidance to help them develop their own solutions. Learning developers are well placed to offer such guidance: many of us are ourselves enthusiastic adopters of new technologies, and our expertise in problem-solving has prompted a diverse range of creative uses. Our experience indicates that guidance on time management and new technologies is most effective when it is creative, relevant and well-informed – and always retains one eye on the goal of developing independent learners.

▶ References

Castell, S., Sweet, O., Haldenby, A. and Parsons, L. (2008) *A New Reality: Government and the iPod Generation* (London: Ipsos MORI/Reform).

CLEX – Committee of Inquiry into the Changing Learner Experience (2009) *Higher Education in a Web 2.0 World* (Bristol: JISC).

Ipsos MORI on behalf of JISC (2008) *Great Expectations of ICT: How Higher Education Institutions are Measuring Up* (London: Ipsos MORI).

JISC (2007) *In Their Own Words: Learner Experiences of e-Learning* (Bristol: JISC).

JISC (2009) *Effective Practice in a Digital Age: A Guide to Technology-Enhanced Learning and Teaching* (Bristol: JISC).

Moon, J. A. (2004) *A Handbook of Reflective and Experiential Learning: Theory and Practice* (London: RoutledgeFalmer)

National Audit Office (2007) *Staying the Course: The Retention of Students on Higher Education Courses* (London: The Stationery Office).

Page, E. (n.d.) 'Using Personal Response Systems to Encourage Active Learning', University of Reading. Available at: www.reading.ac.uk/internal/cdotl/e-Learning/e-Learningcasestudies/cdotl-csPage.aspx (last accessed 29/3/10).

Pickford, R. and Brown, S. (2006) *Assessing Skills and Practice* (London: Routledge).

Prensky, M. (2001) 'Digital natives, digital immigrants', *On the Horizon* 9 (5), 1–2.

Ramsden, A. (2009) 'Using micro-blogging (Twitter) in your teaching and learning: An introductory guide'. Discussion Paper, University of Bath. Available at: http://opus.bath.ac.uk/15319/1/intro_to_microblogging_09.pdf (last accessed 1/09/09).

Section E

Looking Into the Future

18 Looking Back and Looking Into the Future

Michelle Verity and Paul Trowler

▶ Summary

This chapter reviews the growth of learning development and analyses its likely future. It is divided into three linked sections. Each section reflects on issues raised in the rest of the book and considers the trajectory of learning development over time. Firstly, we identify challenges for learning developers as they work to enhance their role and effectiveness for the future. Secondly, we review lessons learned so far about the effects of learning development work (including particular outcomes from the LearnHigher initiative), and their implications for future action. Finally, we offer a longer-term look at the future of learning development work and its place in the academic enterprise, suggesting that a move to 'situationally contingent' provision is the most likely path given the increasing pressure on resources.

▶ Introduction

Until relatively recently, the trajectory of learning development tended to be non-strategic, an ad hoc response to universities' needs and challenges. This meant a lack of coordination and a lack of explicit theorisation and evidence about learning development practices. Actions were based only on implicit theory and on possibly unsound assumptions – for example, that teaching 'study skills' is a 'Good Thing' (whereas some evidence suggests that it encourages a surface approach to learning) or that the best focus for action is the student (the curriculum or the organisation might be better foci). This book is part of a push by learning developers to move away from 'ad hoc-ery' towards enquiry-based practices; this chapter aims to support this push by providing both critical reflections on previous practice and analysis of current and future challenges.

▶ Challenges for learning developers

Conceptualising 'learning development'

Learning development (LD) can be, and often is, perceived as largely remedial, relevant for only part of the student population and not at all staff-facing or institutionally central. Such perceptions 'fix' the role in this location and may become self-fulfilling. Changing perceptions to engage loftier ambitions can be a challenge.

After much debate the LearnHigher partners agreed a description of learning development as:

> an emergent and increasingly recognised field of practice in higher education in the UK. Those who identify with the term are princi-pally involved in areas of work focusing on student learning, work-ing directly with students and in a consultative capacity with other HE staff. This work is sometimes referred to as 'learning support' or 'study skills', but most LD practitioners reject the remedial implications that such terms may carry.
>
> The main aim of LD work is the empowerment of students through the enhancement of their academic practices – such as skills for research, communication, self-awareness and critical thinking – in order that they may benefit as fully as possible from their experiences of, and life beyond, higher education. (Hilsdon, Ridley and Sinfield, 2008)

This raises a number of questions, alternative answers to which provide competing conceptions of learning development:

1   Is it a 'field' in itself or is it integrated into the academic enterprise? (We return to this issue below.)
2   Is the description of interaction with other HE staff as 'consultative' sufficient and correct, rather than (for example) educative, support-ive, developmental?

3   Is the enhancement of that list of academic practices, and more, really feasible?
4   What else should be included under the term 'academic practices'? (And where are its limits?)
5   How should limited resources be prioritised in relation to these aims?
6   How does that set of aims differ from those of academic teachers? (Haven't they always been concerned with learning development, even while teaching 'content'?)
7   Isn't there also a significant role for engagement with organisational policy and processes? (The focus here is on working with students and staff directly.)

The conceptions of the nature, goals and scope of learning development work held by academics, students and senior managers are, in the end, more important than those held by learning developers themselves. No doubt the range is huge, and understandings (some might say stereotypes) are rarely made explicit. Yet such tacit assumptions can have significant consequences, for example in terms of the nature and level of student demand and the expectations of senior managers. They are reified in strategy documents and in performance indicators and so performance comes to be measured against them. Underpinning these expectations are sets of values, codes of signification, which invoke and impose values in relation to learning development work, perhaps seeing it as marginal and remedial – a kind of institutional first aid, or more positively as the jewel in the learner-centred crown of the university.

Institutional integration

The danger here is organisational peripherality. We saw in Chapter 2 that units tasked with learning development functions are frequently (though not always) peripheral to the 'core' academic enterprise in a number of senses. Marginal physical location, lack of engagement with university committee systems and policy-making processes, and only partial integration into the information loop are common characteristics of learning development units and their staff. Cultural, organisational and social marginalisation add to the remedial image that fixes both function and staff in a subaltern role. Countering this is far from easy, particularly given the multi-faceted character of this marginality. One common tactic is to enhance learning development's profile through newsletters, posters, and highly publicised events. But from the perspective of the rest of the university this can just add to 'institutional noise'. Moreover, this approach is directed at 'the university' and so is scattergun in character. As Patton (1997) notes, it is *people*, not organisations, that effect change, and persuading the right people through good data and reasoned argument is a more effective strategy than trying to change 'an organisation'.

Knowing/persuading about making a difference: credibility

To bring learning development to a position where it is more likely to be able to achieve its ambitions it is necessary to persuade, manoeuvre and alter perceptions among real people. Demonstrating the power and potential of learning development practices, embedding and spreading them is not easy. Having credibility, at least among a few senior managers, has been shown to be very important in, for example, educational (or academic) development. The presence of a champion on the top team is very significant in winning resources and getting a voice in policy change, and this was shown by some LearnHigher partners to work well when formalised in membership of a steering group actively involved in learning development work and policy. Demonstrating the beneficial effects of the learning development function is important too. An enquiry-led approach, with good research and evaluation practices, is usually considered necessary in learning development, educational development and in planning change generally. However, because of the multi-causal nature of reality and the dynamic character of higher education (HE), the search for 'impact' in a straightforward sense is misplaced. Rather, changes in social practices (broadly understood) can be identified, as these involve changes in valuing, in assumptions, in codes of signification as well as in more direct and immediate practices (Alvesson and Sveningsson, 2008).

Learning development – a distinct professional community or an integrated function?

Some learning developers express the ambition to be involved in an integrated, professionalised community of practitioners with their own organisation, conferences and increasingly coherent 'interpretive community'. The model sometimes used is the educational (or academic) development community, which, in the UK and elsewhere, has moved strongly in this direction with organisations such as the Staff and Educational Development Association (SEDA) in the UK, the Higher Education Research and Development Society of Australasia (HERDSA) in Australasia or the Higher Education Learning and Teaching Association of Southern Africa (HELTASA) in South Africa, with associated conferences and networks.

The issue here, though, is that increasing coherence among learning developers in different institutions can mean the drawing of lines between them and the wider academic community, including academic teachers and educational developers. Such divisions may be antipathetic to the achievement of the goals of learning development, and can increase the likelihood of the dystopian assembly-line approach to higher education envisaged by Gary Rhoades in his descriptions of Mode III (see below). Perhaps the growth of learning development as a community might itself form part of the problem in the future. The challenge is knowing what to do for the best.

▶ Lessons learned about effects

Important lessons about learning development and its effectiveness can be drawn from the particular experience of LearnHigher. In doing this, we look for those lessons that are of relevance more generally for policy-makers and managers, for institutional top teams, for academic staff, for students, and for learning developers themselves.

Institutional context

Institutional cultures and missions are significant to what can be achieved and what is appropriate for the learning development function in terms of its aims, practices and focus. The literature in a variety of areas confirms our stress on the significance of the institution in this respect (Clouder, Oliver and Tate, 2008; Colbeck, 2004; Hattie and Marsh, 2004; Jenkins, 2004; Lindblom-Ylänne et al., 2006; Zubrick, Reid and Rossiter, 2001). The LearnHigher Centre for Excellence in Teaching and Learning (CETL) provided many opportunities to examine contextual differences because it included partners from traditional research-intensive institutions, post-92 universities (previously teaching-oriented polytechnics) and small, newly designated universities. In institutions where research is the primary concern and teaching and learning, and pedagogic research, are attributed less value, learning developers have struggled to have a voice beyond their immediate vicinity. In many of the post-92 LearnHigher institutions, learning development work and student support is generally given greater recognition and in these contexts partners had greater opportunity to work with colleagues to develop new practices and embed new resources within curricula. The lessons here have been largely for learning developers – they involve deciding what is achievable given institutional priorities, what is likely to work *here*. Institutional managers too might want to reflect on institutional cultures and priorities as reflected in, for example, promotion criteria, committee structures and policy processes and the extent to which these match mission statements and strategic plans for teaching and learning enhancement.

Location of learning development within the organisation

As we saw in Chapters 1 and 2, institutions employ different models of learning development. Some use policy to embed learning development within the curriculum, claiming a contextualised approach (often requiring that programmes demonstrate where learning development needs are met). Some create provision within degree programmes through the delivery of bolt-on 'skills' modules. Another option sometimes seen is the provision of access to 'study support' facilities, either faculty-based, or through a centralised unit. These options have different implications for the way learning development is perceived: as a fundamental aspect of teaching and learning, or a remedial understanding where underperforming students need 'fixing'. Messages about this are conveyed to students and staff, sometimes inadvertently, and these can affect the ability of learning development units to achieve what they see as their role. The messages here are for policy-makers and institutional managers in particular and they concern organisational architecture. The significant questions are: 'Where is the learning development function located, and is this the best place for it?' 'How involved are learning developers in curriculum change and in policy-making?' 'How far do the different goals of the university conflict, and what are the implications of any conflict for student achievement?'

The synergies of collaboration (and the dangers)

LearnHigher grew from an existing partnership between a small number of higher education practitioners keen to share the resources they had developed to support students' 'learning development'. The CETL funding provided the opportunity to formalise this arrangement and expand the network's activities. The 16 universities involved collaborated on a number of projects during the CETL's existence and such collaboration enabled individuals to learn from each other, to develop their expertise, and to build their own capacity.

LearnHigher had goals in addition to resource-sharing, in particular to influence the teaching practices of a wider community and, ulti- mately, to enhance the status of learning development on institutional agendas. Indeed, the network sought to develop its collective voice around learning development as a field of practice. But the develop- ment of a collective voice can silence as well as empower, and a domi- nant voice with a single message can mute self-criticism in relation to activities and outputs. Practitioners come from various professional, cultural and historical backgrounds – they have differing views on what learning development is; what learning developers should do; the constitution of the wider community; what enhanced learning devel- opment status looks like; and whom learning developers should be trying to influence. The lesson here is for learning developers them- selves, and it is: be careful what you wish for – today's solutions can become tomorrow's problems.

Lessons for expanding engagement
The LearnHigher CETL utilised a network model to maximise its reach, employing mechanisms designed to share resources and expertise, to reach new audiences and engage others in its practices. In turn, the 16 partners formed sub-networks with other practitioners sharing an interest in their particular area, often a rich source of dialogue and further pooling of expertise and experience. The size of the partnership and its sub-networks enabled LearnHigher outputs to be further spread. Expertise was captured through a scholarly approach and part- ners conducted practice-led research, published papers and books, and offered presentations at conferences. Systematic evaluation of processes and outcomes was undertaken although recognising that producing evaluation reports alone is not sufficient to engage further audiences. Yet despite its advantages, LearnHigher faced challenges in developing engagement both vertically (within host institutions) and horizontally (across the sector). Learning developers must consider how to engage others in evaluation findings, to develop active engage- ment strategies, and to ensure that their research is both applicable and relevant to others.

Lessons about building credibility
The CETL policy was built on the notion of promoting 'beacons' of good practice as an effective way to bring about change in teaching and learning. Funding excellence has had significant effects; the Learn- Higher experience found that even the relatively modest amount of

funding received by each partner brought with it a level of autonomy within their institution and created opportunity for innovation and creativity that an individual might not otherwise have the capacity for. Capital funding, too, raised the profile of learning development activity. Partners who benefited the most were those in a position to create high-profile spaces for learning development activities, raising awareness amongst students and staff.

Perhaps equally significant, however, was the enhanced status individuals were granted by being a part of this national initiative, generating interest within host institutions and often resulting in invitations to participate in committees and advisory groups with real potential to influence strategy.

Perhaps what the CETL experience taught us most firmly, however, is that 'learning development' should be championed. Not just through the 'individual innovators' (Hannan and Silver, 2000) working from the ground up, but by those with power and influence near the top. Whether champions promote learning development as a specialist set of practices that complement teaching and learning or whether it is embedded as an integral part of teaching and learning throughout course structures and content, its goals are an important aspect of the student experience and require sufficient recognition.

▶ The future for learning development

The learning development function has grown in size and diversified in function as higher education has expanded in almost all countries around the world. This growth has, almost everywhere, set up parallel provision alongside the 'delivery' of the academic curriculum by academics. While in some cases the function has been aimed at enhancing learning across the student body, the more usual pattern has been for it to be remedial.

If that dominant trajectory continues we will see increasing provision and diversification of learning development continuing separately from 'core teaching'. Most learning developers are agreed that this is not the ideal scenario. For them, 'bolt-on' provision of a learning development function has been a compromise, and (especially when seen in remedial terms) a deleterious one. Their preferred future is the integration of learning development with academic provision to provide a seamless experience for all students, who would learn subject content and become extremely skilful in their academic practices simultaneously.

Such a scenario appears unlikely at the moment, at least in the UK, for a number of reasons. Special funding for the enhancement of teaching and learning is under threat as the fiscal crisis bites increasingly hard and priorities turn elsewhere. Universities themselves face a difficult economic future in most places around the world and any function not considered 'core' is threatened. Whether learning developers like it or not, some managers do not see their role as being part of the university's 'core' function, and probably will maintain that view until learning development is no longer located in separate units.

More likely than a general decline of the function, though, is a future which sees situationally contingent provision. As higher education systems globally tend to diversify to include institutions with different missions and distinctive student bodies, learning development is likely to diversify in relation to what is appropriate to the institutional context. Moreover, policy changes and shifting HE agendas will almost certainly require specific learning development expertise to be applied in a 'just in time' way. An example of that is the Scottish Quality Enhancement Framework with its changing 'enhancement themes' which the Scottish universities are required to address. These have included: research-teaching linkages; employability; graduates for the twenty-first century. Similar issues arise everywhere from time to time in the HE policy agenda or as part of the quality assurance systems of different countries. In the UK generally, the push to widen participation has meant an increased need to support less-prepared students. The employability agenda has widened the meaning of 'a university education' and required new expertise in universities. Ideologically driven changes such as the move to 'student-as-consumer' and the international marketing of and competition among universities have done likewise. Student mobility, with its consequent requirement for support for other languages and cultures, will also sustain demand for the learning development function. If only for marketing reasons, every university needs to show that it is a class act, and managers see that learning development can help in this. The increasing integration of ICT into teaching and learning will also see a change in the nature of academic work, foregrounding professionals who are not academics but work alongside them in the teaching and learning process. For Gary Rhoades (2007), the integration of ICT is leading to a 'Mode III' form of teaching and learning organisation, which involves a 'matrix of professional, technical and support personnel' (Rhoades, 2007, p. 1). Teaching and learning becomes, in this model, a multi-professional business with different specialists involved in course organisation, support, delivery and assessment. Mode III, however, is different from the integrated scenario preferred by learning developers. Rhoades sees:

> a disaggregation of the integrated faculty role into a 'virtual assembly line' ... of specialists, focused on separate tasks of instructional design, course content, delivery, support and advising, and assessment. (pp. 2–3)

The social relations of academic production are being driven, he argues, by technological change and by the increasingly entrepreneurial nature of universities worldwide: a form of academic capitalism which increasingly exploits alienated labour.

However, Rhoades' analysis, based on American data, does not apply well to the British or European context. Here the drivers of great significance are wider than just technological change, including policy changes and the need for wider learning development provision than just ICT-related ones. Indeed, his model of the 'dis-integration' and 'de-centering' of the academic's role in teaching and learning is not necessarily a negative thing in the way he depicts, with academics reduced to being 'mere' content experts standing on the academic production line. As we saw above, learning developers, including those writing in these pages, see the potential for a brighter future for both professionals and students. But this book has shown too that Rhoades may be wrong in picturing an increasing role for permanent and expanding non-academic units within universities: 'emergent interstitial units' as he calls them (p. 6). They are in fact in a state of flux and under recurring threat. So if his picture of these professionals becoming a powerful interest group (Rhoades and Slaughter, 2006, pp. 15–16) does ring true, this may be more a result of the perceived need among learning developers, at least, to fight to defend their role in the face of turbulent policies and organisational structures. We can take heart from the critical postmodernist work of Kempner and Tierney (1996) and Tierney (1996), who suggest that a nation's history and cultural context is key to understanding its educational policies and practices, as well as the likely future direction it will take. In short, they eschew Marxist and neo-Marxist notions of 'inevitable paths' driven by technology, and suggest, instead, we look at the particularities of cultural and ideological contexts, developing an understanding of what is valued and what is not. Seen in this light, we expect different paths for learning development around the globe; in the UK we do not expect traditional barriers (and associated attitudes) between academics and non-academics to be quickly broken down. This is not to say, though, that we should not work at that. On the contrary, a critical postmodernist perspective emphasises the crucial importance of actions and agency in changing the world. Learning developers are not powerless in shaping the future of their work, as we can see from this book, from the enduring legacy of the LearnHigher CETL, from the continuation of this work highlighted in the next chapter, and from the individuals who have given so much of their time and effort to the enhancement of student learning. They have made a significant contribution to the future of learning development in the universities of the future.

▶ References

Alvesson, M. and Sveningsson, S. (2008) *Changing Organizational Culture: Cultural Change Work in Progress* (London: Routledge).

Clouder, L., Oliver, M. and Tate, J. (2008) 'Embedding CETLs in a performance-oriented culture in higher education: reflections on finding creative space', *British Educational Research Journal* 34 (5), 635–50.

Colbeck, C. (2004) 'A Cybernetic Systems model of teaching and research production: impact of disciplinary differences'. Paper presented at the *International Colloquium on Research and Teaching. Closing the Divide?* Winchester, UK. Available from: http://portal-live.solent.ac.uk/university/rtconference/2004/resources/colbeck_paper.pdf (last accessed 8/7/09).

Hannan, A. and Silver, H. (2000) *Innovating in Higher Education: Teaching, Learning and Institutional Cultures* (Buckingham: Open University Press/SRHE).

Hattie, J. and Marsh, H. W. (2004) 'One journey to unravel the relationship between research and teaching'. Paper presented at the *International Colloquium on Research and Teaching: Closing the Divide?* Winchester, UK, 17–19 March. Available from: http://portal-live.solent.ac.uk/university/rtconference/2004/resources/hattie_marsh_paper.pdf (last accessed 8/7/09).

Hilsdon, J., Ridley, P. and Sinfield, S. (2008) 'Defining LD' email correspondence, Learning Development in Higher Education Network, Sept. 2008. Available at: www.jiscmail.ac.uk/learnhigher (last accessed 29/3/10).

Jenkins, A. (2004) *A Guide to the Research Evidence on Teaching–Research Relations* (York: Higher Education Academy).

Kempner, K. and Tierney, W. G. (1996) 'Academic culture in an international context', in K. Kempner and W. G. Tierney (eds) *The Social Role of Higher Education* (New York and London: Garland Publishing).

Lindblom-Ylänne, S., Trigwell, K., Nevgia, A. and Ashwin, P. (2006) 'Approaches to teaching are affected by discipline and teaching context', *Studies in Higher Education* 31 (3), 285–98.

Patton, M. Q. (1997) *Utilization-Focused Evaluation: The New Century Text*, 3rd edition (Thousand Oaks, CA: Sage).

Rhoades, G. (2007) 'Technology-enhanced courses and a Mode III organization of instructional work', *Tertiary Education Management* 13 (1), 1–17.

Rhoades, G. and Slaughter, S. (2006) 'Mode 3, academic capitalism and the new economy: making higher education work for whom?' in P. Tynjala, J. Valimaa and G. Boulton-Lewis (eds) *Higher Education and Working Life: Collaboration, Confrontation and Challenges* (Amsterdam: Elsevier).

Tierney, W. G. (1996) 'The academic profession and the culture of the faculty: a perspective on Latin American universities', in K. Kempner and W. G. Tierney (eds) *The Social Role of Higher Education* (New York and London: Garland Publishing).

Zubrick, A., Reid, I. and Rossiter, P. (2001) *Strengthening the Nexus between Teaching and Research* (Canberra, Australia: Department of Education, Training and Youth Affairs). Available from: www.dest.gov.au/archive/highered/eippubs/eip01_2/01_2.pdf (last accessed 29/3/10).

19 Learning Development: Work in Progress

John Hilsdon, Christine Keenan and Sandra Sinfield

▶ Summary

This book has mapped key developments and initiatives in learning development over the last decade, with particular focus on the five years of the LearnHigher Centre for Excellence in Teaching and Learning (CETL). Practitioners involved in the Learning Development in Higher Education Network (LDHEN), the Association for Learning Developers in Higher Education (ALDinHE), and in LearnHigher, have been working to establish learning development as a discipline – and to draw attention to the unique role of learning developers in shaping the higher education (HE) experience. This final chapter highlights some of the exciting developments and challenges which are now emerging.

▶ Introduction

The work of LearnHigher from 2005 to 2010 was generated by its sixteen partners but from the outset one of the CETL's main strengths was its links to the wider learning development network, and the ambition to build on good practice in supporting student learning in the UK HE sector. This period has been especially rich for the evolution of learning development as a community of practice and, we would argue, as a discipline. Many of us have worked in this field in circumstances where we could offer no more than a drop-in service for a couple of hours a week – perhaps supplemented by occasional short study and academic skills courses.

To some extent, this has been a period of 'flying below the radar' of government policies and senior management concerns, which has allowed a flurry of experimentation, action research and the generation of a rich evidence-based practice. Although a wide range of different types of experiences are reported by learning developers, not all of which are positive, for many of us, the CETL era has been an exciting time; and one of great academic freedom. Rather than being seen as a 'Cinderella' service or a remedial unit, as some of our colleagues report, for those with more flexibility in our local circumstances, we have been able to define the emergence of a new discipline. This is historic, and something to be celebrated!

▶ Hard new times

Our mood of celebration, however, is tempered by the economic and political climate. In the wake of recent global financial disruption there are threats of large reductions in funding to public services, with HE in the UK being a particular target for cuts. For the year 2010–11, planned cuts of nearly £400 million were announced (Eason, 2010), and some universities had already started planning redundancies (Morgan, 2010). A new wave of austerity is therefore already on the way, and, for non-traditional students in particular, this means the likelihood of increasing hardship, an inability to afford study and the danger that sources of support may disappear. As our institutions look for areas where 'efficiencies' can be achieved, we are already seeing evidence of support for learning being out-sourced. Some LDHEN members have reported cuts, and, in some cases, posts being eliminated altogether. In anticipation, perhaps, of harsher times, and in order to be more strategic within our organisations, many of us have already developed or extended our ways of working with academic staff across the disciplines: customising interventions and resources and embedding them in particular programmes to maximise impact and effect where possible. Learning developers often sit on learning and teaching committees or within groups which explore transition to HE or ways to improve 'retention'; we may be within working groups focused upon work-based learning or extra-curricular student activities. Some of us are being co-opted into discussions around the development and embedding of blended learning strategies; of student engagement policy and practice; and around developing institutional policies to counter plagiarism. Thus, we see the evolution of complex models of learning development that still work with and for students – but also work with and for academic staff – and for the overall development of successful teaching, learning and assessment practice across an institution.

Times change, but even in hard times opportunities will exist for those with a learning development perspective. Our contribution, as illustrated in various parts of this book, draws upon experience both from the 'chalkface' and from a unique position where we are often in roles mediating between students and other academic staff. In working to help students make sense of academic discourse and practices, learning developers can feed vital insights back into the lifeblood of our institutions.

▶ LearnHigher: moving on, moving up

Despite the threats to HE funding, there is a commitment to sustain the overall LearnHigher project within ALDinHE and alongside LDHEN for years to come, with the hope that more resources may become available to expand its work in the future. The history of LearnHigher illustrates the strength of a committed practitioner network to effect real change. The opening chapter of this book described how we started with an email discussion forum and a 'swap-shop' for learning materials. The learning development community itself produced LearnHigher and will support its future as part of a sector-wide movement encompassing a range of scholarship, research and Continuing Professional Development (CPD) initiatives, with growing links that go beyond the UK and Ireland.

Despite the fact that HEFCE funding ceased from July 2010, the coordinators took an early decision that they would continue to work as a partnership, by re-affirming the link between LearnHigher and the professional network represented by the Association (ALDinHE) and the Learning Development in Higher Education Network (LDHEN).

At its AGM in March 2010, the Association formally agreed to provide an organisational home for LearnHigher, to secure its future as an engine for resource development and research into how students use learning materials. This will include, at least, the maintenance and further development of the LearnHigher website, but there is also an intention to open the partnership to other universities and to re-examine the current division of resources into 'learning areas'.

▶ The strength of the network and association

The JISCmail discussion forum, Learning Development in Higher Education Network, continues to be an informal online 'space' (with around 500 subscribers) for an engaged and interested community of practice. The forum has indeed proved to be a 'treasure chest' (Cash and Hilsdon, 2008) where like-minded people freely share and develop ideas, views and resources. A particular example illustrates this point: a developer who was recently asked at short notice to lead a study skills unit for international undergraduate students wrote a brief email to the list, asking for ideas. Within hours she had received enough advice, materials, and resources to get started, with plenty to sustain her work on the unit. Communications on the list range from day-to-day concerns to ways of influencing institutional policy. For example, sharing our collective wisdom on alternative assessments (one of the online LDHEN discussions from 2008/09) a subscriber collated the responses and produced material for several staff development sessions, and used them to write a whole section in an 'institutional assessment framework' document.

Since its establishment in 2007, a key ambition of the learning development association, ALDinHE, has been to represent the network and its members to government and the Higher Education Academy. A recent submission to the Students and Universities Inquiry enabled the association to articulate the particular learning development message that a modern, accessible and relevant higher education must actively involve students in learning and research partnerships. ALDinHE is also keen to support CPD initiatives to underpin the expertise of learning developers and gain recognition for the field in practice, in research and through publication.

As it has grown, the association has developed a number of working groups to manage functions such as the development of CPD, and the organisation of the annual LDHEN conference and regional symposia. The conference regularly attracts in the region of 150 delegates, and regional meetings provide opportunities for single-issue discussions or initiatives.

In 2009, the association's journal *JLDHE* was established. The first issue contained articles of high quality and thoughtful scholarship, including material by well-known educational developers, Graham Gibbs and Chris Rust. Equally important, however, is the practitioner focus of the journal, offering opportunities for new colleagues to develop their writing skills in a supportive peer-reviewed environment, and to gain experience of publication.

At the international level, ALDinHE has developed links with a number of similar groups, including the academic advisers' network, National Academic Advising Association (NACADA), in North America; the Association for Academic Language and Learning (AALL) in Australia; the Association of Tertiary Learning Advisers of Aotearoa, New Zealand; and the European Association for the Teaching of Academic Writing (EATAW). In embryonic form is an idea being promoted among these groupings to establish an international conference (possibly to be held simultaneously and online in several countries) to bring together representatives of all of these groups around the theme of supporting learning in twenty-first-century universities for global citizenship.

▶ Conclusion

From the stories and examples of practice in this book it can be seen that the learning development movement in UK universities has come a long way, and that undoubtedly it has a long way yet to go. The unifying and underpinning values in our methods and practice are perhaps best expressed by reference to the work of Stella Cottrell (2001), who with Gosling, Wolfendale and others first used the phrase in the 1990s (Wolfendale and Corbett, 1996). A learning development approach is not designed merely to provide support for the 'needy' and does not see students as deficient or in need of remediation. Rather, it is a response to the need for a higher education which is accessible and relevant to all with the ability to benefit. It is therefore applicable to all students, not just groups seen as vulnerable, and it requires flexible and multi-faceted modes of practice. These will include a wide spectrum of initiatives, both 'embedded' and additional to regular university programmes. In all cases, these will be part of whole-institution responses.

Learning development needs to influence all aspects of teaching, learning and assessment, working in tandem with staff from all disciplines, and with students. It implies action on specific learning issues as they arise, but also the development of the ethos of a learning community. So, by emphasising the role of partnership and inclusivity, LD seeks to involve students in shaping programmes of study – as in the student conference initiative outlined in the first section of this book.

Despite the need to 'embed', LD should continue to support, in parallel, those resource-intensive but often outstandingly successful one-to-one services which make such a difference to the student experience. It may now be fashionable to deride study and academic skills programmes – but it is often such provision to which student feedback accords very high praise. Rather than 'either-or', LD promotes an 'as well as' approach, mindful that there are unique advantages for students in having advisers to turn to who are independent of specific courses and their assessment regimes.

We hope that this book has given something of the flavour of learning development – a movement working alongside students to make sense of, as well as to achieve the best in, their studies. We wrote these chapters not only to chart the history of our work but with the intention to inspire and help practitioners to gain influence within their higher-education institutions. We also hope senior managers reading this book will have gained an understanding that learning development staff are uniquely valuable institutional assets – and that harnessing their commitment, energy, expertise and discipline knowledge in the service of real learning will make a positive difference to the life and the success of universities now and in the future.

▶ References

Cash, C. and Hilsdon, J. (2008) *Buried Treasures in a Virtual Community Chest*. Society for Research into Higher Education Annual Conference, Liverpool, UK. Available at: www.srhe.ac.uk/conference2008/papers/0292-John-Hilsdon_Caroline-Cash.doc (last accessed 29/3/10).

Cottrell, S. (2001) *Teaching Study Skills and Supporting Learning* (Basingstoke: Palgrave Macmillan).

Eason, G. (2010) 'Universities' annual funding reduced by £398m', *BBC News*. Available at: http://news.bbc.co.uk/1/hi/education/8427546.stm (last accessed 29/3/10).

Morgan, J. (2010) 'Strike threat as job cut talks break down at Leeds', *Times Higher Education*, 5 February.

Wolfendale, S. and Corbett, J. (eds) (1996) *Opening Doors: Learning Support in Higher Education* (London: Cassell).

Index

institutional default model *see*
socialisation model
international students
and Assignment Success
programme 6, 102–11
and one-to-one academic
advice 97–8
problems experienced by
102–3
International Visual Literacy
Association 184
internet
accessing information for
academic research 230–1
web-based learning development resources 155–66,
204–8
See also e-learning
Internet Detective 204–5
Ipsos Mori 213, 218

J
Jarvis, P. 104
Jenkins, A. 176
Jessen, A. 83
Johnston, B. 79–80
Joint Information System
Committee (JISC) 200, 204,
215, 216, 222
*Journal of Learning Development
in Higher Education* (JLDHE)
16, 23, 256–7
journals, student 175

K
Kempner, K. 250
Kendall, Margaret 205
Knight, P. T. 68, 71, 72, 77
Kolb, David 43

L
Land, R. 23
language, central role of in learning 19
LDHEN (Learning Development
in Higher Education
Network) 4, 13, 16, 19,
206, 253, 255, 258
Leacy, A. 124
LearnHigher 7, 8, 56–7, 124,
149, 156, 171, 178, 179–80,
204, 253, 255
and collaboration 246–7
funding 23, 56
future of 255
lessons learned 245–8
setting up of and functions
3–4, 16, 55
utilisation of network model
247
and visual practices 183,
185–6
learning developers 5, 153
backgrounds and skills 36–7
and career development 23
challenges for 242–5
crossing boundary between
generic and discipline-based
skills 30
interaction with academics
and other university staff
31–2, 35
and recognised qualifications
issue 32
services provided by 29
supporting early student transition 79–89
learning development
conceptualising 242–3
context for 14–16